PAINTING THE BEAUTY QUEENS ORANGE

PAINTING THE BEAUTY QUEENS ORANGE

HONNO

First published in Great Britain in 2021 by Honno Press
'Ailsa Craig', Heol y Cawl, Dinas Powys, Vale of Glamorgan,
Wales, CF64 4AH

1 2 3 4 5 6 7 8 9 10

ISBN: 978-1-912905-47-8 (paperback)
ISBN: 978-1-912905-48-5 (e-book)

Cover design by: Kari Brownlie
Text design: Elaine Sharples
Printed in Great Britain by 4edge Limited

INTRODUCTION

The 1970s were an era of economic struggle, political activism and technological innovation. The radicalism of the Sixties was growing and evolving, but also hitting obstacles and generating conflict in response. Recent history has revised the grim narratives of crisis and stagnation that had traditionally characterised the Seventies, instead rendering them a more positive and colourful time where social and cultural changes offered opportunities and intrigue.

As these positive aspects of the 1970s have been forgotten or neglected until now, so too have the voices of women. There is a particular lack of attention given to working-class women's writing on their own lives; even in history which is conscious of gender, working-class women frequently appear either as exoticised objects of anthropological study, or as sentimental, self-sacrificing stereotypes. While middle-class women can access greater opportunities to evaluate and articulate their own experiences in journalism, literature and film, these platforms have been denied to working-class women, who often find themselves in a double blind spot.

And yet women of all classes played a vital part in shaping the 1970s. Feminism and other liberatory politics continued to flourish in both subtle and militant forms, as women sought broader horizons or greater control over their own lives, jobs and love affairs. In Wales, women organised as workers, took part in political movements, and often held together a fraying social or domestic fabric – a thankless and anonymous task, but one no less political than the paths taken by high-profile individuals like Barbara Castle or Shirley Williams.

This book, then, is a vital illumination of the hidden corners of history and culture. A mix of fiction, memoir and interviews, its contents are moving, humorous, frank and always fascinating.

Behind-the-scenes accounts of Machynlleth's Centre for Alternative Technology and the establishment of a women's refuge in Cardiff, and Barbara Michaels' contribution to the neglected history of Wales' Jewish communities, form a vibrant backdrop against which more personal stories unfold.

The detail in these essays brings to life a different era: political meetings in which "everyone smoked then", the instantly recognisable rock, glam and folk songs that soundtracked these years, and the "brown and orange" colour scheme in which Kate Cleaver paints her recollections, where a comical beginning drops into the racism of the era and the sacrifices made by wives and mothers – and fathers – in hard times. Elsewhere, there are the Laura Ashley peasant dresses fondly remembered by many contributors, the scratchy school uniforms recalled less fondly, and the hot pants and miniskirts, nylon overalls, American Tan tights, or immaculate lipstick and orange spray-tan worn by others. There is the 1976 summer of drought and hosepipe bans, and the 1979 Winter of Discontent. There are the rented colour tellies showing *Carry On...* films, *Whicker's World*, or news coverage of industrial strife and the fast-rising face (and still nightmarishly evocative voice) of Margaret Thatcher.

Mentions of Britain's initial joining of the EU – or EC as it was then – and the sense of expansion and inclusion that some contributors took from it, highlight just what a different time this was. The social instability and industrial conflicts of the Seventies, however, sound an unsettling note of warning throughout the memories of emancipation and discovery that also mark the decade. This overall feeling is captured in pieces like Catrin Gerallt's on 1970s Cardiff, where she describes the era as a blend of bad taste, casual racism and sexism, with a counterposed push for "equality and acceptance".

For many women, these tensions seem to have characterised the Seventies, squeezed between the "everything goes" of the Sixties and the Eighties' individualism and division. In Eluned Evans' contribution, her mother's memories of the Great Depression feed into sympathy for the industrial struggles of the decade, along with sharp analysis of their underlying causes. Carolyn Lewis' account of the intimate, obsessive impact of the 1976 drought on domestic labour and childcare – and of individual betrayal in the midst of a struggling community – is a harbinger perhaps of the "greed is good" individualism that would sweep the country's politics and culture in the decade to come.

The Seventies were bookended by different expectations and possibilities for women. How did this growing freedom and opportunity manifest in the choices offered to women in Wales? While the prospect of a job at Woolworths or as a secretary remained – usually with the expectation that this would only be temporary before the "real" work of marriage and motherhood – the expansion of free higher education to the working class offered many women a path to new experiences. Rona Laycock recalls how her working-class parents "believed Britain was changing" and that education in particular would offer better life chances for their children; they "saw no reason why I should not become an engineer, nurse, teacher or train driver". Conversely, other working-class women, like Sue Bevan, were still shooed away from the idea of university by careers advisors, teachers or their own family. Bevan challenges these assumptions spectacularly in her story, becoming "the first in [her] family to go to university, and [...] go on to do a Master's degree, to lecture at university and to run [her] own business."

These essays illustrate the broad range of 1970s political activity, including Welsh language activism and the peace movement, much of which still resonates in contemporary Wales. As illustrated here, these were both political and personal concerns: Sue Jenkins' vivid portrayal of her schooldays captures the smooth integration of outside struggles for which Welsh nationalists and language campaigners were jailed. In 'A View Like That', Rhiannon Lewis immerses the reader in intimate knowledge of the Welsh landscape and a journey made familiar over generations, echoed in detailed diary entries, all of which feed into a "growing consciousness of what it means to be Welsh". The intrusion into this placid landscape of volatile undercurrents – the politics and direct action of the adult world, and how easily it is absorbed by young adults – identifies language and identity as one of the "minute challenges of self-expression" that teenagers must grapple with as we grow.

For the teenage Sue Williams in 'Chwarae Teg', the central place of rugby within Welsh culture and identity becomes a site of feminist struggle over rules and expectations for young women. Generational differences, conflicts and challenges are a recurring theme in these stories: a younger generation's rebellious restlessness versus an older generation's deference, and the experience of having to rely on peers or personal resources upon realising that older authorities could not always offer you stability, protection or even a fair hearing.

Liz Jones' beautiful piece 'Don't Ask for the Moon' opens with a portrait of Welsh café culture: young people discussing books, film and music – and politics – in exactly the ways that young working-class people are considered incapable of by mainstream politicians. While other contributors found escape and empowerment through university, for Jones this is delayed, and her interregnum illustrates the limited horizons for those left behind, and the sexism and homophobia that limited these spaces even further. This narrow material world, however, is contrasted with the expansive social and cultural horizons enabled by immersion in books and film, the pursuit of working-class glamour, and the escapism allowed by all these things, even if physical escape is temporarily or permanently thwarted.

For Sheila Kitrick, too, education as escape route came later in life, through balancing mature studentship with single motherhood. Her picaresque journey, anchored by commitment to both education and her children, eventually allows her to start a "new life" in Paris. In her similarly striking piece, Sue Davies describes how "[t]he girls in my class were destined for University or motherhood but both seemed like prison sentences to me". She opts instead for an alternative career and gives a fascinating account of her time at sea, during "a time of momentous change in British Shipping, at the cusp between the old ways and the new."

Feminism was one of the "new ways" that spread during the Seventies, bringing in equal pay, changes in the workplace, birth control and greater sexual freedom, but how did it play out in places like Wales? Nic Hafren comments that her father, born in 1930, was "a gentleman sexist which is perhaps the most difficult to identify and the hardest to combat." The stories here deal with both direct activism and feminism's more subtle effects in changing social expectations or allowing individual women themselves to expect, attempt and demand something different. Ruth Dineen's essay opens with her attempt to bridge the gender and generation gap through sharing Germaine Greer's *The Female Eunuch*, but notes how women's magazines also provided political coverage in among the sex and style sections.

As the sexual liberation set in motion by the Sixties took its time to take hold, shocking attitudes persisted towards unmarried or underage pregnancy, told here through stories of scandal, seclusion and forced adoption. Ruth Dineen's 'A Peculiar Pregnancy' illustrates the unfairness faced by young unmarried mothers, as well as the sometimes surprising support to be found in her mother and baby home. Liz Vining's 'Concealment' also addresses the loneliness of unplanned pregnancy and lack of support from a straight-laced society, compared with the solidarity she discovers among the nascent women's movement. Her piece touches on the complexities of social mobility that are so often only discussed in detached academic analyses.

When Carolyn Thomas leaves Wales for university, as told in 'Ch-ch-changes', the alteration of worlds is embodied in alien landscape and architecture as she explores a new realm of theory, culture, sexual fluidity and freedom. Her subsequent return to Wales occasions a further kind of alienation as "everything was changing" in the wider world while, back home, "nothing had changed". She notes how a reluctance to discuss divergent sexualities, combined with a lack of positive representation in pop culture, could leave the liberated less able to communicate with both parents and friends, "adopting an enigmatic attitude to avoid revealing too much".

The keeping of secrets is, of course, often in vain, as community closeness – or gossipy nosiness – ensures that such secrets end up at best intimately shared, or at worst becoming common knowledge. Sue Bevan documents the lack of power and agency of young women in the face of parental, medical and legislative authority, but also shows how secrets, once told, can bring comfort and support through the acknowledgement of shared experiences. In 'Secrets', Philippa Guest explores the tension between intellectual education and the lack of emotional and sexual education in Welsh communities, reinforced by the decade's particular climate of sexual mores, culminating in the intrusion of this repressed knowledge through the downfall of the Bishop of Llandaff. Some secrets don't matter, while some do – but why, and who decides?

Many of the women here felt resolved or resigned to putting up with male violence and intransigence, sexist attitudes, harassment and assault, but they often later gained the confidence and support to object to or actively challenge it. Sue Sky's account of the Cardiff Women's Action Group records the frequent gulf between middle-class activists and the subjects of their activism. It also reminds us that fundraising and bureaucracy for political projects were a different proposition in the days before the internet – but not at all impossible to master. Sky powerfully reveals the practical work and collaboration behind political ambitions and grand pronouncements, and her commitment to centring women themselves in changing their circumstances and providing direct emotional support, rather than acting as a detached saviour.

From alternative communal living in west Wales to a Saturday job in Woolworths, the women here remember new opportunities but also the persistent restrictions of their positions. Actor Sue Jones-Davies' tales of Seventies showbusiness illustrate the peculiar sexist (as well as racist and homophobic) streak that ran through the decade's art and culture: although iconic 1970s productions like *Jesus Christ Superstar* and *Life of Brian* attracted controversy for their rebellious boundary-pushing, they did little to challenge other reactionary conventions.

Similarly, Rose Simpson notes how the decade's radical counter-culture, which inspired many city-dwellers to chase bohemian idylls in west Wales, was not automatically feminist and could unthinkingly reproduce older oppressions, like gender inequalities in division of labour. In 'From Psychedelia to Reality', an inside story of "getting it together in the country", Simpson describes the romantic allure of the Welsh landscape – from the traditional "glamour of Welsh bardic culture and its ancient language", to the more modern dream of a simple life away from the city. But she also shows, as the title suggests, the practical demands and complications of achieving this: the messy meshing of radical politics and local direct action, her own changing identities and definitions, from musician to mother, and her eventual integration into a vibrant local culture and community.

Christine McLennan's 'CAT' forms a useful companion piece to Simpson's, documenting life at the small-scale but deeply innovative Centre for Alternative Technology. Wales' radical tradition of alternative living and green energy is another neglected history which might now, as we face the threat of climate change, offer a path to a more sustainable future. McLennan herself draws these parallels between past and present: "[the 1970s] energy crisis, power cuts, the miners' strikes. It was just dawning on people – the impact that our use of fossil fuels was having on the environment". Her account shows too how differences of class can be significant even within lifestyles based around community, adventure and escape, as well as how language can be both bridge and barrier.

In 'Two Lives', Virginia Isaac recounts another move to Wales from outside, leaving studenthood in Surrey for a farm in the Brecon Beacons. Her commitment to learning the foundations of farm work and taking it seriously engendered acceptance and support from the locals, leading to a self-sufficiency that seems more solidly integrated than that found in CAT. In a community largely insulated from wider political strife – even from the ubiquitous power cuts – she eventually founds Brecon Carreg bottled water, an enterprise which takes her from a simple life dealing with the immediate demands of land and livestock to negotiating with supermarket suppliers and multinational executives. In this and the preceding two stories, what becomes clear is that Wales is not a blank canvas for artists and adventurers from inside or out – but if newcomers engage with what's there on its own terms, showing willingness to learn, then initial differences, tension or hostility need not solidify into an alienating divide.

Meanwhile, more seemingly frivolous or superficial subcultures – from Laura Ashley to punk hairdressing – offered support, inspiration, guidance and confidence to young women looking to find their way in the adult world. Like many subcultural upheavals, punk took its time to reach Wales, but Nic Hafren beautifully documents its arrival in 'Torn Dresses and Rebel Rules'. She recalls the transformative power of the cosmetic ("A mouse could step in and emerge in the cascaded glory of a crazy coloured peacock"), the political power of discovering common experiences across gender, racial and sexual lines, and the cultural power of music as a gateway to art and literature.

Gillian Drake's 'Laura and Me' is a meditation on Laura Ashley, the iconic Welsh fashion house. Now often derided as "milkmaid dresses", the brand nonetheless defined a certain aspect of the Seventies, and this piece illustrates the meaning and significance to be found in the ostensibly trivial. Although fashion is thought of as purely consumption and aesthetics in relation to women, here we see them as entrepreneurs (Ashley herself) and as retail and production workers, but in a "family" environment rather than one of hierarchical exploited labour. Strikingly, the accounts given here are full of well-remembered details of these dresses – colours, textures, falls and frills – showing them as treasured objects that enabled pride in the wearing, variously granting women the ability to securely take part in social occasions, escapist emulation of literary heroines, and democratically affordable beauty.

A similar atmosphere can be found in Jane Salisbury's 'The Wonder of Woolworth', in which a Saturday job – for many women, our first taste of formal employment and an independent income – instils pride and a feeling of maturity and modernity. It also plants the seeds of later feminism, as it reveals the iniquities that mean women earn less than men and married women work a "double shift" of wage labour and unpaid domestic care. The supervision by older women of younger women's dress and conduct works on similar lines to "Mrs Kay" in Lynne Parry-Griffiths' subsequent piece, but in this workplace solidarity triumphs over hierarchy: "My memory is one of collective sociability [...] with older full-time employees looking out for us Saturday girls". Salisbury concludes with a glimpse of her old workplace's current incarnation as a soulless Poundland, "pumping out tinny Musak and with none of the social interactions and polite etiquette that characterised Woolies." "Woolworths [...] is now a Poundland" strikes the same note of melancholy with which Max Boyce, marking the 1970s shift for men from manual labour to a service economy, sang *The pit-head baths is a supermarket now* in 'Duw, It's Hard'.

In 'Painting the Beauty Queens Orange', Lynne Parry-Griffiths evokes a relatively forgotten slice of life in a piece that encapsulates many of this collection's themes. The kind of beauty contest she describes is in many ways another relic of the sexist Seventies – its contestants compared to livestock at an auction and racehorses in starting stalls, identified by their numbers and reduced at one point to "a smiling line of lipstick". But as the narrator herself shows, this is not the only type of femininity available. Instead it is a chosen one, constructed through clothes, make-up and hairspray worn and applied like uniform or armour, and it can be put on and taken off at will. It constitutes a business and industry for the men that run it – and for Mrs Kay who presides over the girls' preparation, enforcing minutely detailed rules and routines of comportment, speech and behaviour – but the girls who take part can also view it as a validating achievement. The narrator admires their talent, nerve and patience, even as she reflects that "when I'm their age I'll be at university with other things to think about".

Finally, Bridget Taylor's 'The Cure' is a moving piece in which the darkness of institutional restriction, directed by social and medical patriarchy, opens up to the light and expanse of the Welsh landscape. This time there are no preconceived ideas of ancient romance or rural simplicity; the narrator enters Wales without expectations, and is acted upon therapeutically by the sweeping sight of Swansea Bay, the majesty of Oystermouth Castle, and the world's-end feeling of Worm's Head. Like so many of the preceding accounts, however much they have been shaped by trouble, trauma or tragedy, the concluding notes are nonetheless those of defiance, contentedness or ultimate triumph.

In these stories, women emerge from a turbulent decade with memories, motivation, and much to look forward to.

Rhian E. Jones

CONTENTS

CARNIVAL CITY

Catrin Gerallt

Stifling heat, standpipes, language protests and the Rolling Stones – the 1970s was a decade of rebellion, of freedom and fun, before the driven 1980s arrived with its padded shoulders and shameless worship of money.

In 1975, at the age of 18, I voted for the first time ever in the referendum on Europe. Thrilled at the prospect of being Welsh and European, I was studying French and spent the summer at a Belgian-based charity, working with volunteers from Europe and North Africa, making friends with a girl from Rwanda who was a nursing student in Brussels, and with refugees from Pinochet's Chile.

It was a time of expanding horizons, of increasing internationalism and diversity. Of hot summers and, for me, of sunlit optimism.

As a Welsh speaker, growing up in 1960s Cardiff had been a confusing experience. There were around a hundred children at Bryntaf, the only Welsh school in the city, bussed from the suburbs in stuffy dinner vans with rough metal floors smelling of grease and gravy spilt from the metal food containers which they carried to school from the council's central kitchens.

My mother was from Pembrokeshire and my father's family from New Quay in Ceredigion, so we spoke Welsh at home. Bryntaf was a warm and happy extension of my close-knit family, but outside school, hardly anybody I knew spoke Welsh. We had Jewish neighbours as we lived near to the synagogue on Cathedral Road: Mrs Jessiman, who lived opposite and who let me play with her china figurines, and Mrs Samuels on the corner, who opened the door to let out clouds of smoke when she fried fish in the kitchen.

My father worked at the College of Music and Drama and had several exotic colleagues like Madame Helga from Hungary who turned up at Christmas in a fur coat, with a bottle of foul-tasting cherry liqueur and Mr Grzbowski who would bring us boxes of cinnamon biscuits and leather purses with the word Praha etched on the flap. In Riverside, my mother taught the children of immigrants from Spain, Greece, India, Pakistan and China.

But, in our stone-built Victorian school in Llandaff, we were in a Welsh cocoon, reciting poems about foxgloves and squirrels, mountains and shining streams. We practised endlessly for the Urdd Eisteddfod, singing about Llanfihangel Genau'r Glyn, Cwm Pennant and the beach at Llangrannog, before going back to play on the scrubby grass of Victoria Park and swim in the chlorinated pools at Guildford Crescent and Llandaff Fields.

Welsh, urban, searching for our roots, as teenagers, we fell easily into the freer, liberal world of the 1970s, benefiting from the protests of the 1960s which had led to the Equal Pay Act, the Sex Discrimination Act and other social reforms.

I didn't know much about the legislation, but I knew that sexism was outrageous and delivered a full-throttled critique of the Miss World contest on the steps of the Central Library when door-stopped by a TV crew while swotting for O-levels. Fortunately, none of my friends witnessed this feminist diatribe on the HTV news. I wasn't particularly political. I loved reading and music: the Stones, Bad Company, Marvin Gaye and anything from Motown. But I took equality as my birthright, never questioning my right to study and work, to mix easily with boys and to have my opinions listened to.

Britain as a whole was looking out at the world. We were travelling more – if only to the Spanish Costas. My mother experimented with exotic dishes like Spaghetti Bolognese and Mexican Chicken and dragged my father out to recently opened Indian restaurants, where he ate egg and chips. A world of new freedoms and experiences.

In 1970, aged 13, I first went abroad without my parents. My three-week stay in France introduced me to teenagers who smoked and lined their eyes with kohl. The family I stayed with fed me raw shellfish, rare steaks, horsemeat and vol-au-vents which, I later found out, were stuffed with calves' brains.

I started wearing eyeliner, coughed my way through a packet of menthol cigarettes and bought the tight-fitting, wide-legged loon pants which, together with my mane of long hair and wooden clogs, made me feel like Jacqueline Bisset, though I probably looked more like a 19th-century bargee.

Inspired by French *joie de vivre*, I read Camus and Sartre and decided that hedonism was far preferable to Chapel puritanism. I planned to settle in the South of France where I would live on Ratatouille and wine and have affairs with men who had the sultry good looks of the smoker in the Gauloises advert.

Before then, I had only been abroad twice. Once to San Sebastian on a two-day sea journey from Southampton and then, in 1969, when I was 11, we drove in my father's battered Humber over the Pyrenees to the thunderous heat of Barcelona, staying in a high-rise apartment overlooking the chemical works at Badalona, which belonged to Pepe, a friend of my parents who had a Spanish restaurant near Mill Lane. We stayed there for a month, getting to know our neighbours and settling into *la vida de la calle*, despite suffering horrendous gastroenteritis when we arrived as my mother, nervous of eating the cured Spanish jamón, fed us ham sandwiches which had been boiling in the boot since we left Cardiff, four days earlier.

I loved languages and wanted to travel, and as the campaigns of the Seventies evolved, my attitude to home became ambivalent. A fluent Welsh speaker, I sympathised with the language campaigners. I wanted bi-lingual signs, a Welsh television channel, equal rights for the language of my parents and grandparents. But some of the activists from the north and west seemed almost as alien to us city kids as the English people who would ask, "Do you really speak Welsh? What's the point?"

Some activists, frustrated by the brick wall response of the Establishment, refused to speak English, regarding all English speakers as oppressors. There was never any serious tension in Cardiff, but in the early 1970s, the Cymry Cymraeg and non-Welsh speakers were two distinct tribes, and when the Welsh swarmed to pubs like the Conway in Pontcanna and the New Ely in Cathays, locals muttered darkly that their pubs were being overtaken by a crowd of hotheads who drank the place dry and talked loudly in Welsh, ruining any chance of a quiet pint in the corner.

But, as Dylan said, the times were a-changing.

Cardiff grew, bringing more people from the north and west to work in the growing media sector, in schools, hospitals and in the expanding local administration.

I heard Welsh spoken on the streets, in shops and pubs, something that never happened when I was younger. And people were starting to mix. Young people discovered the pleasure of mingling with the regulars in working men's pubs, from the Old Arcade in town to the Royal Oak on Broadway; they ventured under the Bute Street bridge to exotic clubs like the Casino and the Casablanca in the Docks, where you could dance in a stifling basement to Gladys Knight and Ike and Tina Turner, funk and soul blasting into the early hours while the ghostly UV light made your bra and pants glow underneath your clothes and the local boys shimmied and spun like Michael Jackson.

1976 had been the year of the drought, the dry reservoirs, the standpipes and outdoor gigs. The year of Status Quo's huge outdoor concert in Cardiff Castle, where our drab, Victorian City took on a West Coast vibe and people started sunbathing in the Castle grounds, kicking off their tight shoes and exposing pale arms and legs.

But the following summers were also, in my memory, drenched in sunshine, culminating in 1978, the year the Eisteddfod came to town. For a week of blazing sunshine, Cardiff became a Carnival City, its parks and civic buildings gleaming under blue skies, diverse communities coming together to celebrate a culture which was, by now, both Welsh and urban.

My friends and I never made it to the official site in Pentwyn. This was before the days of Maes B and Eisteddfod counter-culture, and, while my mother and her friends went off in Welsh flannel shifts to sing a Cerdd Dant setting of Dic Jones' 'Hymn to Autumn', we joined the free and easy unofficial fringe opposite the Halfway in Llandaff Fields.

Young people from all over Wales packed into the pub in their jeans and floating Laura Ashley dresses, looking like exotic birds in the grey sea of locals. They spilled out onto the pavements, drinking pints of Brains and lay on the parched grass in the park, singing, playing guitars, planning campaigns and protests.

Welsh was coming to the city – and we Welsh teenagers were beginning to appreciate its diverse, multi-cultural delights.

Cardiff born poet and musician, Geraint Jarman, brought out his album, *Gobaith Mawr y Ganrif*, combining Welsh rock with Reggae; Heather Jones was breaking out of her pure, Welsh folk sound and starting to rock; hit band Edward H. Dafis had brought out their counter-culture album, *Hen Ffordd Gymreig o Fyw*, satirising the Old Welsh way of life. Bands like Tebot Piws and Mynediad am Ddim were bringing quirky words and funky rhythms to the Welsh music scene. One of the new arrivals in Cardiff, bright young poet Siôn Eirian, who sadly died in 2020, won the Crown at the very young age of 24, bringing a fresh, radical flavour to the centuries-old tradition.

By the late 1970s, the battle for bilingual signs had been won, but Welsh needed to move to the era of punk and hip hop, of comedy, drama and hard-hitting documentaries. It was in 1978 that young journalist, Aled Eirug, stood up in the Eisteddfod Pavilion and heckled Secretary of State John Morris, stunning the crowd of carefully coiffed women and men in suits when he railed against the Government's refusal to engage in the debate about setting up a Welsh language television channel.

At last, Welsh was becoming funky, contemporary – and urban. Siôn Eirian had written *Bob yn y Ddinas*, looking at the seamy underbelly of Cardiff life; Dafydd Huws published *Dyddiadur Dyn Dwad*, the story of a hapless Gog let loose in the pubs and clubs of 1970s Cardiff. Cardiff and Valleys-born people were beginning to learn Welsh – enjoying the friendship and close communities which opened up to them.

It was the year Wales won the Grand Slam, we were taking our first, tottering steps towards devolution and, that summer of '78, there was a sense of celebration, a buzz of creativity and a new confidence.

And Cardiff wasn't such a bad place to come home to. The summer of the Eisteddfod, I fell in love with a handsome, long-haired art student who looked like the smoker in the Gauloises advert – but who was actually from Caernarfon, not Cannes. He lived in a ramshackle house in Roath, shared with artists and actors, and we spent hours in his psychedelic room drinking cheap beer and listening to Dylan, discussing Sartre and Surrealism while the blossom drifted down from the trees outside.

Hardly anybody had a car, but one flatmate had a second-hand Mini and, at the weekend, around six of us would pile in and drive to Lavernock where we would sit on the rocks outside the Captain's Wife, blowing the week's budget on Tequila Sunsets and watching the flaming sun disappear behind the island as we skinny-dipped in the murky waters of the estuary.

My art-student boyfriend won a prize at the Eisteddfod for a painting based on a tale from the Mabinogion. I sent my first story off to an Arts Council competition and was Highly Commended. For that hot summer, life seemed ripe with possibilities.

The 1970s was the decade of bad taste, the three-day week and the Winter of Discontent, but I remember it as a time of equality and acceptance. More working-class children were going to university, many of them graduating from the new 1960s comprehensives. In our faded jeans and Indian cotton tops, with our diverse national and regional accents, we were classless, indistinguishable, equal.

We were, of course, living in an ivory tower. Freeloading students; white, privileged and relatively affluent. Beneath the surface, social discord was fermenting, casual racism and sexism were common – as any quick glance at a sitcom of this time will confirm, but living through the Seventies was a gentler, more reflective experience, looking back to the Sixties' hippy values of tolerance, love and peace, before the madly-driven Eighties swept all that away in its frenzied rush for status and success.

We didn't know it, but we were living through the last days of a soft, green era.

It was the year before Margaret Thatcher came to power, a year when the world was changing. But for that long, hot summer, we were still in the Seventies, stretching out our hands, reaching to the new, European future, claiming equality for women and for our language, young and hopeful under a dazzling sun.

THE SOUND OF WATER

Carolyn Lewis

Sleep deprivation can cause many problems. Not just the physical exhaustion but, after a while, you start to question what you've seen or heard. I know, because that's what happened to me. It was the summer of 1976 and the country was in the middle of a drought. I was aware I was bordering on the obsessive, guarding every precious drop of water: scooping out the contents of my daughters' bath, using it to clean floors and toilets and then sloshing it around my garden, hoping I could keep a few flowers, a few vegetables from withering. Water, water, it was all I could think about.

I was sitting propped up in bed, nursing Bethan, my youngest daughter. She was four months old and, at 3.30 in the morning, I heard the sound of running water. I turned, thinking it was rain, hoping that, at last, the heavens had done what they should have done and sent a deluge to the parched ground. No, it wasn't rain, but I could definitely hear running water. I propped my daughter up on my shoulder and walked across to the window. My bedroom overlooked the back garden, and in the thin, silvery moonlight, I saw the bean sticks I'd jammed into the ground, the fragile runner beans dying of thirst. I'd been so optimistic, so enthusiastic about growing vegetables, feeding my children with healthy food. Bethan's sisters, Katie and Jo, had planted sunflower seeds and now the heads of the flowers hung heavy and torpid, needing a downpour to keep them alive. The girls' swing, stuck in the middle of the straw-coloured lawn, wasn't moving, there was no breeze, no movement at all. And yet, there it was, the sound of water.

The drought had lasted for months and, in the following years, I heard 1976 called 'the drought-filled summer'. That's how it felt, too – as if the drought had filled up every day, every hour with the constant battle to find water, to keep it, to use it for the simple chores that made up my life with three young children. I guarded the water, watched over it like a hawk, trying to ensure that every drop was used properly. A coffee lover, I limited myself to two cups a day and I looked forward to those cups, not wanting to lose what became a small luxury. My daughters, as young as they were, didn't understand my obsessive instructions not to spill anything, not to make a mess. That wasn't because I was fanatical about housework, about keeping things clean; it had nothing to do with that. It was simply because there was no water to mop things up, to wash things down. Children adapt quickly and, before long, they got used to sharing the same scummy bath water, taking it in turns to go first whilst it was still clean. They didn't ask me why I used it to wash floors before, finally, using it to try to resurrect the garden. I knew I had no hope of harvesting my beans after months without rain but I reasoned, that even after being used for so many things, I couldn't afford to waste a single drop.

In 1976, no one had bottled water; at least no one I knew. My neighbours were doing the best they could and, like me, they grumbled about the conditions but we simply got on with it. It was no one's fault. Who could we blame? We queued patiently at standpipes with kettles, buckets and anything else we could use, knowing that we'd have to do it all over again the following day.

I knew the drought was taking over my life but I didn't seem able to do anything about it. It became the first thing I thought about when I got out of bed and the last thing on my mind when, after checking the girls were asleep, I crawled back in. A friend said she'd dreamt about having a shower, letting the water run, shampooing her hair, watching the bubbles on her feet and not once thinking about how much water she was using. I didn't have dreams like that. My dreams were of baked gardens, of a lawn, once green, now crackling underfoot. My dreams were full of a glassy sun in an empty blue sky.

Standing in the queue, I heard muttered voices, gossipy voices telling tales about wasteful neighbours, about people not adhering to the rules the rest of us stuck to. I didn't care about any of that. All I cared about was getting through each day, keeping my daughters clean, trying my best to ensure they had enough to eat and, just as importantly, to drink.

It wasn't just the drought but the never-ending heat. There was no respite and it was doubly hard to explain every day to my daughters why I couldn't fill their tiny paddling pool. Each day they asked and each day I had to say no and tell them why. The reason they couldn't paddle in a few inches of cold water didn't seem fair to them. It didn't matter that their friends couldn't do it either. Each day was the same: a long, hot day with queuing, with holding heavy buckets and kettles, trying not to spill one drop on the way back to my home. Another day with lugging dirty water to the kitchen so I could clean the floor, to wipe down high chairs and remove marks left by sticky fingers. That's what the drought had done, it had filled every day.

In 1976 I lived on a residential street in a suburb of Cardiff where the gardens were long and narrow and, from low walls, we all had a view of each other's properties. We commiserated. We grumbled about not being able to water our beans, carrots and flowers. We watched as tiny seedlings withered and died. We wondered about the man at the end of the road. His garden looked greener than ours. Perhaps it had something to do with the fact that his plot was in the shade. He was rarely seen.

That morning, that early morning feed with Bethan's soft head against my shoulder, I knew what I was hearing. It wasn't rain. It was the sound of someone's hosepipe. A hosepipe. A ban had been in place for months. I stood on tiptoe and looked out. There, I saw a movement. The man at the end of the road was watering his garden. He walked slowly, deliberately up and down the rows of runner beans. I saw how intently he watched the rush of water, his gaze fixed on his hosepipe. That was why his runner beans had sprouted red flowers and mine had died. That was why his lettuces were frothy and green. I hated him.

Bethan is 45 now, she has fifteen-year-old twins and I can still remember the anger I felt at hearing the illicit sound of running water in 1976. I've always loathed confrontations, hated any sort of argument, but that day, after queuing for water and carrying it so, so carefully home, I walked around to my neighbour's house and I told him what I'd seen and heard.

I told him of my frustration and my tiredness as I had tried to do the right thing and he hadn't. I told him it was pointless him denying it, his garden was an oasis of green whilst everyone else's was parched, desiccated. He mumbled something; it might have been an apology. I didn't think it was. I stood in front of him. I held Bethan in my arms and Katie and Jo were at my side. Their eyes were wide as I vented my anger. My fury boiled over as I thought of the ways I'd tried to conserve water, to save every tiny drop, to utilise it, to make it count. As my three daughters watched and listened, I told my neighbour that he'd let my children down, he'd let everyone down, that he'd cheated and I would tell people what he'd done, the way he'd done it: secretly, under cover of darkness. I'd shame him. I felt rage like I'd never felt before or since.

A fortnight later, it rained.

WELSH, FEMALE AND JEWISH

Barbara Michaels

The women who belong to the Jewish community in Wales have always played a major part in fields such as literature, medicine, law and the care sector, but by the Seventies there was already an insidious decline in numbers. However, in cities such as Cardiff there was still a thriving Jewish community, meriting two kosher butchers and a delicatessen – even some more rural areas, such as Pontypridd, could boast a kosher butcher. By the Seventies there were the two synagogues in Cardiff which are still in existence today providing both the pivotal hub and the premises around which Jewish life revolves. Minutes of the Cardiff New Synagogue (subsequently renamed Cardiff Reform Synagogue) Ladies' Guild, a women-only volunteer group organising religious, fundraising, social activities, food for the festivals and acts of *tzedakah* (charity) for their meeting on May 12th 1975 refer to 'a number of forthcoming charity events and initiatives such as the Treasure Hunt and annual Garden Party.'

I spoke to some of the Jewish women who are still in Wales today – read their stories below. Others who were here at that time include the Cardiff-born 1970 Booker Prize-winning novelist Bernice Rubens, who died in 2004. Much of Bernice's writing reflects the tight-knit immigrant Lithuanian Jewish community in which she grew up. She is quoted as having said: 'Most of my books are about survival and that is a Jewish area.'

Described by an interviewer from the *London Evening Standard* as 'Exotically swarthy, gypsily beringed, small and plump,' Bernice drew on her Jewish upbringing in novels such as *The Elected*

Member, published in 1969 – the story of a Rabbi's son Norman Zweck who becomes a drug addict at the age of forty-three.

Truda Bell, now in her early seventies, remembers how it was bringing up her son and two daughters in Cardiff, back in the days when there was a thriving Jewish kindergarten:

'On my marriage at the age of 20 I moved to Cardiff, leaving my parents in Manchester so I was without family support, my husband's parents being frail. I had a wonderful sister-in-law and we had children of similar ages. Within a period of 12 months, I had two children, a boy and a girl. As a young mother I looked forward to the day when my eldest could attend kindergarten.

'Two wonderful ladies, one Jewish, Aunty Faye, and one a practising Baptist, Aunty Pam, ran the kindergarten at Cardiff United Synagogue, then in Brandreth Road.

'As Aunty Faye lived around the corner, she collected Jonathan and later his sister from the house before 9 am and returned them at noon, in her distinctive white mini with huge brightly coloured flowers along one side. The other children were collected from home and returned in a minibus. There was a fully equipped kindergarten room on the synagogue premises where the children could play, draw and paint, play with sand and water and do jigsaws.

'There was also a bonus in that Aunty Faye and Aunty Pam taught them Hebrew blessings, which the children learned by heart. On a Friday morning, in preparation for the commencement of the Sabbath on Friday night, one girl would be mummy and light the Sabbath candles saying the blessing, and a boy would be the daddy and say the blessing for bread and wine (in this case, grape juice). All the children joined in and looked forward to their turn to be mummy and daddy.

'By the time my third child was born in 1975 after a gap of five and a half years, my older children were in school. When my daughter was ready to attend kindergarten in September 1978, Aunty Faye was seriously ill, sadly passing away in the October, but Aunty Pam continued in her role until well into the Eighties.

'In its heyday, the kindergarten had 30 children in attendance. Today, the Cardiff Jewish community is so small that the number of children between the ages of 3–5 at any one time can be counted on the fingers of one hand.

'Long gone are the days of the Cardiff Jewish Kindergarten. Now their religious grounding comes from the home alone.'

Doreen Bloom, now in her eighties, was born in Cardiff and has lived there all her life:

'I was brought up at a time when the Cardiff Jewish community was probably at its biggest, numbering around 3,500. We were a close community, around whom most of my social life revolved. With four children, the Seventies saw a very busy time in my life. There were occasions where Jewish children, both in primary and high school, did face some incidents of anti-Semitism, but they were mostly minor.'

Doreen belonged, and still belongs, to Ziona ladies' group. Now known as Cardiff Ziona WIZO, the group is part of the Women's International Zionist organisation which raises money to help underprivileged women and children of all denominations in Israel. An important part of Jewish female society in mid and south Wales today as it was when it was started in the late Sixties, the group was originally titled Young Ziona. Having dropped the 'young' from the title when it became inappropriate to the age of its members, the group still holds regular meetings and fundraising events, albeit on a smaller scale than formerly.

'We used to run quite large fundraising functions – fashion shows and shows starring showbiz personalities such as Alfred Marks and David Jacobs, but, with decreasing numbers of members, this is no longer possible.'

Miranda Kitchener is fourth-generation Welsh:

'My maternal grandparents, my parents, myself and my husband Michael, my daughter and son-in-law – all Welsh, and married at the Cathedral Road synagogue.' She writes:

'My family moved to the city of Cardiff from the nearby beach resort of Porthcawl when I was 16. Many families were doing the same – moving from small towns and villages to the capital so that their children could hopefully meet Jewish partners. Cardiff was thriving with several Jewish youth clubs, a synagogue and shops. A new synagogue was opened in Penylan, an area that many upwardly mobile Jewish families had moved to. When I got married in 1961 the synagogue, in Brandreth Road, was overflowing and on High Holidays seating spilled into the hall behind.

'In 1962 the late Dolly Reuben, Bernice Reuben's mother, invited some young marrieds to a meeting. She was chairman of WIZO and knew all the top brass. She had been running a WIZO group in Cardiff for years and also started a second group for the next age group down. She felt it was time for us youngsters to form our own group (we were in our twenties). Twelve of us got together and Cardiff Young Ziona was born. Several of us are still much involved and have raised many thousands of pounds for women and children of all denominations in Israel. I was the first treasurer. We had a commitment to raise £50 a year and we were terrified.

'Through the Sixties, Seventies and Eighties and up to the present day, Young Ziona (now Cardiff Ziona WIZO) has thrived. Over the years we have organised many functions and I firmly believe that we added greatly to the social and cultural life of Cardiff Jewry. In the synagogue's kitchens, we catered ourselves for functions and put on dinners for up to 200 people with entertainers who were appearing in the local theatres.

'There were also shows organised with our own talented casts. Many lifelong friendships were made then. We worked hard raising money, including on every New Year holding an amazing fancy dress party fuelled with champagne cocktails.'

Despite now living in London, Miranda keeps in close touch with her many friends in Wales via the London branch of Welsh Women's WIZO.

Judy Simove, Miranda's cousin, arrived in Cardiff in 1970 'As a Jewish newly-wed.'

Judy and her husband Maurice celebrated their golden wedding anniversary in 2020. Still living in Cardiff, they are active members in the life of the community:

'Like so many of my female contemporaries at that time, I was an "import". We had come to "join-in-matrimony" some of the local men who had businesses or professions based in the town. I was particularly lucky in that Miranda introduced me to her circle of friends straight away. This is one example of how belonging to a minority group has great advantages. Instant extended family!

'My husband and I purchased a house which, unknown to me at the time, was not only close to the synagogue, but only three doors away from the Rav [1], an Orthodox Rabbi of great religious standing. His wife was quoted as saying: "They are very brave living here!" Now, though I was always proud to be Jewish, my

---

[1] Note: 'Rav' is an alternative word for 'Rabbi.'

adherence to the rules of the faith was far from observant. However, this proximity did not stifle my behaviour. In fact, I did not see the Rav for nearly a year!

'We have three children – two sons and a daughter. Both of our sons were born in that house and later on, when they were about three years old, they were scooped up by the obliging minibus, and taken to the wonderful Jewish kindergarten every week-day.'

Of major importance to the Jewish women doing their utmost to run their homes in accordance with the rules of Jewish Orthodoxy was the availability of meat and poultry killed according to the laws of their religion.

Avril Blasebalk's grandmother Sarah Krotosky and her husband Abe opened their butcher's shop in Pontypridd at the turn of the twentieth century. By the Seventies, owing to insufficient demand in Ponty the shop had already moved to Cardiff, first to Wood Street, then to Bridge Street, where Sarah ran the shop with the help of her sons Gaby and Arnold. Once again, in 1986, an expanding city centre forced a move, this time to City Road, Cardiff, finally closing in January 1992. Now Jewish customers have to rely on fortnightly deliveries from London for their supplies.

THE JLGB

Growing up in Wales in the Seventies, girls were encouraged to join the JLGB – the Jewish Lads and Girls Brigade. The Welsh branch of the Brigade was formed in Cardiff in April 1977, with Laurence Cohen as Captain and Laraine Salaman and Trudi Harris as leaders, all of whom are still living in Cardiff. A couple of years later a junior unit was formed, which is still extremely active. Laurence Cohen writes: 'I remember those years with great fondness as do our children who were born and educated in Cardiff.'

Judy Cotsen is Chair of Pencare, the charity which looks after the Jewish residents of Penylan House, first set up more than 50 years ago to assist those of the Jewish faith needing care. She tells us how much has changed since those early days back in the Seventies:

'It was very different back then from the way it is today. The home was full and was only for Jewish people. Very often there was a waiting list. There was a very large dining room where everyone ate together, it was very much like a retirement home. The residents then would come into the home often in their sixties to enjoy retirement and be looked after. The home was very much the focus of the community.

'Twenty years on, with a diminishing community, the number of people coming into the home was very much reduced. It would have been difficult to survive, so it was decided to take in people who were not Jewish. This was a huge change – but it worked. Everyone mixed well.

'It was, however, the beginning of a huge change. By 2012 the home was struggling, the building needed a lot of work, so it was sold to Linc Housing association who agreed to build us a home within their home where we would have all kosher facilities.

'Nowadays we have very few Jewish residents, partly due to the decrease in the community, families moving away and also older people are now fitter and living a lot longer. We have a number of people in the community well into their nineties living an independent life.

'Penylan House is now very much a nursing home, a world apart from the good old days when the home was an extension of the community.

'Volunteers have always played a big part in the running of the home, but there was no risk assessment or health and safety concerns back then. Volunteers would go into the kitchens and cook for functions, and there were outings for which a volunteer would drive the minibus.'

One of the drivers was **Renee Woolf**, who still organises social events for the handful of Jewish residents, their families and guests. Renee remembers:

'A favourite outing was to Porthcawl, for tea at one of the seafront hotels. There was one occasion when I was the driver when we went to the wrong hotel. I didn't realise what had happened until tea was served – with ham sandwiches! (Jewish dietary regulations do not allow ham to be eaten.) I had to get everyone up and out of their seats to the other venue. On another occasion we were halfway back to Cardiff when we realised we had left one of our wheelchair residents behind, and had to turn round to get her.'

THE CONTINENTALS

Many of the Jewish people who had escaped from Nazi persecution, not only from Germany but from Poland, Czechoslovakia and Lithuania, landed up in Cardiff just before the beginning of World War II. Among them was Doris Moritz, who passed away aged 95. Doris and her husband Alfred, who became Professor of Classics and subsequently Registrar in 1975 at Cardiff University, were among those who came over on the *Kindertransport*. Others, who came later, were Holocaust survivors, rescued from Hitler's death camps. Many stayed in Wales and made their lives here.

Terry Farago, now in her nineties, still lives in Cardiff:

'I was born into a middle-class Jewish family in Budapest. By 1943 there was open anti-Semitism in Hungary. Aware of the escalating threat to their lives, my parents nevertheless delayed leaving until it was too late.'

Herded onto cattle trucks filled with others in the same situation, the family were sent to Auschwitz concentration camp. Months of being in 'A living hell, starving and miserable' followed. Work saved her from the gas chambers and eventually, in May 1945, Terry was freed. She went back to Budapest, married and lived there for ten years before correspondence with a refugee girl living in Cardiff led her, with her husband and young son, to emigrate to Wales. She has been living in Cardiff ever since.

Holocaust survivors **Anka Bergman** and **Edith Salter** both escaped from Auschwitz and became part of the Jewish community in Cardiff. Edith passed away in 2011 and Anka two years later. Their stories are told in *Fragments*, by Frances Rapport, former Professor of Qualitative Health Research at Swansea University, who is now living in Australia and a Professor at Sydney University.

I was privileged to meet Anka when I moved to Wales in 1996. She was always happy and smiling, despite any health problems as she got older. To me she epitomised the spirit of those who survived the atrocities perpetuated during the Holocaust. It was, I guess, that indomitable spirit that enabled them to survive.

When I arrived in Cardiff twenty-five years ago, I didn't know a soul other than my uncle and aunt, Dr Harry Rapport and his wife Gwen, my late father's sister, who then lived in Brandreth Road, but I felt at home immediately. There may not be as many of us here as there were back in the Seventies, but for those of the Jewish faith who live in Wales, there still remains a wonderful sense of community – of belonging. Although much has changed since the Seventies, that is still the same.

I must stress that by far the largest number of the Jewish community in Wales are in the south Wales area, the majority of these living in Cardiff, which is where I live, and it is the Jewish community in that area which is the subject of my article. There are also small groups in north and mid Wales, but to the best of my knowledge there are no synagogues still in existence. An excellent source of information on these areas can be found in *The Jews of Wales* by Cai Parry-Jones.

The JLGB (Jewish Lads and Girls Brigade) in Cardiff, 1975, following the Brigade's return from summer camp. There were only three girls in the Brigade at that time up until a junior unit was formed in 1979, when more joined.

Telephone : 28797

Est. over 70 years   Wales' "only" Jewish Butcher

A. KROTOSKY
48 BRIDGE STREET - CARDIFF

EVERYONE "MEATS" EVERYONE IN KROTOSKY'S, WHERE WE TRY TO DO THE IMPOSSIBLE IMMEDIATELY, ALTHOUGH MIRACLES TAKE A LITTLE LONGER

Only the finest quality Beef, Welsh Lamb and Veal available. Our Poultry is Fresh Daily

Smoked Beef		Continental
Sausages	Stockist of	Worsht
Worsht	Bloom's	Viennas
Selection of	Frohwein's	Saveloys
Delicatessen	Hebrew National	Frankfurters
Stocked		Liver Worsht

WEEKLY TERMS

Back in the Seventies, observant Jews bought all their meat and poultry from the Jewish butcher's shop Krotosky. Nowadays everything has to be ordered from London, with deliveries every other week.

21

Cardiff Ladies
Luncheon Club

Many of the ladies who attended meetings of Cardiff Ladies Lunch Club in the Sixties and Seventies were members of the Jewish community. In the larger photograph (top left) you can see seated on the right my aunt Gwendoline Rapport (my late father's sister). Auntie Gwen's husband was a doctor – Dr. Harry Rapport. They were married just before the start of WWII, and immediately after they were married my uncle, a medical officer in the Army, was sent out with the Forces fighting in Egypt. They did not see one another for four and a half years. My aunt was a qualified pharmacist and when the war ended and he came back to open a practice in Cardiff, she worked alongside him, making up the medicines he prescribed in the back room of their house. She was a great character and, although approaching her eighties when I arrived here in 1996, was immensely helpful in introducing me into the Jewish community.

Jewish weddings can be quite formal. Lynne and Philip were married at Cathedral Rd synagogue in 1969, with a reception afterwards at Bindles in Barry. The reception was originally to be in City Hall, but had to be altered when it became unavailable owing to arrangements for the investiture of Prince Charles.

DEAREST MOTHER AND DAD

Eluned Evans

This is the story of my mother – an American who married a Welshman and came to make her life in Wales. The story is told through the letters she wrote to her parents, especially those she wrote between 1970 and 1980.

Phyllis Kinney was born on the 4th of July 1922 in Pontiac, Michigan, but has spent over 64 years of her life in Wales. She was the only child of James and Lois Kinney and was always extremely close to both her parents. Her first connection with Wales was made when she went to Michigan State University to study music. It was there that she was introduced to Welsh folk songs, learning to sing them in English, by her music teacher Gomer Llewelyn Jones. She was later awarded a fellowship to study voice at the Juilliard School of Music in New York, and became friendly with the family of Rev. Cynolwyn Pugh, minister of the Welsh Church of New York.

It was Rev. Pugh who, in 1947, encouraged Phyllis to come to the UK to become an opera singer. He gave her introductions to a number of musicians and conductors, including Sir John Barbirolli, as well as to members of the London Welsh community. It was through Barbirolli that she joined the Carl Rosa Opera Company and through Janet Evans, with whom she stayed in London, that she met the Welshman she would marry barely a year after she arrived here – Meredydd Evans. One year later, their only child, a daughter, was born. They were married for nearly 67 years, until Merêd's death in 2015 and, other than the ten years between 1950 and 1960 (eight of which were spent back in America), they lived their whole married life in Wales.

Phyllis had been brought up in a very different world, living a cosmopolitan life in an affluent country. In post-war middle-class America it was taken for granted that a woman would eventually marry and raise a family. This was particularly so in the late 1940s and 1950s once the men returned from the war in Europe and later the Korean War.

This domestic role was not what Phyllis had planned for herself. She wanted to be a professional opera singer. Although her feelings changed somewhat once she married and had a child, she found that trying to juggle family and domestic responsibilities with a professional career came with enormous challenges. It was not until the 1970s, and all the changes that decade brought about, that Phyllis began to find her 'voice' again and establish a place in her own right within Welsh culture.

Throughout her years abroad, Phyllis wrote regularly to her parents back home giving them news of her activities and those of the rest of the family including her daughter and grandchildren. The 1970s was both an exciting and a challenging decade for her and the family with changes in almost every aspect of their lives and this was reflected in her letters to her 'Dearest Mother and Dad...'

Reading these letters home, a number of themes emerge which reflect both Phyllis' personal life and the changes within wider society. Domestic life with its juggling of work commitments and family responsibilities, increasing engagement with Welsh culture and language, an enduring interest in American and British politics, and the struggle to find time for personal and research interests all made regular appearances in the letters.

In 1970s Britain, domestic work was considered by many to be menial and inconsequential – an unacknowledged and unregarded background noise to the lives of most men. Politics, industry and the media were, with a few notable exceptions, the preserve of men. Women were rarely encouraged to take part and, when they did, were often made to feel unwelcome. It took courage for women to stand up and make their voices heard – and particularly so for women over the age of 40.

It is clear from Phyllis' letters throughout the 1970s that she was, like so many other women, much more than 'just a housewife'. She was the painter and decorator, cleaner, cook and bottle washer, hostess to hordes of visitors, nursemaid to her grandchildren and nurse to the adults. She was also the family's 'life admin' manager dealing with bills, arranging repairs, dealing with the utility companies and looking after the finances. On top of all this, she was also teaching in Cardiff, Bangor and Caerleon, as well as becoming more involved in research work and Welsh language radio and television. Not surprisingly, the frustration of trying to keep all these balls in the air occasionally spilled over into her letters to her parents.

14 Feb 1975 – 'I've spent this week working hard, in part to make up the lessons and lectures I missed last week [she had been ill]. And sometimes it seems as if so much of life is spent these days just "arguing" with people – trying to get them to come and fix the TV or returning something that doesn't work properly. Honestly, I said to Merêd, if some of these people who are supposed to make things or fix things came to me for voice lessons and I did as bad a job on them as they do on mending my things —- they'd all be hoarse for the rest of their lives!!'

In 1969 Phyllis became a grandmother for the first time and from that point on the juggling act intensified. I had married a student at Sussex University and in June had given birth to a daughter, Kathryn. Over the next decade the support my mother gave us was immense as she regularly, and uncomplainingly, came to our rescue by providing childcare whenever it was needed and giving us occasional, much needed, financial support.

13 May 1970 – 'Here I am on a train again, going to Brighton this time, ... I had hoped to have a week at home but Eluned wanted to bring the baby back to Cardiff while Peter's exams are on as she keeps waking up in the middle of the night and they're both a bit haggard. And since she's got my car which is 14 years old – and since the baby is so mobile now – she asked me if I would come down on the train and drive back with her. So here I am, on a train again for the 6th time in 4 weeks.'

Phyllis often found herself, suddenly and without warning, with a houseful of family and friends to feed and accommodate. My parents' house was a fairly standard 3 bedroom end-of-terrace but it was not unusual for there to be anything between 4 and 13 people visiting at any one time. My father was a very sociable man who came from a large family – and by the middle of 1971 they had two grandchildren, Kathryn and Gareth, so when we came to stay it meant finding room for four of us.

13 October 1971 – 'Well, the "tumult and the shouting dies, the captains and the kings depart" and this is the first free 5 minutes I've had since I last wrote you. Honestly!!! For the past 10 days we have had Eluned, Kathryn, Gareth, Jac and Lil (Merêd's brother and sister-in-law) all staying in the house, and then last weekend we also had Peter [Eluned's husband] and 2 friends of his ... all staying here! I nearly went mad. And I've never been so exhausted in all my life. However they have all finally left, and Merêd and I are alone in the house for the first time in 5 weeks... I figured that Merêd and I have been on our own in this house exactly 3 weeks out of the last 6 months – since April 15. And they don't come one at a time either. Last Thursday while Jac and Lil were staying with us, Merêd's cousin Francis turned up because he had never met Jac so I asked him to stay to dinner

and while we were having dinner – 6 adults and 2 kids called in to see us and 15 minutes later 2 more people came. And it's been like that for the past few weeks.'

Even at the end of the 1970s, this was still the case although by then my parents had bought and renovated a house in Cwmystwyth, near Aberystwyth. It was, clearly, enjoyable but exhausting!

18 July 1978 – 'By now we have settled back into our normal life – not quite as busy as term time but there's still plenty to do. And of course in the fine weather everybody decides to go for a drive in the country and visit Merêd and Phyllis! Last Sunday was a glorious day and 13 different people called. I was up and down every minute dishing out tea and biscuits.'

Economic upheaval and industrial action became part of life for everyone during the 1970s and its effects became a regular theme in Phyllis' letters. She was extremely sympathetic to those on strike as she understood the kind of financial pressures many people were facing. She was 7 years old when the Great Depression hit America in 1929 and, although her father managed to keep his job, it was at a greatly reduced wage, which led to the family house being repossessed as he couldn't keep up the mortgage payments. However that didn't make it any easier to live with the disruption throughout the 1970s.

8 Dec 1970 – 'Well it's all rush, rush, rush these days with Xmas coming … and in the midst of it all the electricity workers are having a go-slow, which means that we are having power cuts at the most awkward times! And with no warning whatever. Yesterday I was up teaching at the Training college when the lights and electric power went off at 2:40 and didn't come back

on again until 5:00. And then when I came home to get Merêd's dinner, there was another cut between 5.15 and 7.00 p.m. And we are only just getting over the garbage men's 5-week strike.

In January 1971 the postal workers went on strike and it meant that there were no letters being written to, or received from, Phyllis' parents between 20 January and 7 March 1971. This was particularly hard for Phyllis because her parents' health was quite poor at that time. The only way of communicating with America during that period was via the telephone, which was prohibitively expensive, or by telegram.

The miners went on strike twice during the 1970s – from 9 January to 28 February in 1972 and again during much of February 1974. In addition, January 1974 saw the introduction of the Three-Day Week. All of these figured large in Phyllis' letters to her parents, who were clearly worried about the situation here.

14 Feb 1972 – 'We are in the midst of a miners' strike (in which I must say I think the miners are fully justified as they have been very shabbily treated by the government) as the strike is now entering its 7th week it's really beginning to bite. The power stations have so little coal left that they are having to ration electricity by making massive power cuts every day. Today it is the turn of our district and we are without power today from 10 – 2.00 and from 9.00 – midnight tonight. Fortunately, we have a gas cooker which means that we can cook and make hot-water bottles to clutch in the icy atmosphere; but although our central heating is gas-fired, it is unfortunately pumped by electricity so that when we have a power cut, the heat goes off. But we are considerably better off than those people whose homes are all-electric, which includes Eluned. She and Peter and the children have all had this exceedingly unpleasant flu which is

going around, and they couldn't shake it off. So on Wednesday after I finished teaching I drove down to Brighton and brought them all back with me. I think they will probably be better off here until this strike is settled because in their all-electric flat they have no means of alternative heating or cooking when the electricity goes off.'

16 December 1973 – 'We on fixed salaries have sat here and watched the government carefully controlling any raise in wages while allowing prices to skyrocket – and last year many companies who were allowed by the government to raise their prices made record profits. And because there is so little profit-sharing with the workers here, very little of those profits went to the workers in extra wages. So of course, there is great bitterness. And it is, as usual, the general public that will suffer. So far Merêd and I have been OK, but if the gas men go on strike I don't know what we'll do. We don't know whether Eluned, Pete and the kids will get home for Christmas because the train men are running a go-slow; they can't hire a car because of the petrol shortage; and they, poor lambs, have only electric heating so when there are power cuts there is no way for them to keep warm. Oh, well, I suppose we'll survive somehow!'

10 January 1974 – 'It is true that things are very bad here economically and I think we may be in for a recession. The Prime Minister, a very stubborn man, has obviously decided on a real showdown with the unions, even if he throws millions of innocent people out of work to do it... For what it's worth (and I'm usually wrong!!) I think Ted Heath will have to settle with the miners, very much against his will, because the general public's sympathy is with them – they have a dangerous and unpleasant job which is now vital to the country's welfare in view

of the oil crisis – and if Heath called an election now as he would like to do, it is by no means certain that he would be re-elected. In fact, if the Labour Party were not in such disarray, the Tories wouldn't stand a chance. Let us pray that somehow, somewhere, someone will act responsibly and get this country on the right road once again.'

In 1973, my father had left his job as Head of Light Entertainment for BBC Wales and taken up a post at Cardiff University's Extra Mural Department as a lecturer. This changed both my parents' lives for the better. My father was much happier – doing a job he loved – and they had more time to follow their interests both separately and together.

From 1974 onwards life became more settled for Phyllis because she and Merêd had sold the Cardiff house and moved to a small flat in Llanrhymni on the outskirts of the city. They had used the money from the house sale to buy the house in the village of Cwmystwyth in mid Wales. They bought the house with the intention of moving there once Merêd retired, and spending weekends and holidays there in the meantime. Their peace was soon shattered however, when, in July 1975, only months after the renovation of the Cwmystwyth house was finished, my marriage ended and, at my parents' suggestion, I moved to live there with the two children. The move turned out to be a positive one for all of us although it meant more travelling back and forth between Cwmystwyth and Cardiff and increased financial pressures for Phyllis and Merêd.

20 Oct 1975 – 'Well, here we are, back in Cardiff again. The autumn season is now beginning to be very busy indeed ... especially as I am now fully into my teaching in my three different jobs. On Monday morning we drive back from Cwmystwyth;

Tuesday I leave for the [Cardiff] University at 9.00 and finish at 3.00; Wednesday I am at Cardiff Training College from 10.00 – 4.00 (with no lunch break); Wednesday night I lecture on folk music from 7.30 – 9.30; Thursday I teach at Caerleon from 10.00 till 3.30 (again, without a break); and on Friday morning I am at the University from 9.30 till noon. So I am really busy, and of course as soon as I finish on Friday we high-tail it down to Cwmystwyth to be with Eluned and the children.'

Reading the letters written throughout the 1970s it is noticeable that the tone becomes more relaxed and playful as time goes on and there is a sense that Phyllis was reshaping her domestic role to make more room for her personal and professional interests. It's also very clear that her relationship with her grandchildren became a very important part of her life. Her letters are chatty and full of wonderful descriptions of the children and their activities. This description of the children when Kathryn was just 3 years and Gareth barely 1 year old is typical of Phyllis' descriptive style and her desire to keep her parents in touch with their great grandchildren's progress.

5 June 1972 – 'When I tell you that Eluned and the children have been here with us for almost a fortnight, you will realise why you haven't heard from me … [when he first arrived] poor little Gareth took one look at all of us and decided he did not want to belong to our family or have anything to do with us. He was cutting some very nasty teeth and he yelled bloody murder for about two hours after being put to bed, and then just to show who was boss, he woke up at 4.30 in the morning and yelled some more. Fortunately Kathryn behaved very well, but poor old Gareth had a very trying weekend – to say nothing of the rest of us. By Tuesday the teeth had come through and by Wednesday

he was back to his usual sweet easy-going temperament. He is just beginning to walk – that is, he walks everywhere if he has just one finger to support him, and he walks around the furniture as long as he has a single corner to hang on to, but he is still a little shy of letting go completely. Mind you, he's a big boy, so that when he falls there is a lot to get bruised. He weighs as much as Kathryn and is nearly as tall! And he is incredibly beautiful. His hair is dark brown and curling and his eyes are dark sapphire blue and he has a dimple. Kathryn is just darling. She seems to have got through that very difficult patch and is delightful to have around. Her hair is very long now and still very very blonde and beautifully curly, and her eyes are grey, and she is such a loving little girl. She is crazy about music and loves to come and listen to my singing lessons and will sit there as good as gold. She is full of mischief of course and has her naughty moments but she has matured a lot in the last few months.'

The 1970s was also the period during which Phyllis began, most intensively, to engage with, and contribute to Welsh language and culture, as her letters reflect.

22 March 1972 – 'I am beginning to publish some of the Welsh nursery school songs I composed for that TV series for the under-fives. They will appear (some of them at any rate) in a magazine for Welsh teachers and then I hope to collect about 20 of them in a book [*Caneuon Chwarae Cyf. I* in 1972 and *Cyf. II* in 1974]. And it's a really time-consuming job getting them ready for publication: making very simple piano arrangements for teachers with no special musical training, adding guitar chords for those who can't play the piano at all, copying out carefully and checking spelling etc. But I hope they will be useful to Welsh teachers as there is almost nothing of that type available in Welsh.'

9 July 1973 – 'A week from today I leave for Aberystwyth to spend a fortnight on this crash course in Welsh – and I do hope I come back spouting Welsh like a native because I have been invited to take part in a radio quiz on music – in Welsh!!! – and there will be a pilot programme the day before we fly to America and if I'm good enough they will make a series of it. So keep your fingers crossed that my Welsh will improve to the necessary standard as I would really love to do it.'

By the end of the 1970s, Phyllis' Welsh was so good that she was taking part in a wide variety of Welsh language programmes on both radio and television, including the music quiz on the radio which proved very popular. She was also adjudicating in eisteddfodau and writes that during the 1976 Urdd Eisteddfod, she adjudicated a number of competitions in Welsh. In the same letter she mentions that she had been interviewed for an article in the *Radio Times*. 1976, of course, was the Bicentennial year and Phyllis wrote and presented a series of Welsh language programmes on BBC Wales called *Y Tir Newydd*.

11 May 1976 – 'Next Tuesday we start recording the first two programmes in my TV series and we will be doing two a week for the next 5 weeks so there is lots to do.'

Phyllis' research interests were also developing during this period and would eventually bear fruit with her book, published in 2011, *Welsh Traditional Music*. In a letter of 1973, she mentions work she and Merêd were undertaking for The Welsh Folk Museum at St Fagans. It was later published as *Caneuon Llafar Gwlad Cyf. 1 /Songs from Oral Tradition Vol. 1*.

30 April 1973 – 'Speaking of folk music, Merêd and I were given a most interesting job which we started over the Easter weekend.

The research dept. of the Welsh Folk Museum has been collecting folk songs on tape for years. Now they have decided to publish a book of some of the best of them, but of course they must first be written down ... Our job is to listen to the tapes of these singers – some of them are very old – and write down in music, what they are singing. Then we compare it to the existing transcription to make it true to the singer and yet easy to read. Hard work but very satisfying!!'

Merêd's letters to Phyllis had always been in English (with the odd word or phrase in Welsh) but by 1973 he was writing to her in Welsh with the occasional explanation of a word in English. From then on almost all their letters to each other were in Welsh only. In August 1976 Phyllis was delighted with a letter Merêd wrote to her, in Welsh, from the National Eisteddfod while she was on a visit to see her parents. Translated, it reads:

4 August 1976 – 'The world and his wife have been asking after you and praising your television programmes. "Phyllis has really carved out a niche for herself" said one. But honestly, there have been loads of people singing your praises. Last night John Gwilym and I had dinner together and he was remarking how high the standard of your Welsh is.'

Phyllis grew to see herself as someone who could be a bridge between Wales and America – interpreting Wales to Americans and America to the Welsh. This was particularly so during the 1970s with the era of Nixon and Vietnam in America and industrial strife and economic chaos in the UK. Throughout her life, Phyllis has always maintained a lively interest in the politics of both her adopted country and the country of her birth. In the letters to her parents she often wrote about the political situation in the USA and her feelings about the political direction in which the country was heading. During the years from 1952 to 1960, when we had been living in America, she had been a staunch Democrat, campaigning for Adlai Stevenson who stood against Eisenhower in 1956 and later for John F Kennedy (although we had left the USA before the election of 1960 which Kennedy won). She had also been a fervent supporter of the Civil Rights movement and of Dr Martin Luther King Jr in particular. Her faith in the political system of her homeland was badly shaken following the assassinations of President Kennedy, Dr King and Bobby Kennedy. So, she found the election of Richard Nixon in 1968 very worrying.

> On 13 May 1970, she wrote – 'I don't know what to say about the terrible things that are tearing America apart, though I must say it would be hard to find a worse president [Nixon] than you have at present. However, I pray he won't get killed because [Vice President] Agnew really would be the rock bottom. I don't see any easy solution – there has got to be patience and understanding on all sides and those are two items that everybody in the US seems to be short of – especially the president.'

She was also fairly clear-eyed about the difference between politics in America and the UK.

> 17 July 1972 – 'Of course people in this country are highly amused at hearing McG[overn] called a radical because compared to OUR radical politicians he's very much in the centre. But of course any one of our radical politicians would give Americans a heart attack!!'

36

Although her parents had voted for Richard Nixon in 1960 and again in 1968, Phyllis was never a Nixon supporter and was appalled by the whole Watergate scandal, as this letter demonstrates.

27 October 1973 – 'I don't know what to say anymore about Nixon. It certainly seems as though his sacking of [Special Prosecutor Archibald] Cox was because he was afraid of what Cox was turning up with regard to his campaign financing and some of Nixon's backers. In a funny kind of way it has been a surprise to me – although I thought Nixon would "walk over his grandmother" to become President, I didn't really think he would be such a fool as to indulge in the kind of shady financial dealings that could be brought to light in this way. I would have thought he owed the office of the Presidency more than that. He is obviously not prepared to resign, and unless they turn up more shady stuff, the Senate will be loath to impeach – but what a terrible thing for America to have over 3 years more with a man whose ability to govern is so very crippled. ... We were all sickened when we heard that Cox had been sacked, and when [Attorney General Elliot] Richardson resigned after that it left only one man in the government that people have any respect for – and that's creepy old Kissinger! ... Nixon has lost all respect of people over here – even the papers that supported him at the start of the Watergate affair have turned their backs on him now since his refusal to be held answerable to any court. Even after his turnaround on the issue of the tapes, the fact that he first stated that he would not release them to the courts has sickened everyone!'

Nixon must have been a hot topic of conversation when, as she regularly did, Phyllis visited her parents. As they became increasingly elderly and frail, she went over to the US much more frequently.

During the 1970s Phyllis' parents experienced a lot of health problems: falls, chest problems, prostate troubles and hip replacements. It was very difficult for Phyllis, their only child, to be so far away from the parents she loved. Her parents moved home twice during the decade, with their last move, in September 1974, being to a retirement community called Carolina Village. Phyllis had urged them to move to Wales so that she could look after them but they were concerned that the Welsh climate would make their health problems worse. So it was a great relief to Phyllis to know that they would have support when living in Carolina Village, especially as there was a health centre on the premises. In a country with no national health service, it was important for them to be living in a community where they would be cared for if they became too infirm to stay in their apartment.

Phyllis was extremely close to her parents, making regular visits to Carolina Village until their deaths, within 6 weeks of each other, in 1986. In December 1976 my mother and father, along with myself and my children, were preparing to celebrate Christmas in our new home in Cwmystwyth. We didn't have a phone in the house at that time – we finally got one in June 1977 – so Phyllis couldn't phone her parents on Xmas day. At the end of her Christmas letter home, she wrote:

> 'Well, my loves, I do wish we were going to be together for Xmas but at least it is nice to know that you are with friends and not rattling around all by yourselves. You know how much we will be thinking of you on the big day. Much love to all our dear friends at the Village. I think of them all so often with warm affection – and of course my deepest love to you both.'

My mother, Phyllis Kinney, battled hard to make a place for herself in her adopted home. She never stopped being an American but she was open to embracing Welsh life and did so with enthusiasm – particularly Welsh culture, language and music. From her letters to her parents, it is clear that, for her, the 1970s were a time of discovery, of consolidating much of what she had learned about herself in previous years and developing further the skills and interests that she already had when she came to Wales. During their many years together, she and my father developed a true partnership, working collaboratively, to share with others their love of Welsh music. But for my mother, the 1970s was a formative decade during which she found her 'voice'.

A PECULIAR PREGNANCY

Ruth Dineen

I heard Jack come in, stumbling down the dark hallway, rummaging in the kitchen. The clink of bottle on glass and the slam of the living room door.

Hours later it was the smell of smoke that woke me.

The source was a book on his bedside cabinet, set alight by the cigarette he'd carefully balanced on the now smouldering cover. Germaine Greer's *The Female Eunuch*. Not his natural choice of bedtime reading. Jack was an ex-RAF pilot. Late 50s, handlebar moustache, a selection of cravats and a serious drink problem.

No, the Greer was mine, an eye-opening discovery I'd loaned him after one of our 'women's lib has gone too far' conversations. Jack, a lifelong bachelor, assured me that a woman's destiny – and happiness – lay in motherhood and wifely service. My current discontent with my lot was all the evidence he needed.

I was certainly discontented.

I was 22 years old and six months pregnant. More to the point, I was single. One or the other would have been fine but the combination was seriously problematic. I'd been forced to leave a good job in London and, as a consequence, had to move out of my flat. Jobless and homeless in quick succession. And needing to be hidden from the world – to 'keep my options open'.

I was sent to live with Jack, a wartime friend of my father's, in a bungalow in Teddington.

Which was how I came to be standing there in my baby-doll nightie, about to throw a glass of water in the general direction of the conflagration and his head.

Jack was kind and amiable but generally drunk. I was sort-of appreciative but increasingly irritated. Setting light to Germaine was the last straw, I decided. I needed to find alternative accommodation.

Serendipity. The previous day I'd bought myself a women's magazine – *Cosmopolitan* probably. An interview with Goldie Hawn, advice about how to get and keep your man, and a piece about male pin-ups adorned with photos of Burt Reynolds without his trousers. Strange, the things you remember.

There was also an article about the closure of mother and baby homes in the UK. According to the author, their demise was due to lack of demand since we were now living in a time of female liberation and moral freedom. Not in my bit of Wales we weren't, and, I suspected, not in Burnley, Bromley or Belfast either. However, there was one home still going strong in Monmouthshire. St Anne's Convent – a refuge for unmarried mothers run by a silent order of nuns. That unexpected juxtaposition was strangely pleasing. And there was a phone number for Sister Dolores who was in charge of the home and who, presumably, did speak.

Having had his sleep wetly interrupted, and been repeatedly told off all morning, Jack was snoring on the sofa by mid-afternoon. I took the opportunity to call St Anne's from the hall phone.

An Irish brogue. Friendly but distracted.

Hello. Sister Dolores here. How can I help you?

I was whispering, afraid of waking Jack.

Hello, Sister. I'm pregnant.

I'm sorry. Awful line. Awful. What did you say?

I'm pregnant, Sister. Pregnant.

Noooooo. Sorry, my dear. Can't hear a word.

I'M PREGNANT, SISTER!

Oh, that's lovely. Lovely.

It seemed that this was an exclusive sort of unmarried mother's home. Normally girls would only be admitted after a referral or interview but in my case Sister Dolores was willing to make an exception. Apparently, I sounded like a nice girl.

Within the week I was a resident, in a dormitory with other fallen souls. Louise Lucinda Lewis from Hackney, one of seven children by three fathers who'd all been given names beginning with 'L'. Janani, a nurse from Sri Lanka, abandoned by her boyfriend and clearly distressed. Illiterate fourteen-year-old Charmaine who'd been in and out of care all her life. Silent Georgina. And Molly – clever, pretty, funny. Pulled out of school in her GCE year and packed off to St Anne's for the duration. Her child was going to be adopted it seemed. No choice and no discussion.

My first meeting with Sister Dolores was on the following Sunday in the small convent chapel. She arrived to a head-craning rustle of delight from our lumpen congregation, looking like an illustration from a story about everyone's favourite pie-baking grandma.

She spotted me sitting uneasily at the back alongside my besuited boyfriend – afternoon visits were allowed on Sundays.

Hello! I'm Sister Dolores. You must be Ruth. And who is this beautiful young man?

The beautiful young man was dumbstruck.

Tommy, I said.

Hello, Tommy! And what are the two of yous giving up for Lent?

Swearing. (The first thing to come in to my head.)

I'm bloody glad to hear it.

She cackled and moved on. Not your usual sort of silent nun, it seemed.

*

Daily life at St Anne's was dull but not unpleasant. We all had cleaning tasks: scrubbing the enamel baths with special pink scouring cream, bleaching loos, wiping down surfaces, dusting and floor-sweeping. Serving rotas. Washing up rotas. Drying and putting away rotas.

Every fortnight we changed our sheets. This was a particular joy – the rubber undersheets we slept on created their own overheated microclimate which a hot summer exacerbated. Sheets didn't stay fresh for long.

The regularity of our lives was soothing. After lunch was cleared away we had our official work. Fixing hair slides on to cards, three on each side; sorting coloured beads in to plastic packets; putting leaflets into envelopes and sticking down the flap by wetting it with a small orange sponge that sat in its own special water tray. We only had one of those per table so we'd sometimes use our tongues until they were gummed up by the taste of the glue. Made from bits of cow, Molly said. Louise shrieked. I was sceptical but it turns out she was right.

Late afternoon, with permission, we were allowed to walk to the town for a wander around Woolworths or to sip a cup of pale tea at the one café. Sitting there among the unfallen and disapproving, among the twinsets and petal hats, felt like a revolutionary act at a time when we and our shame were supposed to stay well hidden.

St Anne's overlooked Chepstow Racecourse. A gate led out onto sparse woods and a grassy slope. On Sundays after church we were free to do as we pleased. And what we pleased, at least on sunny days, began with the arrival of the boyfriends – also sparse – and a trip to the races.

As a kid I'd had a dressing-up box. It was a wonder. Filled with my mother's old dance dresses, scarves and shawls, a deep blue embroidered silk dressing gown, costume jewellery, beaded handbags. To my huge delight it turned out that St Anne's had the equivalent – a dressing-up wardrobe, stuffed full of pregnancy clothes left behind by previous cohorts of the fallen. Chiffon, lime sateen, elasticated waists and floral polyester figured strongly.

Molly, Louise and I were regular Sunday visitors, mixing and matching, styling and discarding. Eventually, dressed to the nines, we'd set off through the woods, boyfriends in tow. Molly's boyfriend brought spliffs the size of ice-cream cones; Louise brought cod-liver oil, having persuaded us that regular slugs would bring on a speedy birth. I brought salami, my pregnancy obsession. Biscuits and bananas completed the picnic. At the time I felt the scene had a certain *Déjeuner sur l'herbe* elegance. Clearly it was good quality pot.

Mid-afternoon Louise would insist on an 'encourage the birth' session. The three of us would take an extra gulp of oil and run up and down the hill several times, scarves, beads and swollen bosoms wobbling wildly. I still wonder what the race-goers made of the sight.

*

I wasn't nervous about giving birth. I'm an optimistic soul and always assume that everything will turn out well. But I was nervous about the obligatory shave and enema routine. Girls had returned from the experience with tales of humiliation and, more significantly, weeks of itching ahead of them as their pubes grew back. I was determined to avoid that if I could. I planned to delay my arrival in the hospital for as long as possible so that there wouldn't be time for anything but the birth itself.

My waters broke in the middle of the night and contractions began almost immediately. I was excited. I left the wet bed and went quietly downstairs, clutching my stomach and gulping great breaths of air with some vague notion that this would help. I tried to time the contractions by the grandfather clock in the hallway but got distracted. I crept back to the dormitory to get a cardigan. I hummed songs, thought about pink babies in fairy-tale pink cribs, walked up and down the corridors. Sat. Stood. Crouched. Curled over.

I held out until dawn and then went to wake the maniacally cheerful resident midwife.

I remember kindly ambulance men; a labour ward in a windowless basement, empty except for me; a young male doctor who told me in passing that it didn't hurt that much and to be quiet; my feet up in stirrups for the longest time; an irritated midwife; my yelling baby; lots of stitches.

But no enema and no shaved pubes.

I was quite the heroine when I got back to St Anne's. I sat in my salt bath on my rubber ring and felt smug. A win against the system.

*

A week later Louise Lucinda returned to London with her son Valentine, named after his ultra-cool, ultra-hip musician father.

Georgina's baby was stillborn. At the time that seemed much worse than adoption. Perhaps Georgina thought so too but it was hard to tell. She was thirteen years old and simply overwhelmed.

Janani dressed her dark-haired daughter carefully and then put her in the nursery. The adoption agency took her away. We sat and cried together.

Charmaine was determined to keep her desperately wanted child. I doubt that there was a happy ending however. All of us were under huge pressure to 'be selfless' and let our babies go, and Charmaine had no one to speak up for her.

And Molly went back to school. We are still in touch. She was eventually and joyfully reunited with her daughter, herself a single mum at sixteen.

*

As for me and the pink baby of my imaginings...

He turned out to be a boy, and the best thing that ever happened to me. No bull.

45

CONCEALMENT

Liz Vining

It could be argued that my political thinking was subconsciously kick-started on the day I was born in Aberdare, July 1953. Due to an outbreak of measles, the local maternity ward had been closed so Mum was to give birth in her parents' house. When the time came, Bampi and Dad were banished to the kitchen to boil kettles and make tea on demand. My 16-month-old sister was with an Aunt. As Mum's contractions intensified the midwife was summoned. When she arrived, the formidable Nana Lil recognised her as a diehard Labour voter. There was no way Nana, a staunch Tory supporter, was going to let this Red over her doorstep. An argument ensued and, only when they were drowned out by the desperate pleas from my mother, was she allowed into the house to deliver me.

A few years later, after working since age 14 in the dangerous and frightening conditions at the local coal mine, Dad, a qualified electrician, seized an opportunity to escape and relocated the family to Penarth.

At age 18 I was living at home with my parents and was about to complete the Foundation Course at Cardiff College of Art with a plan to go on to study Fashion and Textiles in Loughborough. This wasn't going to happen.

By now through hard work and determination, Mum and Dad had managed to climb up the social ladder – starting a small business, owning their own home, becoming active members of the local Rotary Club – but their values were still deeply rooted in the tightly structured religious south Wales valleys working class (but Tory voting) culture they had come from. It was fully expected that I, like my older sister, would go into office work, or possibly nursing, or, in their wildest dreams, teaching. But I knew this was not the future I wanted.

In defiance of my parents' wishes, I had applied for a place on the Art Foundation course in Cardiff, and as soon as my acceptance letter arrived, I left school. Despite the pleas of my teachers and my parents, I was determined to leave straight away and sit my A levels externally. I hated the stifling atmosphere of school and took on various part-time jobs to fill in the time before college started in September 1971.

On Tuesday 27th June 1972, without a backwards glance or explanation for my tutors or other students, I walked away from that exciting and creative Art College life I had fought so hard to be a part of.

The day after my leaving college was meant to be one of celebration, a joyous coming together of two families, supposedly every young girl's dream. My wedding day. I should have been excitedly looking forward to it, but I wasn't. I was terrified and physically and mentally exhausted. Because it was expected of young courting couples and probably to appease my parents, my boyfriend and I had become engaged the previous year and a date for our wedding was set.

In the early months of 1972, having been seriously ill with glandular fever and viral meningitis, I had lost a lot of weight. This meant missing several weeks of college and required me to provide a certificate of good health in order to resume studying. My mother decided to accompany me to the consultant's office where I was asked to describe my symptoms, one of which was missed periods. This was glossed over as being normal with these types of illnesses, but I knew there was another reason. With my mother in the room and as an unmarried teenager, I wasn't going to confess to being sexually active. I knew I was pregnant. I didn't confide in anyone except my fiancé although he simply dismissed the idea and thought it unlikely due to my weight loss. We never spoke of my being pregnant again. As the months passed, I became adept at concealing the growing bump from family and friends by holding my stomach in, jeans secured with elastic loops and wearing loose smock tops. Thank goodness for Seventies fashion.

Despite it being contrary to my newly developed free-thinking Art college mindset, we carried on with the plan to marry: Wednesday, 28th June, 10am, St Peter's, Old Cogan, Penarth. Early morning, midweek, fewer guests, it made sense to us. Our preferred choice of venue would have been the registry office but this was a compromise for our conservative religious families. His, Italian Catholic; mine, Church in Wales.

In the weeks previous, I had pre-empted my mother's desire to shop in the bridal department of David Morgan's store Cardiff and taken a solo bus trip to Bath. Laura Ashley came up trumps: three voluminous, milkmaid style maxi dresses at £6 each. Two dresses for me to aid the concealment and one for my bridesmaid. A pair of white Dolly shoes for £4 and another £4 for a Playtex corselette to trim the silhouette. My parents were thrilled by my thrift. The previous year, my sister's bridal outfits had set them back over £200 – a huge amount of money at the time.

On the morning of the big day, I was up early, dressed and ready to go before my parents and bridesmaid had a chance to start fussing around me. An anxious practice session in front of the bathroom mirror, checking the angles, remembering to hold my stomach in and to keep my bouquet in the right place.

The ceremony itself passed without a hitch but all I could think about was trying to keep the bump hidden. The furious kicking from inside me was a constant reminder. Photographs and then on to Mark Manor for the reception where the best man, ironically named Mr Stork, gave a suitably risqué speech which, after a few drinks, even the more strait-laced elders enjoyed. It was then my father's turn. Once all the usual pleasantries were out of the way he announced with great pride that he and Mum were to become grandparents for the first time. My eyes darted around the room and my blood ran cold. Had all my hard work at hiding my pregnancy been in vain and why was he telling everyone? He then went on to explain that it was my married older sister who was expecting. I could breathe again.

Later that day my new husband and I drove to Swansea in our barely roadworthy Mini to start the next chapter of our life. No honeymoon for us. He had found a job as a graphic designer on the *Swansea Evening Post* at £20 a week which had enabled us to secure a mortgage to buy a small house with an outside toilet, no bath, no hot water, no gas and barely any electricity.

Just hours into that first evening as a married woman in our new home, I heard a knock at the door. A neighbour, about my mother's age, welcomed us to the area and asked if I would like to go to Bingo with her. A sweet gesture but still only 18 years of age and seven months pregnant, I politely declined her offer. Instead, I went to bed alone and cried myself to sleep.

We had very few visitors over the next few weeks, and with increasingly more to hide we avoided trips back to Penarth to see our families. My husband had the distraction of going to work each day, but I spent most of my time on my own with my thoughts in a house with very little in the way of basic comforts. I felt desperately lonely and was paralysed with fear about what was to come. Maybe hoping it wasn't really happening and that it would simply go away, we still hadn't discussed the pregnancy or even acknowledged that we would soon be parents. There was nothing in the house to suggest a baby was on the way except, hidden in a bedside drawer, were a bottle of TCP, some cotton wool and a pair of scissors. Having avidly read a set of vintage medical books, I had naively convinced myself that I could deliver the baby on my own and worry about the consequences later.

August arrived and with it a surprise visit from my older sister. It was obvious that she was happily pregnant and joyously displayed her slightly swollen belly whilst talking "baby this" and "baby that". Then, in a way that only older sisters can, she looked at me and said, "Ooh, you've put on weight". That was it, it was my cue to let go, to out myself. "We're having a baby, soon," I blurted. "But nobody knows and you mustn't say anything." She was surprised that I hadn't told anyone, shocked that I hadn't been to any antenatal clinics and astonished that I wasn't even registered with a GP. We made a deal: she would keep quiet; I would visit a local doctor and then tell Mum and Dad the news. A few days later, I registered at a local surgery. At the appointment, after a cursory examination and a reprimand, my new GP diagnosed that I was approximately 5 months pregnant and that he would write to the local maternity unit for an urgent appointment. I didn't dare tell him that I knew the birth was imminent and left with a prescription for iron tonic. On the way home I phoned my parents from a call box to tell them that another grandchild was on the way and that the date would be confirmed after I had been to the antenatal clinic. That would buy some thinking time.

The next day, Saturday, we took a trip in the Mini to Llangennith and on the way home visited the summer funfair on Oystermouth Road in Swansea. Although I was completely exhausted, my husband asked if we could go for a drink in the Cross Keys pub so he could watch a bit of the Munich Olympics on the telly. Because we didn't have a TV at home, I reluctantly agreed. In the pub I began to feel unwell, fidgety and nauseous and was only vaguely aware of what people were talking about. There was something about the USSR cheating at basketball. For the life of me I couldn't understand why this was important after hearing the reports of the shocking terrorist attacks and murder of Israeli athletes that had taken place just a few days earlier in the Olympic Village. Eventually I had to race to the toilet where I threw up and wet myself. I didn't realise at the time that this was my waters breaking. The next 24 hours were spent with intermittent stomach ache until the pain became unbearable. By Sunday midnight I could barely breathe. Reality was dawning; I was in labour. We drove to the rather grim looking maternity hospital in Mount Pleasant, which was originally the old Swansea workhouse.

On arrival, the night nurse took my details but couldn't find anything in the files. An avalanche of angry questions followed. "What antenatal clinic have you been to?", "Where are your records?", "Why aren't you registered?" After I had tearfully given her the required information the father-to-be was dismissed and told to come back in the morning and he happily left.

Still crying in fear and in agony, I was led into a side room and told to lie on the narrow bed. Then, without warning or explanation, a cloth strap was put around my midriff above the belly to effectively tie me down. My legs were put up in stirrups and the nurse, without even looking up, examined me internally, shaved me, and gave me an enema. "Not long now. I'll be back in half an hour." Laying there, unable to move, I could hear weeping, wailing and screams from adjacent delivery rooms. It was as if the ghosts from the old workhouse were still haunting the place. The maternity unit was obviously understaffed, busy and I was not alone in my misery.

And so the night passed with an occasional visit from the duty nurse. The pain was getting more excruciating with each contraction. Was this the punishment of women by God that I had been told about in church as a child? I really thought I was going to die, but was told to stop crying and that I was just being a "silly girl". At around 7am two student nurses about my age were ushered into the room and told to keep a watch for any changes. They simply ignored me and sat on the windowsill chatting and giggling about what they had been up to over the weekend. Eventually, at 9.30, my husband reappeared, obviously hoping it would all be over but at this point I didn't care. I just wanted the baby out of me as quickly as possible. I was high on pethidine and given gas and air at intervals but neither did anything to relieve the absolute agony I was suffering. A midwife eventually appeared, did another internal and announced she was going to perform an episiotomy. I had no idea what this was as my vintage medical books had made no mention of it. The intense searing pain as she sliced into me was unbelievable, but with one extra push my baby was born: a beautiful healthy 6lb 6oz girl. In an instant, all the agony, all the fear was gone and with an almighty rush of euphoria, my life was changed forever. I felt invincible.

Except of course, there was just one more hurdle to cross. The parents had to be told that they had become grandparents several months earlier than expected. That was hubby's job. Two days later, Mum arrived at my bedside brandishing a Black Forest Gateau accompanied by Nana Lil dressed in her best fur coat and matching AG Meek handbag, hat and gloves. Nana rushed over to me, smothered me with lipstick kisses and out of Mum's earshot whispered, "Who's been a naughty girl then? Don't worry dear, it happens to the best of us". It was at that moment I realised there was a club with secrets and codes that no one told you about but into which I had just been initiated. I was a mother.

Post birth my stomach was very quickly back to its pre-pregnancy normal; all those months of holding my pelvic floor up and my breath and tummy in had paid dividends. The worst part was the haemorrhoids and the multitude of stitches inside and out which throbbed painfully. It would be years before I was fully healed physically and psychologically.

At this time, new mothers were kept in hospital for a two week "lying-in" period to recover from the birth and to be instructed in the new ways of bringing up a baby. Great emphasis was placed on the importance of bottle feeding: it was healthy, it was hygienic and it was the modern way. Even at my young age this made absolutely no sense to me and I was determined to breastfeed my baby. I was the only one on the ward to think this and the nurses constantly lectured me and did their utmost to persuade me to use a bottle.

All the other babies were fed at four hourly intervals during the day and taken away to the nursery at night. I insisted and fought for my baby to be next to me at all times so that I could feed her on demand. This was very much frowned upon by the staff who were convinced that a strict regime was paramount (and probably more convenient for them). As a compromise, I was allowed to breastfeed but only if I did it privately, with my chair facing the wall and curtains drawn around the bed. I couldn't wait to get out of that hellish place.

Although happy to be discharged, the grim reality of our basic home life returned. I missed running hot water and the luxury of soaking in the hospital's deep Victorian slipper baths. A top and tail flannel wash in a small bowl was not the same. We bought a traditional tin bath from the local hardware store to be used a couple of times a week. It took an age to fill with saucepans of hot water and so the baby was bathed first, then me, then hubby, then the laundry. Domestic bliss.

Late summer drifted into autumn and in the colder weather our one-bar electric fire was not enough to keep us warm. The answer was to collect and burn scrap wood from the local builder's yard and coffin offcuts from the funeral director's workshop across the road. Despite having very little money and no luxuries we liked our quirky little house and saw its potential, so made plans for an extension and applied for a housing grant from Swansea City Council and the future looked a bit brighter.

A few months later devastating news arrived. The plans and grant application had been rejected because the house had been condemned under a compulsory purchase order for a road widening scheme. None of this had been revealed at the time of purchase and a long legal battle ensued. It was finally settled in 1979 with a £500 compensation payment when it was discovered that the previous owner was a local councillor who knew full well we were buying a condemned house. The road widening scheme never happened.

During this time, I had met another young mother who told me with great enthusiasm about a weekly women's group which she thought I might be interested in. Rather than stay at home worrying and getting depressed, I decided to go along. I'd always thought of myself as being politically aware but how wrong I was. This was a baptism of fire and an eye-opening experience for me. It was the newly formed Swansea Women's Liberation Group.

Events and discussions, lectures by and for women. I loved it. Oppression of women, domestic violence, unequal pay and conditions, abortion rights were all highlighted and discussed. The most memorable event was an intimate self-discovery session where with speculums and mirrors we were encouraged to examine ourselves. This was taboo breaking and incredibly liberating; my mother would have been mortified.

An offshoot of the SWLG was SWAC (Swansea Women's Abortion Campaign). A group of us attended the 1975 NAC (National Abortion Campaign) London rally to protest against the 1975 James White amendment to the Abortion Bill which was seeking to roll back the rights that women had fought for. "A woman's right to choose" was our mantra. It was exhilarating. I felt alive and excited marching with like-minded women, our Swansea banner held high. Despite the jeering and harassment from the priests and nuns and members of SPUC (Society for the Protection of Unborn Children) lining the streets we were determined, with the many thousands of other campaigners, to fight this bill and keep our hard-won rights. We did win; the amendment was scuppered.

Back in Swansea, the SWLG continued its work to educate and inform, and I was proud to be a part of that group enthusiastically attending meetings, protests and parties. However, my still very basic home life had become grim. My husband had been made redundant, we were desperately poor and our will had been broken by the ongoing legal battle with the Council. In May 1977 we'd had enough so packed our meagre possessions into a few tea chests, boarded up the house and moved back to Penarth where employment and comfortable rented accommodation were available. A new chapter of my life was set to begin.

The emotional impact of having to hide my pregnancy and the trauma of giving birth in 1972 had deterred me from having another baby so much that when I became pregnant in 1989 it was something of a shock. This time however, I would be ready. I was informed and I was vocal in my demands. The time spent in the 1970s with the SWLG had given me confidence as a woman to speak out and not be fobbed off or silenced. Ready to give birth but before being induced, I demanded and had an epidural and forbade the midwife from performing an episiotomy. I stayed in control throughout the pain-free birth of my second daughter and this time I was encouraged to breastfeed.

I am still passionate about women's rights and am an active campaigner for CAPH (Campaign Against Painful Hysteroscopy) and supporter of Sling the Mesh Group.

FIRSTS

Kate Cleaver

Can anyone remember their first word? I suspect mine was something like 'mum' or 'dad,' I couldn't say for sure, but what I do remember is being told by my parents about my first public word. You see my parents were worried when I was a child. I didn't hit all those milestones you are meant to. I mean I hit most, but I never crawled. My mum says that my main form of locomotion was the bum shuffle. I went straight from that to walking. Of course, research now suggests that the inability to crawl is linked with dyslexia and dyspraxia, so it is hardly surprising I couldn't do it when I was a kid. My first public word is important, more so perhaps than others as I started to speak and hit my talking milestone, got a vocabulary of about ten words and then stopped talking.

Nothing.

For months.

I saw specialists. Nothing wrong, they said.

My parents worried.

I watched everything. I don't remember this, but it is what I have always done so I'm expecting it happened.

Then one day I was in my high chair and, although I don't remember either, my mum says it with a quiet reverence that makes me think it occurred as they say it did. I had chips I believe and according to mum I was a messy eater but an efficient one. I have always liked my food, never turning down something tasty.

'Can you pass me the tomato sauce?'

That was me.

My parents were shocked. I was no longer silent, nor was I limited to a series of single words. I had gone from ten words to a complete sentence structure and a pretty decent vocabulary. I hit the milestone. Blew it out the water. It was probably my first microphone drop. So, you can imagine that they had great expectations for my first public word in front of my dad's family.

I was a short child, very short, so there was the immense underlying cuteness of me being in a frilly pink and grey dress with princess sleeves. We are going back to the late Seventies here so please think more frill and less practicality. It was a special occasion though. I was meeting my dad's mum as a walking child and not a babe in arms. It was big for my parents. As my mum says, I was becoming a little person with a personality. So, I am tottering around and my Aunt B gives me a packet of crisps. Not the greatest snack for a small child but I got them. The packet was as big as me almost and it took concentration to keep them from dropping to the floor.

At the time I was not terribly well coordinated and the worst happened. It dragged on the floor and I put one tiny patent leather clad foot on the edge of the packet. That slippy plasticky foil pulled from my hands and I watched as those crisps spilled. I stood there a moment with my tiny hands on my hips surveying the damage and then said something in a voice that carried in the now quiet room. There must have been at least twenty plus relatives there.

'Shit.'

That is it, the first public word I uttered. The word I spoke in front of my dad's mother. There was a moment of silence and then an audible intake of breath from twenty mouths. And then my mum and Aunt B's laughter.

It is a wonderful memory and one that is retold. One that is laughed at. I love it. There are others: the first time I realised I could draw; the first time I wanted to be a writer; the first time my dad became redundant... That one was big for me. Dad had worked for a tractor company; he was and still is a mechanic. It was the years of Thatcher and he lost his job. In my diary in school I wrote about him going on the dole. And I drew a picture of him. I think he was half brown and half orange... The brown pen had died after I had only coloured in a bit of him, so I picked orange for the other colour. Before that day I hadn't seen much of my father. He would be travelling all around the country fixing massive tractors. It is one thing I like Thatcher for. She gave me back my dad. Of course, as an adult I can see that the stress my parents were under with my dad out of work and no money was incredible, but as a child it was great. Dad would make breakfast and put the oven gloves on his head, turning him into a dog. It was so much fun. It was a time of laughter and music, and the fact I remember it as that shows just how hard my parents worked to keep it that way. We didn't have much food, and we – they had two kids by then – would feel hungry a lot. I never knew that my mum would just not eat. Dad would be out working at whatever he could. Fixing cars on the quiet.

'I'll eat with your father.'

Then when dad came in she would smile and give him the rest of the food.

'I ate with the kids.'

In reality she would eat what we left with a slice of white bread, dry. Hunger hurts.

One of my first memories is my waking in a room that smells of incense and damp. The damp was everywhere. It permeated the chair that I woke up on. It is strange about memories, that they never run in sequence and they are always snapshots. You can get a few frames of a movie but never the beginning or the end. Essentially that is what happens with this one. I can smell the damp in the chair, a strangely comforting smell that is musty and fragrant. I'm guessing that my mum used some thing on the chair in order to hide the smell. The coarse texture of the rough weave of the tiny white and brown checks. I used to run a finger along them, brown, white, brown... I woke on that chair. That is my first memory and from speaking to mum I must have been three or four. I do know I was tiny and didn't move. I knew that the chair was a bit high, so I waited.

Brown.

White.

Brown...

It is here that my fear of fireworks started. There were two racist firsts in that property in the north of Stafford. My parents had brought a house after they got married and it was an unpleasant place. Full of damp and tiny. My dad wasn't the DIY type then, but they had no furniture, so my mum brought a grey file filled with *Reader's Digest* projects. How to turn orange crates into a coffee table... My dad became very good at DIY but those first years were a nightmare of minimalistic poverty. My parents had moved from London. The lack of affordable housing had forced them out and they had ended up buying where they did because of money. They didn't factor in Stafford itself. Now, I left the place in 2000 and have pretty much tried to never go back, but when they bought it they had no idea that they were buying in a white supremacy area.

My parents' first house, my first house. There had been high expectations, but people got in the way. Mum remembers this one and although I do, it is a more distant memory and entwined with a much younger one. Dawn French, the comedian, lived with her then-husband, Lenny Henry, in the Dudley area of the Midlands, and I remember sitting with my parents and watching a stand-up where Dawn got into being part of a mixed-race couple. It was funny but tinged with bitterness and sadness. At one point she started talking about having shit smeared on her front door. Mum and Dad had grimaced and my memory had tugged at me. I asked if that had happened to us and my parents had nodded. The vague memory crystallised. Dawn was miming someone holding a dog up and using it as a living piping bag to write on her wall. Ours was less creative. Someone had smeared it on the front door and pushed some through the letterbox. It is my mum's worst memory.

What always troubled me is that they must have had their hands covered. I have had dogs, I know it stinks and acts like a semi-solid, so I can't see them being able to do that without getting their hands and arms covered. How do you do that? How do you hate someone so much that you are willing to cover yourself in dog shit in order to get your point across? As far as I know, as soon as my parents found out the mood in the area, they stuck to themselves and set about making a plan. My parents are great at plans. They have three running at the same time. If one fails they have the next. There was a plan. For me, the dog shit was not anything that worried me. After all, I didn't clean it up. One day it was there and later it wasn't. My life was very focused on my parents and I do know they were unhappy.

As a child it was the firework through the door that scared me. The smell of burning and smoke... I woke I guess from the bang, but despite this the memory is like a silent movie. I see my dad coming down the hall from the back of the house and the garden. It is foggy in the hall and there are smoke swirls. My dad is walking slowly, almost as if he is in slow motion. His movement is deliberate and he is holding his hands funny. I know I'm scared and silent. It is as if my voice and hearing have been stolen. The smoke swirls, grey blue and smelling of sulphur and black. Dad's hands are red. He is holding them awkwardly.

The snapshot is a nightmare, but it is only a snapshot. I had to talk to my mum in order to find out what had happened. She told me about the letterbox opening with a loud snap and then the fizzing sound as the firework was pushed through, only to lie like a fish out of water for a second on the welcome mat. Before springing into the air. Then my father caught it without thinking and wrestled the live firework outside before it exploded. I guess he reacted without thinking. That evening he saved us from a fire. Saved me and mum. But he burnt his hands. They burnt his hands.

After that day plans moved fast and pretty soon we were moving into another house. My first move. Still in Stafford but out of the National Front area. Working class and a sprawling old council house became home. There were problems. No heating or electric upstairs. But from the moment I walked in I felt safe. That house was set on a corner and although a semi-detached, was set far enough back that you could see anyone who came to the door.

I even remember the number of the house, 61, and the postcode and the five-digit telephone number. Yes, I am that old. I have a feeling that if the house had been structurally sound we would have stayed there. As with all good things, it didn't last, but until I was doing my GCSEs it was home. No fireworks and no shit. People looked but they didn't say or do anything.

I always wanted to be liked, but I was socially inept although that was more to do with my neurodiversity than my colour, I think. I was reading in the front garden. There were these huge plants that grew under the front window. I have always loved horror movies, and books and one of my favourites was *The Day of the Triffids*. Those wonderful moving plants. The first time I realised that monsters could be benign and slow moving. I was lying in the grass that was a little too long and staring at the words on the page. I'd not long been reading and it was amazing how the words could make a movie in my head. The triffids above me waved in the air and I know I was smiling.

'You!'

Someone called out and I looked over at the path. It was slightly higher than where I lay so I could see that there were three girls there. All white. I recognised them from up the road a way. They were older than me.

'What?' I asked. I was a little annoyed as the plant had been about to catch someone.

'We wanna see inside,' the redhead asked.

I noticed a few things about these girls. They were all in short skirts, they were all thin and they all had on way too much make-up. I guessed they were about fourteen.

'Why?' I asked.

'Because.'

It is at this point that most people would have picked up their book and gone inside. But I was a curious creature and these people intrigued me. I had forgotten about the firework. My life was a safe one. Nothing could hurt me inside the fence. This was home.

'Okay,' I said and got up. They appeared shocked but the ringleader laughed. It wasn't a pleasant laugh.

They came to the gate and I opened it. I did not invite them in. They stepped over without needing an invitation. Not vampires then... I have always had problems with understanding what is reality and what is fiction. It has to do with the autism and at this age, about twelve, it was riding me hard. I would read something and then believe it. Looking for clues in everyday life. The triffids in the garden had never moved so I assumed that they were not as in the book. Probably the wrong type.

The girls walked to the front door, a brilliant electric blue, my mother's choice and a favourite colour of mine.

'Just push,' I said.

They walked in. We had changed the inside a bit so it wasn't quite like other houses in the street but they started to make themselves comfy.

I went to the kitchen and filled a jug with ice and squash.

'Thanks,' another said.

And this is where memory gets fuzzy. I can see the ice melting in the jug, the orange of the juice. I can feel myself taking a sip from a glass, the acid on my tongue and the cold as it slides its way to my stomach, but I don't know what happened. I don't know what was done. The whole day is a blank. I know I let them in at about ten in the morning and that my mum came home at three. But I don't know what happened. I may never know. My internal movie clicks on and my mum is telling me off that I shouldn't let strangers in the house. I feel like I want to say they are friends but they aren't. I think Mum must have driven them out. My face feels strange. Sort of raw. Had I been wearing make-up? Then I was back to the normal routine. A few things changed. I never took friends home. I never lay in the front garden again and I never spoke to those girls again. They never spoke to me. Instead they would turn from conversations and walk away as if they didn't see me.

What happened?

My world of firsts is littered with love and hate: white, brown, white. I suppose it is strange and these things don't happen to everyone. But they are my reality and it wasn't until I was much older that I realised it was different from other people's.

I saw a clip on the internet of Muhammad Ali. He said as a small child he asked his mum why Angel's Food Cake was white and Devil's Food cake was brown. Why do all the bad connotations have to be black or brown? But in my life the bad has normally occurred because of the brown. It has taken an awful long time for me to grow into my skin and embrace and be proud that I am a lady of colour. I may stand with one foot in my mother's 'fish and chips' culture, but my other foot is firmly planted in a world of colour and dance. My wardrobe contains jeans and t-shirts, but also scarves filled with hand embroidered gold, individual inset mirrors and bells. Instead of hiding behind one culture or the other I accept both the brown and the white, they are both me, and I am both of them. They are what makes me. Colour does not define me; it is me.

SECRETS

Philippa Guest

My hand dithered over the shampoo bottles in Rawlings' Chemist, Llandaff Village High Street. Weighing up the various options, I remembered that the Sunsilk advert had told me a girl's most important secret is her shampoo. The next stage in the decision-making process was to ascertain whether I was greasy or normal. Normal was obviously the more appealing of the two descriptions, but I was conscious that in recent weeks my scalp had been exuding more oil than in its previous ten-year existence – a situation probably exacerbated by the fact that I kept combing my fringe downwards to see if it had reached the tip of my nose. With a quick glance in the plastic mirror on the shelf above, I decided that the more complimentary of the two adjectives probably fitted me better as a person (regardless of my hair); I grasped the slim, beige bottle and presented it cheerfully to Mrs Rawlings, who had been observing my indecision patiently from behind the counter.

The Llandaff of my childhood did not seem to be a place to harbour secrets. In the chemist, if someone had a verruca, a sticky eye or constipation, it was fine to announce the predicament loudly, and no one would flinch. In the Church in Wales Primary School, if someone's Dad liked to drink, we knew about it and thought nothing of it if we saw him staggering over the kerb outside The Butchers Arms. In this popular pub, friends and regulars discussed the rugby and the cricket with a sense of camaraderie that kept the same crowd coming back night after night. As kids we valued the sense of togetherness within our community, and we listened keenly to adults' conversations, from which we gained a basic grasp of people's lives and current events.

However, it would probably be fair to state that in the deeper, more complex world of human relationships, I was a complete innocent. Despite all our primary teachers' wisdom and skills, not one of them ever taught us about sex. As we were a Church school, there were daily religious assemblies with prayers and the curriculum consisted of a very thorough grounding in the three Rs. We also enjoyed some wonderful musical opportunities, including membership of the Cardiff Junior Schools' orchestra, if we could scratch out the scale of G on our violins, and singing complex popular songs in huge choirs at the annual Schools' Concert in Sophia Gardens Pavilion. I could sing the alto of 'Jesu Joy of Man's Desiring' before I was eleven, yet I have no recollection of lessons about love or emotions; in those complex developmental aspects we were self-taught and very naive. If any of us knew anything about sex, the knowledge had been acquired from pets, birds or insects, and tended to be sketchy or euphemistic. In my experience, sexual relationships were not mentioned in the presence of children, and never shown on television during our waking hours. I acquired a number of prejudices by osmosis, including the notion that it was shameful to be an unmarried mother. I had no idea why that might be the case, so I surmised that it might be because the woman was too 'twp' to find a man to marry her!

At the heart of the village, nestling by the river Taff, sat the Cathedral, a place where people turned for sanctuary or solace – a holy place intended to give respite from the vagaries of human existence. However, churches not only serve mortals, they are also staffed by them, and in the mid-1970s a scandal of great magnitude hit this institution, shaking Llandaff's respectable society to its very core. The media enabled the shock waves to spread far and wide, testing the foundations of people's faith, and causing pain and heartache to those who worshipped there.

I can trace the beginnings of this scandal to early 1972, a time just before Mrs Thatcher snatched the free milk that used to bubble so brilliantly when we blew down our straws. About thirty of us were on the bus returning from Guildford Crescent Swimming Baths, a Victorian gem in central Cardiff. Plastic bags were not yet in general usage, so the boys' damp bathers were folded within towels to emulate Swiss rolls, while the ponchoed girls hid their costumes in trendy wicker paniers with flowery plastic coverings, like a troupe of Little Red Riding Hoods. School uniform was only for secondary schools, so we always wore our home clothes and girls rarely wore trousers. That afternoon, Standard Four were laughing at Mr Gruffydd, a fearsome Welsh-speaking teacher with a dry sense of humour, whose reminder that "Pibellau gwag sy'n gwneud y twrw mwyaf!" had little effect. As usual, he was sitting at the back of the brown double-decker in a seat adjacent to what appeared to be an Emergency Exit. To our joy, someone had graffitied the words 'Ejector Seat' above his head. On reflection, Mr G had probably chosen that seat to prevent any of us from releasing our classmates onto the Western Avenue roundabout. Weaned by Daleks, and nurtured by Captain Scarlet, *Thunderbirds* and the Moon Landing, we had space travel in our blood, and the notion of our grumpiest teacher spiralling out into the Universe appealed to us. The *Dr Who* theme tune rocked the bus, and poor Mr Gruffydd temporarily lost control of his 'empty vessels' – a rare occurrence.

We entered the school chastised, unshowered (there were none), chlorinated and marginally less energetic than when we left. To our surprise, the headmaster, Mr Penhallurick, his moustache twitching, met us at the door and directed us into the school hall to tell us some news that had evidently delighted him so much that he wanted to share it with us immediately. There were no school newsletters in those days unless dinner money was required; if anything was to be communicated, we were told to inform our parents, a method much given to errors and miscommunication.

That afternoon, Mr Penhallurick wanted us to let our parents know that a new Bishop of Llandaff had been appointed, the Right Reverend Eryl Thomas, currently Bishop of Monmouth. He was returning to our diocese, where he had been an acclaimed Dean throughout the Fifties and Sixties, and he was respected by everyone who knew him. This was exceptionally good news for the school and the whole community. We must let our parents know that we were lucky to have the return of such an inspired and committed spiritual leader, who would work tirelessly for the Diocese of Llandaff.

Judging by the lack of reaction, the news was unremarkable for most of my classmates, but I was an exception. As a Llandaff child born and bred, I had known Bishop Eryl all my life, and I loved him like an uncle. After a trip to the Holy Land, he brought me a small, gold cross from Bethlehem, which I still cherish. My parents thought the world of him as a pastor and friend, and I had grown up with the knowledge that he had masterminded and overseen the huge task of restoring the Cathedral after it had been wrecked by a German bomb in January 1941. As Cathedral Dean, Eryl had welcomed the Queen to the re-opening ceremony in March 1960, a legacy that was still fresh in the memories of our family and friends when I was a little child.

As Mr Penhallurick had predicted, Bishop Eryl's renewed presence in the diocese was met with happiness and hope by all those involved in the life of the Cathedral and Church Schools. He did not disappoint – large numbers of us attended church and were confirmed in the three years that followed his return, and the life of the diocese once again flourished under his guidance.

Meanwhile, my journey towards adolescence continued in an unexceptional manner. I left the safe confines of the village school and became slightly rebellious, testing boundaries at home where I felt it was safe to do so. I can vividly recall my father's horror when he came home for his cooked lunch to see 'Fuck Off!' neatly emblazoned in my best, copperplate handwriting on our wipe-clean kitchen noticeboard. The felt pen clipped to the side of the board had somehow proved too much for me and propelled itself into action independently of any conscious decision-making, fitting its message assertively between my mother's scribbled 'processed peas' and 'pay Mr Jenkins'. The words radiated out, cartoon-style, a raucous, bold affront to my parents' decency. Both Mum and Dad stood dumbfounded, regarding me as if I had just walked off the set of *The Exorcist*. I knew 'that word' was rude – very rude – but I tried to state in my defence that my friend Anthony had told me it was a secret to do with a man's trousers, so I didn't realise its import.

My mum decided to enlighten me. After my poor dad had returned to work and mum had washed the lunch plates, she sat me down at the dining-room table, looked me in the eye and proceeded with an explanation:

"A man has a little hosepipe and a lady has a rose garden. When they would like a baby, the man uses his little hosepipe to water the rose garden and that is when the baby is made. You have seen pregnant ladies, so you know that the baby grows inside the lady's tummy for nine months until it is born. The rude word you used is to do with the watering process. I won't say it and I don't want you to write it or use it again – people won't think you are a nice girl if you say it!"

Unusually flushed, she carried on with her chores while I con-templated my father's perished, rubber hosepipe, which my friends and I had attempted to use as a skipping rope. It was certainly not little, as it stretched right across our perfectly square garden, frequently springing leaks that frightened the dog, or cascading off the outside tap like an uncoiling serpent on the attack. As for a lady's rose garden: I hadn't got one, didn't want one, and decided it sounded far too prickly a prospect to entertain. Growing a baby inside my tummy was an abhorrent idea.

The next time I looked at the kitchen noticeboard it had been wiped so clean that not a smudge remained. I hated processed peas, but I hoped Mr Jenkins received his pay.

One day in 1975 I returned from secondary school to find my mother ashen-faced and shaky, trying to make sense of something she had had whispered to her in the High Street. Once more she sat me down with her, but this time I think it was for her sake rather than mine. Bishop Eryl had been arrested. She felt there had been a terrible mistake. She thought perhaps his enemies (what enemies?) had been spreading lies about him in an attempt to take his important role away from him. It was impossible he had done what they alleged, unless some medicine he was taking had made him behave in a way that was completely out of character. It was incomprehensible to all the people who thought they knew Eryl that he could be capable of committing a 'crime' that involved sexual encounters with men. The hushed and tragic shock waves that spread through Llandaff were worse than those generated by the World War Two bomb; that, at least, had been perpetrated by an external enemy. How was it possible such a loved and respected man could find himself at the centre of such controversy?

I was just fourteen and I decided I would have to find out for myself. With an intense sadness, I read the newspaper reports that pulled no punches, and the situation temporarily broke my heart. I learned the legal term 'gross indecency' and I could not equate the version of heterosexual sex I was just beginning to see as the norm with a man's desire for another man in such a risky and public setting. Was it about the excitement of risk-taking, a rebellion like my kitchen noticeboard moment, a secret outlet from the pressure of religious calling? Or more simply, had Bishop Eryl decided that he fancied men? In the mercifully more enlightened twenty-first century, the events would hopefully have had a different outcome. As it was, the Church in Wales swiftly used its ejector seat, and a priest who was arguably one of its finest clergymen spent the next twenty years assisting in small, 'out of the way' churches.

As paragons of 'respectability', my parents decided that they had to cut all contact with their former friend, on the grounds that they felt he had let everybody down so badly. I think the truth was that my father chose not to accept homosexuality, and my mother was hurt by what she saw as a betrayal of trust. I was a teenager who did not think anything much, the hurt soon becoming obscured in the mists of adolescence. However, as an adult I have come to feel differently, and the sadness is reawakened whenever I look at that little gold cross from Bethlehem and ponder the prejudices and personal choices that led to the demise of such a talented man.

The last time I set eyes on Bishop Eryl was in 1984 at my father's funeral in Llandaff Cathedral. As I left with my family, I saw Eryl kneeling towards the back of the church, dark-suited and anonymous, a crushing look of sadness in his whole demeanour. My dad had been one of his best friends, and Llandaff Cathedral was always his beloved church.

WOMEN BLEED

Sue Bevan

Valentine's Day 1972, and all I want is to bleed.

Growing up in the Welsh Valleys of the Seventies was full of contradictions. We'd heard of the Summer of Love and women's rights, and contraception was supposed to be freely available. We had choices, at last. The second wave of feminism had brought radical change, we read. Abortion was legal. Women finally had agency over their own bodies, their lives.

That's not how it felt for me.

Like many others, our small town of Mount boasted little to occupy youngsters back then. Pinball down the Bracchi's; a disco once a month in the church hall if you were lucky; dangerous liaisons behind the bike shed. Raised in a loveless family, I spent my teens looking for love. What I found was sex. I can't say it was hiding exactly, and by fifteen I was pregnant. I didn't tell my parents, of course. You didn't tell them anything. It only caused rows. In any case, maybe I was wrong; maybe being sick every morning was down to the stress of constant walking on eggshells in our house. Or maybe it was the diet to squeeze into those hotpants from Ponty market. It was probably school pressure, I told myself, or hormones, or all of the above. So no, I definitely wasn't pregnant. I couldn't be, wouldn't be. And as long as I kept telling myself that, it might even come true.

But that's not how pregnancy works.

I must have been about four months gone when Mam obliquely half-broached the subject. One dreary Sunday afternoon she was watching a wartime romance on TV, working her way through a stack of ironing. This was her chance to raise why I hadn't asked for money for jam rags for months now.

"I've been paying myself," I lie in an instant, turning away to hide my flushed cheeks.

"What with?"

"Pocket money, okay?"

It was more attitude than I'd normally ever dare.

"Well, don't. Ask me next time, all right?"

I head for the door, desperate to escape further scrutiny.

"Did you hear me, Susan?"

I've heard her all right. She's heard me lie, too.

Next morning, she marches me down to the doctor's. We wait outside the drab surgery in gloom and drizzle, queuing up beside men coughing their lungs up from years down the pit, women with backs stiffened by factory line work and domestic labouring. These were the days when washing machines and hoovers were still luxuries.

A neighbour stands ahead of us, spotting us arrive.

"All right there, Ruth?" she calls over.

"Can't complain."

"This your youngest, is it?"

Do I imagine her eyes drifting to my stomach? I lean into the damp stone wall, pulling myself upright in a pathetic attempt to shrink my expanding waistline. It makes no difference; my school skirt hasn't done up for weeks now. I have no waistline. Even my duffle can't hide it. Feeling sicker than ever, I fill my head with song lyrics, trying not to think. The damp has seeped through to my bones by the time the bolt on the surgery door slides across and those of us there early enough pile in. The rest will wait outside for now. Mam and I sit side by side on one of the solid oak benches surplus to chapel requirements.

Eventually the doctor pops his head around the door,

summoning us into the only examination room. Our neighbour's eyes follow me as we head in.

"See you, Ruth!"

I bet she does. I bet she sees everything. I smile, hoping to keep her on side. It's futile. She was never on side in the first place.

A kindly man, Doctor Lewis has been our family physician for years. He tells us to take a seat and is straight down to business. How he can help, he asks. Only by turning the clock back, I think. But in any case, he's not addressing me. The only time he does is when he has to ask me a direct question. Even then his eyes don't meet mine. My mother tells him I've been missing my periods. He asks me to pop me up on the couch. I lift my skirt when I'm told, and I'm telling the truth when I say I can't remember when the last one was.

"Five, six weeks ago? Or more?"

"More maybe."

"Two, three months...?"

"More. I think."

My voice trembles as I stare at the tar-stained ceiling. Doctor Lewis examines me robustly, pressing this side and that, poking and prodding, applying his stethoscope to listen for a second heartbeat, checking the development of this brand new person I refuse to accept is growing inside me.

Have I felt any movement ... here, for example?

"No," I lie. Or maybe not lie. I'm willing it to be true.

Am I sure?

"Yes."

Of course I've felt what turns out to be a five-month baby's first movements. I'm just too terrified to admit it to myself, and I absolutely can't acknowledge it to anyone else. That would make it real, and that's unthinkable. A tear fills and overflows my eye, but I wipe it away and neither of them sees because I'm oddly invisible, a non-person.

Have I been feeling sick at all?

"No."

Not in the mornings, maybe?

"No."

Finally he steps away and washes his hands, and I know he's about to confirm what soon I won't be able to hide any longer.

"Well, Mrs Jenkins," he says, "... she's definitely pregnant."

There's a fleeting silence that opens a bottomless pit, and I fall in.

"Four, five months I'd say, but it's hard to be precise without knowing the dates."

"Right, Doctor."

My mother's voice isn't her own. It's thin and weak.

Doctor Lewis tells me I can get up now, and he takes his place back at his desk, jotting a few notes. Leaning back in his broad oak and leather office chair, he meets the desperate eyes of the diminutive woman in front of him.

"Have you thought about what you'll do?" he asks her gently.

I might as well not be in the room as he adds, "It's too late to do anything about it now, of course."

Suddenly I'm hot and the room is closing in. I focus hard on the second hand of the large, black-framed wall clock. I must not make a spectacle of myself. I must not faint. Tick ... tick ... tick. The voices are distant now.

"Yes, Doctor. She's going to stay with her sister. In Plymouth. It'll be adopted down there."

"Ah. Right. Good."

He makes another note, and a small part of me wants to cry with relief: they're not going to just throw me out on the streets after all. But the bigger part wants to fight, to scream that they have to listen, I have to be heard. Ask what I want. Just ask me!

He's writing again.

"Plymouth, did you say?"

"Yes. Her sister lives there. It's all been arranged."

My body, my baby. "All been arranged."

I say nothing. You always say nothing in our house if you've got any sense. I haven't got much, clearly, but I've got enough to know when to hold my tongue.

The walk home from that surgery is the longest half-mile of my life.

That night my mother makes me hot chocolate. I lie on the settee with my head on her lap, watching but barely registering the final episode of *Please Sir!* And for the one and only time she strokes my long dark hair, and with a tenderness I now know comes only with the territory of being a mother, however rough the terrain might be. Lying there I'm relieved I'm facing away, so she doesn't see when I finally let the tears roll down my face and soak into the nylon of her navy blue skirt.

Early the next day Dad loads the car he's borrowed from a workmate, while Mam makes sandwiches for the long drive. It's tinned salmon, a treat usually kept for day trips to Barry or Porthcawl in the summer holidays. But this is January in Mount, and the biting wind whipping up the valley makes it feel like the sun will never shine here again. By nine we're locking up. Little do I know that this will be the last time I'll step foot in that house.

Curled up on the back seat – it was the days before seatbelts – I rest my head on the shawl Granny crocheted me a lifetime ago. I've tossed and I've turned all night, and I'm feeling weak. I imagine they've barely slept either. Pulling my duffle around me I let the car radio drift over me as Dad turns the cold engine over. The New Seekers want to teach the world to sing, but the atmosphere in that car is as far from perfect harmony as you get, with Mam stone-faced and Dad knowing his place. He lights a Woodbine and takes a long drag before putting the car into first and releasing the handbrake.

As we pull onto the main road Nilsson's 'Without You' is on the radio, still number one in the charts. I try not to think about whether the sorrow shows in my own eyes but maybe Dad sees me in the mirror because he turns it off with, "I don't think we want that."

He changes up to third, the fag dangling from his lip, the car filling with smoke.

"Leave it on," Mam snaps. "I like it."

"Not now, okay?" Dad braves it. "I've got a headache."

I brace myself. It's going to be a long, long drive.

At half past eleven we cross the old Severn Bridge and turn south towards The West Country. I look back and watch Wales become a distant horizon, wondering if I'll ever be back.

Next morning they're up early and can't get out of the door fast enough. For the next four, terrifying months my sister will be the only mother I'll know. My parents have already taken two days off work because of me – the second thing I feel guilty about. The first is the small matter of ruining their lives. The next time I see them I'll be the fifteen-year-old mother of their eight-day-old grandchild. With bright blue eyes this baby will be the spit of my dad. "A proper little Tom," my brother will say when he comes to the hospital. Not that they'll ever know. They won't ever set eyes on the baby. They don't see the point in 'upsetting people', aka them, so they're not there for my antenatal checks or when I'm given the due date. They're not there when the doctor makes an emergency home visit because my urine test shows my excruciating back pain is a severe kidney infection, and the baby might be at risk. They're not there when, just weeks before I'm due, I buy newborn clothes this baby will wear when we finally leave the hospital after the eight days I'll have her, and they're not there when Braxton Hicks contractions scare the life out of me, or when I wake with a start at night, petrified by the too-rapidly-approaching birth, or when I buy the bracelet that will go with my child when s/he goes to 'more suitable' parents so there's something of me to have and to hold when I'm not there anymore. When I labour in agony all through the night, alone in a side room because that's what you do to under-age girls to teach them a lesson, they're not there. No one is. And when I take my newborn in my arms and swear I will never let her go, there is nobody there but me. And her, my beautiful baby girl.

They will eventually reappear only after the baby has gone and it's time to drive me back home. Without my child. 'Home', where I'll sob into my pillow by night and by day, where no one will listen and no one will hear. Where the world is deaf to young women like me. Girls, just children themselves. Children torn from their child.

The day I give birth to my first-born, June 5th 1972, the funeral of the Duke of Windsor – the former King Edward VIII – is being held at Windsor Castle. I imagine everyone glued to their TV screens. My whole class will be at school sitting their O Level physics exam, but I'm a bit busy with applied biology, discovering the relief of gas and air; learning experientially how an episiotomy feels; finding out how it is to have legs strapped into stirrups to be stitched back together with insufficient anaesthetic, trussed like a turkey at Christmas. And T. Rex tops the charts for the second week running, with lyrics about babies and a wild rock'n'roll child, taunting me when all I do is turn on the radio.

I name her Alison. Choosing it tears me apart. It should be a name I like, but not so much that I'd want it for a child I might one day be allowed to keep. Not my favourite name. They'll probably change it, in any case, her 'proper' family. So Alison it is.

For eight days I nurse her, feed her, bath and change her. I burp her, revelling in her vomiting formula over me, even though I long for her to suckle. Slowly, painfully, my melon breasts shrink when I take

77

the pills that will dry them out. It's excruciating, these breasts fit to burst, spilling my milk, when I have so much to give and I'm denied the gifting.

At night I creep into the nursery, and in the dimness of the nightlight I lift all eight pounds five ounces of her out of her cot, cradling her in my arms as I tiptoe her back to my bed where we lie together in the quiet, eternal dark. Whispering her lullabies I kiss her eyes, her nose, her tiny fingers, trying for all my life to be silent, to move unnoticed, attract no attention. We have to be quiet, or else. But I can't be quiet enough. A nurse arrives and scolds me, tearing her from my arms.

"Please. Don't take her. Please!" I beg.

But I'm fifteen and it's clear: I have no voice.

"It's not safe, Susan," she says sharply. "You might roll onto baby."

She turns to take her back to the nursery.

"Alison," I say.

"Sorry?"

"Her name. It's Alison."

I would never roll onto her. Because that would mean closing my eyes, drifting to sleep, and I'd never waste that precious time. I simply cannot stop gazing at this beautiful baby girl who came from my loins. Yes, I tell her in the dark, you're the spit of your grandad. A right little Tom, and he'd love you, if only he'd see you.

Another day. Bath, change, feed, burp her ... Bath, change, feed and in between I cwtch her to eternity.

In the bed next to mine is Janice. Seventeen and Cornish, she's just given birth to her second child. This adorable baby boy with a shock of red hair will be adopted too, just like the baby girl she's already lost to adoption.

"Don't have nothing to do with it," she tries to warn me. "It's easier. Trust me."

But her words fall on deaf ears as I bath the baby and cwtch her, kiss her and sing, cwtch her and rock her, then cwtch her and feed.

In the blinking of an eye, it's Day Eight. Of course it was always going to come. In the real world time doesn't stand still, no matter what's going on in my head. In my world we stand together forever, side by side and arm in arm, warriors against every injustice the world can throw at us, trying to tear us apart. But in the real world I don't have the strength to fight.

When the moment comes to leave the ward, my social worker insists it's best if she carries 'Baby' down in the lift. I'm left, flat-bellied and leaden-footed, to carry only the pain.

Back at my sister's house, our parents pack me back in the car and we head home. Dad lights up and starts the engine, Roberta Flack on the radio: 'The First Time Ever I Saw Your Face'. It could have been written with exactly that moment in mind, but I'm beyond listening. That line, though – the one about joy filling the earth and lasting – that line I can't fail to hear, and no matter how impregnable this armour I've built around where my heart used to live, it kills a big part of me.

I remember next to nothing about the summer of 1972 except the music. June, July, August ... they come and they go, and all I recall is the songs.

Here's the laugh, though: while I'm away giving birth, my parents move house. No, really. They do. Just like that. To somewhere the neighbours won't know I'd been sent away, won't be speculating why that was, putting two and two together and making four. It's a semi instead of a terrace, and the other end of town. The thing is, it's only a mile, and everyone knows everyone else's business in any case, so there really is no point. For me, though, it's another disorientation. And okay, yes, I'll be going back to school, but it will be into the re-sit class, with the kids who failed maths and English. And since I'd been thinking about a career as a maths teacher maybe, I'm like a fish out of water. Most of my old friends left school at sixteen – staying on is a luxury few can afford – so they won't be there when I walk through the gates on that first day, and I don't know the kids this end of Mount, so nothing will be familiar except this crushing weight of the secret I have to keep. Even when every cell of me screams I should howl from the rooftops that I want my baby back, I'll say nothing.

Cracks start appearing.

It's September, and I'm back in school. But I'm not just in the wrong year group. I'm in the wrong life. No one here knows what I've gone through. Or that's what I think. School's been told I've had 'nervous exhaustion', 'exam stress', whatever. Ironic, given I'm one of those sad kids who loves exams, sailing through. But asked about my long absence, missing my O Levels, I'm word perfect every time. Of course I am. My mother's made it clear, on pain of death, that I'll never tell anyone. So I don't. Not even my best friends, and they don't push it. But I'll just say to any young person out there with a friend who might be in my kind of situation, do. Push it. Get them talking. To you, to an adult they trust, to anyone. Because believe me, they need to.

As for teenage me, I keep on smiling, laughing, developing a reputation as a bit of a joker.

"You should be onstage," my new school friends laugh when I regale them with funny stories. "You're such a comedian."

Yes. I know. I find it a better mask than tragedy.

Breaktime. The radio's on in the sixth-form common room. It's a year since Elton topped the charts, but Tony Blackburn's still playing 'Your Song'. This song is her song, our song, and it floors me. I rush out to the toilet and lock myself in a cubicle, my fist in my mouth to muffle my cries. Then I wash my face and head up to double Economics, all smiles, mask replaced.

Evenings I sit in my unfamiliar bedroom and listen – proper

listen – to Joni Mitchell, 'Little Green', on the album I bought with my birthday money a fortnight after watching her disappear in the back of a social worker's car. I can only hope, pray, she will have the kind of happy ending Joni wished in the song for the baby she lost to adoption, when she signed the papers, when her child was given a new family name. I play and replay it until the grooves in the track are as worn down as I am with the weight of it all.

And I wonder what they've named her.

There's no counselling for girls like me, no support on offer. It's Dad who takes me to Cardiff on the bus weeks later to sign the final papers. The hard stuff in our house is always delegated.

We're called into the mahogany-lined magistrate's room and I try to control my nausea. The enormous desk is designed to intimidate, I suppose, as the whole thing's meant to be. An elderly man reads me the details of what I'm about to sign away, should I put my name to these papers.

"Is this really what you want, Susan?" he asks in a gentle paternal tone.

In my head I say, "Do you know my mother?"

But the answer lies in the fact that he's asked in the first place, so I pick up his fancy fountain pen that I don't really know how to use, and sheet by sheet I sign, and in signing I erase every right I would ever have to know if my child is alive or dead.

Next day I'm back at school. It's all over now. I develop a way of functioning, sure that my secret is safe, my reputation untarnished. Until the Christmas party. A friend's parents have rashly left us the run of the house. Typical teenagers, we illicitly drink anything we've got our hands on: lager and black, cheap cider, martini and advocaat, but thankfully not in the same glass. Some hit the harder stuff. Some drink more than others. I drink little, acutely aware that actions have consequences.

Late on, the 'fittest' boy around tries it on with me, and to be fair

I don't resist a good snog. But when he gets too fresh, I put on the brakes. No, I'm not going upstairs with him, and no I'm not going out the back, either. Or anywhere else. Or any further. He pushes it, but I make it clear it's not happening. He just doesn't get that no means no.

"Ah, come on. Why not?" he spits, not used to not getting his way. "We all know what happened to you, in any case."

It's like a bomb's gone off as he turns and heads off to hit on somebody else, unbothered by leaving me in pieces. I run upstairs and lock myself in the bathroom, mascara streaking my face, and utterly inconsolable as I collapse onto the cold, hard floor. A girlfriend has seen me fly out and she's outside the door now, pleading for me to open it. But I'm gulping air between convulsions of tears when I hear a wailing come from somewhere close by, deafening and primal. Then I realise it's me.

"Please, Sue," she implores, "... just open the door. Please. Let me in, come on."

Who knows how long I'm there. Time's become so elastic in these turbulent days-cum-weeks, but at some point the wailing subsides and instead I'm sobbing with tears and snot and make-up all over my face and hands. I think I'm going to throw up now, and it's not down to alcohol.

"Sue, let me come in, come on. Just open the door," she says. "I need to tell you something. Please."

There's a moment when I can breathe without sobbing again, but my whole body shudders instead.

"Listen," she whispers through the door, "... it's not just you, okay?"

I don't know what she means, but she adds, "It happened to me, as well."

Someone's thrown me a lifeline in a vast bay of quicksand. I don't even know I've reached out and grabbed it, but slowly I'm pulling myself to my knees, hands trembling as I slide back the latch and, exhausted by the effort, fall back to the floor. Easing the door open my friend slips in, and then we're wrapped in each other's arms on a bare tiled floor, weeping like babes for the children we've lost.

We never speak about it again.

Social Services promised a letter telling me how Alison's settling in with her shiny new family. And a photo, they said. They'll send me a photo. For days I wait for the post. Days turn to weeks. I write to ask for news. Nothing. I wait some more, then weeks turn to months. Finally, one morning, a letter falls onto the mat, and it's addressed to me. I open the brown envelope to find a distressingly standard letter. The baby is thriving. She has an older brother. Her dad is an engineer and mum's a hairdresser. She's happy, growing well, and very settled.

They have renamed her Helen.

My stomach rises to my throat, strangling me. Even her name has been taken. Every trace of anything I ever gave her has been erased, as if I never existed. I fold the letter back into the envelope, and there at the bottom is a single photograph, the thing I've been waiting for all that time, a photo I've built my days and my nights, my weeks and my months around, and now I have it in my hand. When I see her there in her pink lacy dress with a mop of fair hair and my Dad's blue eyes, I weep all over again. It's her. My baby girl. I thought I'd cried a river dry, all that chasing and waiting and holding my breath, so very afraid it would never arrive. Afraid – petrified – that in time I would forget her face.

It would be decades later when I'd learn that a mother never forgets her child's face.

September 1975, and my father packs the car. Again. My mother and I slide in between the towels and sheets, the records and clothes, boxes of food, and books, forests of paper and bags of pens, and Dad drives us back over the old Severn Bridge into England. Again we turn right and head south, but this time I can't wait to get away. This time we're heading for Hampshire and a new beginning, a chance to reinvent myself. Because by some miracle I have actually managed to secure a place on a degree course in Economics and Politics at the University of Southampton.

A working-class Valleys girl, I'd been told by the career adviser not to bother applying.

"Go for a secretarial course. You're well-organised, and you've got good people skills. You won't get an offer from Southampton, and even if you do, you won't get the grades."

I'm the first in my family to go to university, and I'll go on to do a Masters degree, to lecture at university and to run my own business. I'll win international writing prizes and become a published poet and playwright.

I've chosen an all-female hall of residence. We unload the car and check out my room. My parents don't hang around. They wouldn't know why they should. But as Dad says goodbye, his body stiffens, fighting back his tears. Hugging me tight he tells me how proud of me he is, and then, embarrassed he retreats down the corridor, lighting a fag as he goes. He will die of a massive first heart attack on New Year's Eve the following year. He'll be forty-nine. Mam hurriedly puts her arms around me and pats me repeatedly on the back. She never did learn the art of hugging.

"Write soon."

Her voice shakes, a crack in it. Then she turns and walks away. Never once did she look back.

As they drive off, I watch from the window until the car disappears, then I set up my record player and slip a vinyl out of its sleeve. It's Janis Ian. 'At Seventeen'. At that age, the truth she learned was that love wasn't meant for ordinary girls like her. And me?

I'm seventeen and some. And I've learned that women bleed.

Decades later, I'm returning to Mount. It's almost fifty years on and I'll be performing my award-nominated solo show telling the story of losing my child to adoption. I'll be telling it in my own words and with my own voice. I'm a theatre-maker these days, and I run my own company. I write and I perform, I produce and direct, and in between I sweep the floor. This is me coming to Mount to confront my biggest fear. I'll be telling the tale that's been told in South Africa and Sweden, New York and Edinburgh, Boston and London, and more. But this – this coming back to where it all began, this coming home – this is a challenge like no other.

"Storytelling at its very best," the reviews have said. "Sad and sweet and beautiful all at once." "Masterful." And it's these and the audience response, along with any strength I might have gained from a life lived, that will carry me into that space. I grew up in a house in which the standard response to expressing an opinion was, "Who do you think you are?!" Finally I'm here to say loud and say clear, "I don't think anymore. I know who I am."

I drive over the new Severn Bridge and along the M4. At Cardiff I turn north and make my way up past Ponty. It always feels like a homecoming as I head up alongside the River Cynon to Mountain Ash.

I arrive early at the venue, taking time to prepare the space and ready myself. I put on costume and make-up, psychological protectors of my heart, and then I'm set to look my home town right in the eyes.

"Home." Quite a four-letter word.

The event has sold out but we squeeze in all who turn out. Half my class from school are here. So too are my extended family. For many it's the first time they've seen me perform, except maybe the sixth-form play long ago. But Lady Bracknell this is not, and I'm no Oscar Wilde.

They line the bar and get their drinks and, in a wonderfully leisurely Valleys way, eventually they settle down. It's all of fifteen minutes late by the time we're ready to go, but no one seems bothered by minor details like that. Drawing myself up to my full five foot six, I take a moment for their eyes to meet mine, and then I tell them the tale of my teenage self, sent far away to have the child I'd be denied the right to raise and to know, and how the story went from there. I weave fact and fantasy, tears and laughter, and yes, there are tears and laughs from them too. Thankfully in the right places. From my class. My family. The community I grew up in. And then, when the last words have left my lips and I take my final bow, the entire audience gets to its feet and gives me a standing ovation. In my home town. Where I was never to wash my dirty laundry.

And I breathe.

CHWARAE TEG

Sue Williams

On that warm day in the spring of 1973, Elaine and I had just changed into our sports kit for netball practice. We were fifteen. While we waited for Mrs Jones our PE teacher to arrive, we used the time to perfect our passing. I was Goal Shooter, one of the two positions in a team of seven allowed to aim balls at the net. Elaine, a natural athlete, could play in any of the other five. I'm tall, at five foot nine, and our speciality was for Elaine to hurl hard and very high passes, not straight at me but to one side. Then I would leap from an unexpected direction, catch the ball over other players' heads, and score a goal. Sometimes I would use a flick of my hand as a directional signal to Elaine, but often she just knew, in that instant, which way I was about to move; we had practised together with such repetition that we had developed an understanding not of words, but of movement.

I was in mid-air when I heard my name being shouted, by a voice I recognised but which, at the same time, didn't sound like itself. Turning my head towards the shouting, I missed my catch and landed empty-handed. As the netball bounced away behind me on the tarmac, I watched Mrs Jones march down the path from the main school building. By this time, she was yelling Elaine's name as well as mine, and waving a piece of paper. She ordered us both into the changing rooms.

'NOW!'

We obeyed. The rest of the team stood around, astonished.

It was not normal for teachers to shout at us. They didn't usually need to, in a girls' school that was, according to a *South Wales*

Evening Post feature that appeared many years after the school had closed, 'famed for its legendary discipline'.

Some purpose-built secondary schools had already been established in Swansea by that time, but ours, Llwyn-y-Bryn – the name translates into English as 'Hill Grove' – had started life as an elegant mansion built within spacious grounds. Situated towards the brow of a hill overlooking Swansea bay, it had become a school – originally private – in 1888 and had suffered bomb damage in 1940. A pick 'n' mix collection of added buildings now scattered the site. Scraps of shrubbery and a few trees remained, although the main greenery consisted of an expanse of fastidiously manicured lawn overlooked by the bay window of the headmistress, Miss Havill's, office. The only onsite sports facilities comprised an old-fashioned gymnasium and two tarmac netball courts located steeply downhill from the original house, the lower one doubling as a tennis court in summer. The netball changing rooms were dark and musty, positioned as they were in the space underneath the school's most quirky extension: a wooden edifice that appeared to be built on stilts. It contained classrooms and was known as 'the verandah' – which it might as well have been, so cold were its rooms in winter.

In 1968 I had passed the Eleven-Plus exam and placed this school as my number one choice. I was the only child from my council estate to gain admission to it. This meant that instead of crossing the road from home and walking about fifty yards to go to the primary school, I now had to catch, alone, the number 93 bus and travel four miles into the town centre, followed by trekking up a long hill. Perhaps because I was the only local kid to get in to Llwyn-y-Bryn, my parents had never been sent information about school transport: the girls I first made friends with in my class all lived on the opposite side of town, and it was weeks before I found out about the school bus that passed the top of my road every day.

Plenty of other instructions had arrived through the post,

however: I had to wear a navy pinafore dress, white blouse, green and white striped tie, plus what turned out to be a very itchy green serge beret and blazer. My mother, bristling with pride that I had got in to what she considered the best school in Swansea, had taken me into town on the number 93 to a shop I'd never been inside before: Sidney Heath, a small family-owned department store in Castle Gardens. It sported an impressive Tudor frontage that my eleven-year-old self thought was genuine, and its interior was richly carpeted and hushed. The instructions for PE kit read:

Gymnastics: White cotton vest, navy knickers with white cotton lining, towel and polythene bag; large shoe bag (16 in. by 16 in. when completed); gym shoes marked with name on outside.

Each article must be clearly marked with the owner's name.

Thankfully we only had to do gymnastics – which I hated – for our first year, and thereafter started netball, which I loved. By 1973, when Elaine and I were the butt of Mrs Jones' anger, the school had seen sense about navy knickers, and whilst they were still required for PE, we now wore green skirts over them.

I stepped out of the spring sunshine and followed Elaine into the understairs cupboard of the changing rooms, mentally running through any rules I might have broken. Which didn't take long: I was hardly ever in trouble, and I was certain this was not one of the rare occasions when I'd done something wrong. I reasoned, therefore, that whatever it was must be Elaine's fault, that I was being blamed by association. Elaine was much feistier than me. She hadn't started at the school aged eleven but had arrived later, when her family moved to Swansea from High Wycombe. English girls were a rarity, and always seemed to be wiser to the ways of the world, far more sophisticated than those of us who had grown up in Swansea (as had most of our parents). Usually, the English girls left again after a couple of years when their fathers changed jobs, but Elaine's family ended up staying.

'I have just...' Mrs Jones had become red in the face, visible even in the gloom. I could see she was trying desperately to maintain self-control, struggling in her fury to formulate words. Elaine and I glanced anxiously at each other. This was not the Mrs Jones we knew and liked – the newly-wed who was young, slim and blonde, whom we regarded as the prettiest teacher. If I had known the term at the time, I might have said she was in danger of spontaneously combusting. We shuffled our feet, waited for Mrs Jones to make sense.

'Miss Havill...'

Oh, no. Suddenly it was clear why Mrs Jones was behaving like this: she'd been dragged over the coals. But what about? Miss Havill addressed school assembly every day, but rarely spoke to pupils individually, and never did any teaching. It was meant to be the job of the Deputy Head, a physics teacher, to dole out punishment. Whatever was coming would be serious.

Mrs Jones had recovered the ability to speak. She was telling us that she knew we were the ringleaders. She was asking, how dare we go behind her back like this? How dare we place her in the position of being hauled in to the Headmistress' office? How dare we take it upon ourselves to form a school rugby team?

In retrospect I should have known what she was talking about, but in that moment I genuinely didn't. I stayed silent.

'It's not a team and it's nothing to do with the school!' Elaine was protesting.

What was nothing to do with the school?

'If it's nothing to do with the school, why have the Welsh Rugby Union written to Miss Havill?' Mrs Jones thrust the letter at us.

We took a couple of steps towards the light of the doorway. As my eyes flicked down from the insignia at the letterhead and along the lines of typing, I began to understand.

I've always been obsessed by sport; I was brought up on it.

Encouraged by my mother, my dad used to take me and my little sister with him when he went to watch the Swans play football at the Vetch Field. In 1970 I'd appeared – the only time before or since – on TV, on Welsh *Match of the Day* as a member of the crowd, standing in front of a stanchion on the mostly empty terraces, waving my black and white scarf. Elaine was just as obsessed as me: we were both in the school hockey team as well as netball, and, for my last Christmas present, my parents had paid for me to join Swansea tennis club. However, apart from Billie Jean King, all of my sporting heroes were male. The truth was that nobody was famous for playing netball or hockey. Not even the best in the world were shown on television; between us, Elaine and I couldn't have named a single international player. By contrast, *Match of the Day* showcased football every Saturday, and the BBC televised the rugby Home Internationals in February and March each year. Not only that, but a matter of weeks previously, on January 27th 1973, the Barbarians – in other words the British Isles – had beaten New Zealand for the first time ever, in Cardiff. It had been a comprehensive victory where, in the opening minutes, Gareth Edwards had scored a famous try that even today is widely considered to be the greatest in the history of the game.

The sports we played at school were netball, hockey, tennis and rounders. The sports we talked about at school were football and rugby. These were often the subject of argument between me and Elaine, because she fervently supported England. She had by far the upper hand with football, but when it came to rugby, her fervour was not rewarded by the performance of the English team at that time, who often finished bottom of the Five Nations championship. The Welsh team, by contrast, had dominated world rugby since the beginning of the decade, and seven of them were in the victorious Barbarians side. Six of those Welsh players had been involved in that famous try.

This is how rugby permeated the ether. Both my parents were fans. And plenty of the girls in school, including some who didn't like either hockey or netball, wished we could have a go at it – not that we ever seriously considered this a possibility. But suddenly, that had changed. Our friend Barbara, the hockey team goalkeeper, had gathered us around to explain that her father, one of the Swansea rugby club coaches, would be happy to introduce us to the sport – as long as our parents didn't object. Object? When I told my mum and dad, they were thrilled.

One weekend soon afterwards, some having travelled by bus, others by car, one or two on foot, a crowd of us had converged on a playing field in the Townhill area of Swansea then, as now, known as 'The Ganges' because of its tendency to flood at the slightest hint of rain. Most girls, but not all, were Llwyn-y-Bryn pupils. Barbara's father, arriving with a professional-looking net bag full of rugby balls, had put us properly through our paces. He had us running around the pitch to warm up, performing various exercises, doing passing drills. He also spent time explaining the rules – unnecessary in my case, since they had already been drummed into me by my father. I fancied myself as a kicker, and in my memory was the last one off the pitch that day, using every dying second to keep on kicking for goal, my rugby ball the last to be returned to the net bag. Every one of us wanted to carry on training. We agreed to return in a fortnight.

Ten days later I was standing in the half-light of the verandah changing rooms, scanning the WRU letter for any mention of the players: Gareth Edwards, perhaps? Phil Bennett, or my namesake, JPR Williams? But I had never heard of the men whose names were inscribed at the top of the page, nor the signatory. To this day I have no idea who wrote it, but I remember its words clearly. It stated that by forming a team the school were putting pupils at risk, because rugby was dangerous for young women. The WRU wanted to be assured it would be stopped.

But you can't stop us, was what I was thinking. It's not illegal. Straight away I questioned myself. Perhaps it really wasn't legal for females to play the sport. But surely Barbara's father wouldn't have been willing to break the law?

What neither Elaine nor I could have known was that women had been playing rugby since at least 1887, when the first instance is recorded, of a girl in Enniskillen, Northern Ireland: she scored a try for the school team in which she played alongside her brothers. There are various isolated examples, around the world, from the end of the nineteenth and beginning of the twentieth centuries. We will never know the real picture, given the huge gaps in the recording of women's lives over time, but suffice to say that from about the 1960s, teams were being formed, especially in Australia, France and England. Fixtures had begun to be played. Later, the USA would be at the forefront.

I can't say that either Elaine or I were aware of it in 1973, but it had been three years since the Equal Pay Act became law. It would still be two years until the Sex Discrimination Act, which was to set up the Equal Opportunities Commission, but it was a time of great change. My mother's views on what I would later recognise as gender politics are a good illustration of the conflicting attitudes that abounded at the time. Having left school at fourteen without qualifications – she had not been permitted by the education authorities even to sit the Eleven-Plus examination – she did shop work before training as a shorthand typist. She taught me and my sister that it was wrong to have sex until you got married; she did not hold with the view that married women should give up their jobs, but on the other hand she was adamant that when you had children you had to stop working. It was therefore right that men were paid more for doing the same jobs as women, because they had families to support. I would like to claim that I was annoyed by this circular reasoning, except that would be untrue. I think I just accepted it. But the fact that even my mother, a relatively uneducated person, could be delighted that I had the chance to play rugby, only serves to highlight exactly how retrograde the attitudes of certain men in authority were at the time.

Mrs Jones had taken the letter from our hands.

'Do your parents know about this?' she demanded.

'Yes,' Elaine and I both said.

'Barbara's father is training us,' Elaine added.

This made matters worse. The next words Mrs Jones spoke were in the form of orders. The rugby was to come to an end. No arguments. Elaine and I were to tell everyone immediately. Miss Havill was writing to the WRU to assure them the matter had been dealt with.

Elaine was standing her ground. This isn't fair; it's up to us what we do outside school. But something inside me knew it would be pointless to protest. Although our school excelled at sport – we would become netball league champions that season – and Elaine and I both knew we were good players, we hadn't even been allowed to attend county trials, because this was our O level year. The school, heavily focussed on academics, held that we would be unable to handle county representation – which ended at Easter – alongside studying for exams that didn't start until late May. Against this background I knew that no one would be prepared to defend our right to play rugby. Indeed, the people in supposed authority over us – women – were all capitulating because a man nobody knew had written a letter. I could feel my insides tightening with the injustice of it, and being screwed yet tighter by the worry of how to explain to the rest of the girls. What would we say to Barbara, let alone her dad?

I needn't have worried. As if by magic, the whole thing fell away. Barbara's father had already been got at by what my future, politicised self would probably have described as the forces of reaction.

Neither my nor Elaine's parents thought what had happened was fair, but there was never any suggestion they would make a fuss. The following year, our Lower Sixth, both Elaine and I got into the county side. I was also selected to represent Wales and, in 1974, I played against Northern Ireland in Cardiff. So I did have my moment of glory, but not in rugby.

In the autumn of 1975 Elaine went to Hull for university, I to London. After graduation we lost touch. When I was living in London in 1981, my boyfriend, a postgraduate at Imperial College, came home one day and told me that Imperial had formed a women's rugby side.

I felt suddenly, painfully jealous. I cried. I had trouble explaining to him why – perhaps because I missed those friends from school. Perhaps because things had moved so far forwards that what had happened to me, and Elaine felt, only eight years later, practically Jurassic.

In 1982, Imperial College Ladies went on a tour of France. In 1983, the year in which the Women's Rugby Football Union was formed, I had my first child. After working as a probation officer in London, I moved back to Swansea in 1992. I played club tennis and squash for a number of years. As for rugby, which I never played again, the first women's Six Nations championship took place in 1996.

In the early 2000s, when I worked in government, two things happened at around the same time. I was appointed to the Sports Council for Wales, and, via Friends Reunited, I found Elaine again. During my six years on the Sports Council, I entertained many staff and board members with the story of how, aged only fifteen, I had been barred by the Welsh Rugby Union never having played a single match.

As for Elaine, she had become a teacher, not to mention a martial arts black belt. By the time we resumed contact she was living in the

USA, having retrained as a veterinary surgeon. Latterly, she has become possibly the only Ivy League professor of veterinary medicine to support the English rugby team. I'm not sure she realises what the Welsh words 'Chwarae Teg' mean, but what I do know is that – thanks in part, perhaps, to what happened on that day in 1973 – she and I share the same profound commitment to fair play.

NOT IN SMOOTH WAYS

Sue Jenkins

My father was very proud of his Give-A-Show Projector, though he couldn't afford many slides for it. As a child I got to sit in our lounge, with the curtains pulled, and look at images of Niagara Falls – over, and over, and over again. A coalminer's son from Fforestfach, he knew he would never get to see the Falls – a trip to London to stay with Auntie Doris Morris was as exotic as it got for our family – but this was a good second best. My father was very proud of me too, especially when, in 1968, I passed the Eleven-Plus, so I could go to Llwyn-y-Bryn.

Llwyn-y-Bryn High School for Girls was for the crème de la crème, the crachach: the journey of high honour lies not in smooth ways embroidered in green thread on the white badge – and etched on our insides. In One North, we wore our uniforms proudly. Although the beret was compulsory, Miss Havill and her cohort were curiously insouciant about hem lengths: unlike with previous generations, there was no longer a ruler measuring height from the floor, so my gymslip was short, very short. And there was the ritual debobble-ising of the beret, the ensuing hole an opportunity to express our burgeoning creativity and practise the embroidery skills we were acquiring in double needlework with Mrs Beese.

In class, we were required to sit in alphabetical order. Towards the end of the first year, a new girl joined. Her surname came just before mine in the alphabet. In our intake there was already Vicky who was black, Helen who was Jewish, Lynn who was tall – we embraced diversity. But this girl was not only late, she was also English. So, we were mean to her. And she was meaner back. She could inflict a lethal dead leg. So, we stopped being mean to her.

She was afraid of nothing, well except for Miss Ivy Davies and the torture chamber of French verbs, of course. She would conduct daring, unofficial experiments in the Chemistry Lab. She would perform exquisite manoeuvres on the top netball court, while I looked up from the bottom court, relegated to a position where I could do no harm. She stepped enthusiastically into the bus that would take us up The Ganges to play hockey in those hideous boots, while I tried to hide. We were also bussed to another hell hole, Swansea Baths: 'No Heavy Petting', cautioned the sign. After our swimming lesson, she would strip off the regulation black bathing costume and stand naked, while I attempted to shower in my towel. She was to become the obvious choice for a leading role in the school play, *The Princess and the Swineherd.*

There was scant formal sex education at Llwyn-y-Bryn. The little word 'no' was considered more than adequate instruction. I hadn't the first clue. Members of Two North gathered earnestly around the blackboard in the Biology Lab for my benefit. Beverley and Moira fashioned a diagram of how to insert a tampon. What? They must surely be having me on ... again. I imagine Miss Nock would have folded her arms atop the shelf of her breasts, and frowned deeply, had the chalk outline and arrows not been wiped away in the nick of time.

Memories of slipping out of school at lunchtime, when it wasn't allowed (our berets abandoned long since), to buy pasties from Eynon's with money earned from our Saturday jobs. There was always ready employment in the shops in town for High School girls who had done their Maths and English O Levels a year early. I allowed customers to try out lipsticks on me on the cosmetics counter at Woolworths; she sold bicycle tyres at Halfords.

The Sixth Form came, and with it the concept of promotion: from the striped tie to the plain green one; access to the windowless common room; becoming prefects. My cousin, four years older than me, was studying for his degree in jail, incarcerated for fighting for the Welsh language, while we spoke the Queen's English, our accents rendered classless from the constant repetition of "I just want to listen to new music which is pure beauty to the ears", and with 'aitch is the eighth letter of the alphabet' in indelible ink on our brains from writing it a hundred times in our blue exercise books. To this day, hearing 'haitch' gives the jolt of an electric shock.

Then more riotous adventures, learning to drink alcohol, time off school to take our driving tests (she, the natural driver, failing for no obvious reason; me passing first time, despite committing the ultimate sin of rolling backwards on my hill start – the examiner was a friend of my father's). Driving gave us freedom, the thrill only heightened by the threat of that tiresome invention, the breathalyser. Seven of us on pedalos in Paignton. Kissing boys. Gathering at Jane's house, her parents away for the weekend again. Walking on the beach at Pennard with our friends, some no longer alive, and with our dogs, still alive in our hearts. That legendary party of Mark's...

Sitting in the Latin Stock Room with Mrs Hughes: it was an easy game, distracting her from Caesar's Endless Gallic Wars by getting her to dip into the vast and worldly caverns of her brain. I do remember enjoying special, serious moments in that tiny room, talking about poetry, Catullus a favourite. "Lesbia, and her pet sparrow – that's where it all started," I can still hear her saying, a twinkle in her clever eye. It was getting more serious between us. My mother smelled a rat. "Are you having an unnatural relationship with that girl?" I looked her in the eye, and I denied her accusation. We sat our A Levels. Our university applications went in, and we left Swansea, separately.

That was in 1975. We never would have dreamt back then that, four decades later, we would be able to marry. Our wedding was at Niagara Falls, and it was witnessed by another old Llwyn-y-Bryn High School girl, whose name came just after ours in the alphabet.

A VIEW LIKE THAT

Rhiannon Lewis

Picture the scene if you will: a school bus, already old-fashioned even in 1978, leaving its garage at TM Daniel in Cardigan to begin its early morning journey. It motors along Gwbert Road, Radio 1 blaring with the latest songs from the charts. The sun is rising behind it as it travels west towards the coast.

Just when you might be anticipating picking up speed beyond the 30mph speed limit sign and experiencing the lurch in the stomach at the sudden drop in the road before descending to the wide-open vista of the sparkling estuary, the bus takes an abrupt right turn and climbs the hill. Leaving the outskirts of Cardigan behind, it roars past the sign pointing towards Ferwig because, although the tiny village is one of its intended destinations, that particular road is too narrow and tortuous for this 40-seater vehicle. It climbs quickly past farmland, the gnarled and leaning trees testifying that, at over 300 feet above sea level, this is a more open landscape, where the curlew still returns to its summer nest on Rhos Tŷ Gwyn. If you turn to glance behind you now, you will see, from the right vantage point, the Teifi Estuary and Cardigan Bay shimmering in the morning sun, the town of Aberteifi waking from its sleepy slumber, Llandoch's terraces clinging to the hills in the distance and, further still, the outline of the Preseli mountains, lilac-coloured. You might not realise it, but the fields you can see over the gorse-topped hedges are owned by farming families who are probably ploughing the land their grandparents ploughed before them.

And just as you're beginning to settle into your journey, two miles out of town the bus stops with a screech of brakes to pick up a passenger from the end of a farm lane. She wears the navy uniform of Cardigan Secondary School and carries, for one so slight, an unfeasibly large leather satchel stuffed with books, which has been fashioned in the only proper place to buy satchels, Geler Jones. She is 15, and a farmer's daughter. Her parents farm 36 acres that are still capable, at a push, with much grit and determination, of sustaining a family of four children.

The journey continues, past other farms, some larger, some smaller, winding eventually past the excellent village school which, despite having only 20 or so pupils, is still open; past Siloam chapel where this teenager will probably be reading a psalm or two in the Sunday service, singing a solo or even sitting in to play the organ if the official organist is unavailable. Other school pupils are picked up from the front of their houses or the end of their lanes.

After a day at school, the journey takes place in reverse. This time the bus travels the length of the estuary first, climbing the hill from Gwbert, past the Cliff Hotel and up towards Ferwig from the direction of Cardigan Bay, dropping the children at the village and eventually (first on in the morning, last off at the end of the day) our by now exhausted teenager returns home.

There will be chores and homework and television, of course. But since January, this teenager has been keeping a detailed diary. Not merely a snapshot, for at well over 100,000 words for 1978 alone, these daily scribblings grow to become something more like a saga. The entries cover all the subjects you would expect from an average fifteen-year-old: anxieties about homework, endless analysis of friendships and friends, first loves and all the excitements and disappointments that are inherent in them, future hopes and aspirations, and the tension of trying to grow into a responsible adult whilst having one's wings regularly clipped and one's time on the phone strictly monitored.

There is something else too. It runs like a silver thread, much like that bus, weaving its way through the fabric of a world that comes vividly back to life on reading the diaries – the growing conscious-ness of what it means to be Welsh and to speak Welsh. Sometimes it is expressed explicitly, sometimes it is only hinted at between the lines – glimpsed, as it were, like the distant sea between the hedges and the golden gorse.

Our teenager is so keen to begin writing her diary that the entries begin on Christmas Day, 1977. 'At last! I have been longing to write in my new diary since the day I bought it.' So here's the first surprise – that it begins in English, despite the fact that home, chapel, and the immediate farming community around her are almost entirely Welsh-speaking. At this stage, there is no analysis of why she begins in English, although there is plenty of discussion on the subject of keeping one in the first place. 'After considerable thought I have decided that I shall write to you (my diary) as I would write to an old friend. It feels more … well, personal, if you understand me.'

And this 'old friend' needs a name.

'Your name will have to reflect your personality as does every name. You will be (or are, I should say!) very considerate, thoughtful, understanding. There to listen to all my problems, and share my happy times. That's the whole purpose of a diary really, isn't it?' After some debate, the 'old friend' is named Phyllis, inspired by the fact that this girl is still starry-eyed after a Christmas production of Gilbert and Sullivan's *Iolanthe,* where Phyllis, one of the characters, is described as an 'Arcadian Shepherdess and Ward in Chancery'.

And what a good listener good old Phyllis proves to be, because even by December 27th our diarist is complaining that she should have bought a Page-a-Day diary; she is already making daily forays into the Extra Notes section at the back, and will eventually supplement the pages with reams of additional paper.

Of course there is a simple explanation for the use of English, although she will not really have thought much about it. Despite the vast majority of her school teachers being Welsh-speaking, and at least half the children coming from Welsh-speaking homes (for every three Welsh-speaking streams entering the school in 1973, there are three corresponding English-speaking streams), the content of her lesson is, more often than not, in English. Subjects such as maths, the sciences, geography are all taught through the medium of English. However, when approaching teachers with a question after lessons, pupils are just as likely to ask them in Welsh as in English. It is what is sometimes described (disparagingly, by some) as a 'natural Welsh school'. Using English comes naturally too, as is the ability to switch between languages, depending on the context, or to whom one is talking.

On the whole, there is an unselfconscious self-confidence in all Welsh things. She has English-speaking friends, Welsh-speaking friends and others whose language at home is Polish. If you ask her whether she thinks her education might be improved by removing her to a Welsh-medium school (if such a thing existed in her area at the time), she will see only disadvantages, the loss of different per-spectives, the loss of wider horizons and more specifically, the loss of valued friendships. Her English-speaking friends don't feel like a threat to her Welsh world. Any 'threat' to the Welsh language is still somewhere over the horizon, beyond the range of the school bus.

But things are afoot. Things have been afoot for quite a while. The form tutor she had on entering the school in 1973 has since been in jail for damaging public property. These are no random acts of vandalism, but targeted protests against the powers that be. Members of Cymdeithas yr Iaith, the Welsh Language Society, want equal status for the Welsh language; they want a Welsh television channel. The sight of road signs, daubed in green paint, is commonplace; television masts are dismantled. Behind the scenes, no doubt, the school must tread a precarious path. It must nurture a generation of pupils who are capable of obeying the 'rules'. But at school and at home, the attitude of adults towards such events is a quiet, tight-lipped support and tacit admiration. The Welsh-speaking English teacher says, knowingly, 'Desperate times call for desperate measures', and our teenager understands exactly what he means. This is not to say that she doesn't grumble with the best of them when *Top of the Pops* disintegrates into a fizz of black and white dots. 'Oh, Cymdeithas yr Iaith is at it again.'

Then all of a sudden on April 19th, after attending a careers convention, this:

'I want to teach Welsh or at least go to a college & get a degree in Welsh & go from there!' Then, before the entry finishes, this:

'Oh, and by the way, this is the last time I'm going to write in English. Due to circumstances of my own choice, I will now write in my mother tongue. The reason I haven't done this up till now is that I felt Welsh was almost impossible to write as one speaks it. The solution is to speak how you write, i.e. better! My spoken Welsh (and my written for that matter) needs improving, so what better way to do it.'

The following day, she is indeed writing in Welsh. This, translated:

'It's quite odd to be writing in Welsh now after some months writing in English but I will get used to it, I hope. The purpose of all this, is to enable me to write Welsh more easily and less stiffly than I do at the moment and to come to use the language as it should be used, not some half 'mish-mash' of words from every other language under the sun! It dawned on me, some time ago, that language isn't an impersonal thing, but something which is a part of every person, and everyone can choose to make the best they can out of that, or to ignore it. I am the language, and every Welshman or Welshwoman can keep the language alive, or see it die. And I, for one, will not lose it without some resistance. Ah! I sound like someone from Cymdeithas yr Iaith philosophising here! It would be sad, don't you think, to see something so beautiful disappearing for ever...'

Fighting talk for a teenager who is not yet 16.

It's clear from the entries that follow that she struggles to write as she speaks. Come to think of it, when has she ever seen her own 'tafodiaith' (dialect) written down? Words more common in her textbooks make a brief appearance: 'efo' (with) instead of 'gyda'; 'tatws' (potatoes) instead of 'tato'; 'trio' (to try) instead of 'treial'. There are long passages that sound more like they're emulating (badly) a novel by Kate Roberts. Initially, there is a lack of confidence, or perhaps a lack of awareness that a colloquially written sentence such as, 'We ni wedi mynd i'r dre i brynu tato newy' (We've been to town to buy new potatoes), is perfectly correct, even though one might not want to write it in an O-level essay on Taliesin. And just when our focus has been drawn right into the minute challenges of self-expression, the lens pans out again to the bigger picture. At the end of a long entry describing how she is enjoying a day home alone when the rest of the family has gone to the Royal Welsh, this, added almost like an afterthought:

'Wales is to get its own exclusive channel! Another success for the Welsh Language Society.' The word 'gorchest' used for success is an interesting choice. A word more commonly associated with military success or victory on a rugby field than political achievement.

The 'gorchest', however, is far from a done deal, and Gwynfor Evans will eventually have to threaten a hunger strike to ensure that the Thatcher government doesn't renege on its pre-election promises. But for now, all that is in the future, and just as the country must jump over its hurdles, so she has hurdles of her own to leap over – the all-consuming O- and A-levels.

The view from the trundling bus broadens out. By the entries of early 1980, there are new developments. The burning of English holiday cottages has begun back in 1979. On 13 March 1980, this:

'There is a rumpus regarding the programme about burning cottages that was on *Nationwide*. The police say that it has put their arrangements/enquiries back by 7 weeks – great! I hope no one catches the people.' But there is no further discussion as to why catching 'them' would not be a good thing and, within half a page, the entries return to more pressing matters: driving lessons, who is now going out with whom, and the prospect of revising Donne, Wordsworth and *Doctor Faustus* all in one evening.

Then suddenly, as if a range of glowering mountains becomes visible for the first time through a too severely trimmed hedge, there are images of Russians invading Afghanistan, Tito being toppled in Yugoslavia. She has serious conversations with her friends about, what seems at the time, the very real prospect of being called up to fight in a third world war. Her parents, both born just too late to fight in the Second World War, seem privileged to have been spared an actual front line, and their comments about the hardships of cheese rationing begin to sound a little hollow. Despite the almost daily lecture of 'work hard, get good results so you can get a good (i.e. clean, i.e. one that doesn't involve staring at the arse end of a cow on a daily basis) job', it occurs to our teenager, for the first time perhaps, that her future world may not turn out to be an improvement on her parents'; things might not always get better.

And for all the successes of the Welsh Language Society closer to home, the A-level Welsh teacher still feels the need to goad us with comments such as, 'The Welsh language will be dead by the time you're grown up'. It is a deliberate tactic, of course, and, even at the time, she can see it for what it is. Saying something is out of bounds to a group of idealistic sixth-formers is always guaranteed to raise the hackles and before we know it, this 17 year old is a card-carrying, paid-up member of Cymdeithas yr Iaith. Of course, she won't be taking any action. Whilst her parents consider it laudable for other people to break the law to protect the Welsh language, she knows very well that she will be skinned alive if she tries anything of the sort. What would 'people' think?

Not surprisingly, for one who spends so much time in a chapel, God is a very real presence throughout the diaries and is often referred to as something which has, potentially, a huge influence: 'I hope God will allow this to happen...', 'I wonder what God has in mind?', 'If only God would tell me what to do!' But on the whole, God is a benign, forgiving presence. He isn't half as scary as the 'people', whoever they are supposed to be. And the parents can be even scarier than that, because the carrots in a 1970s upbringing are far rarer than the sticks.

And soon, there is a new and painful lesson: to every action, there is a reaction. On the face of it, supporting a cause, albeit innocently and only on a membership card, might seem fairly innocuous. But her on-off English boyfriend sees it as a personal dig. Why does she want to join an organisation that hates the English? She tries to explain that the aim is merely to achieve equal status, not obliterate. But the damage is done. Something else goes up in flames and, this time, the fire hasn't been lit by Meibion Glyndŵr.

Soon the A-levels are over and she must venture further afield, to Aberystwyth University to study English, Drama, and, you guessed it, Welsh. She's made it! Now all those hopes and aspirations for the future can be fulfilled. But no sooner has she unpacked her mug tree at Pantycelyn Hall and is signing up for countless fresher events, than she is greeted by a conversation that goes something like this:

Sophisticated Older Student (in Welsh): What's your full name?
Our Teenager: Rhiannon Mary Davies.

S.O.S: No, it isn't.

O.T.: Sorry?

S.O.S: Your name isn't Mary. It's Mari. You're in Pantycelyn now. Next!

It is a brand new experience, this feeling of not being Welsh enough. After all, her mother has spent years studying family history and, in all the 400 years' worth of evidence she's gathered, hasn't come across anyone who has lived much further away than Pembrokeshire – and north Pembrokeshire at that! The edge of her family's known universe stretches in a modest arc around from Carmarthen to Penrhyn Coch with the occasional intrepid deviation to Machynlleth and Dinbych-y-Pysgod. More to the point, both her grandmothers' names had been Mary, and you couldn't get much Welshier than them! But she does find herself wondering whether she should change it, unofficially. And what about the Davies, could that become a Dafydd? And while she's at it, why not add an 'ap' in there too, just for good measure!

Undaunted, and still gripped by language fervour, she signs up to become a voluntary Welsh language tutor. Thousands of English students turn up at Aberystwyth every year and many of them are interested in actually learning Cymraeg. She will be playing her part, drawing people in, creating brand new Welsh speakers who will, in turn, carry the torch for Wales and its beautiful language. The lessons start well. The students are keen. They turn up at the hall once a week. She makes them tea and offers them chocolate biscuits; they make progress with pronunciation.

But then, one day, they turn up despondent. She wonders whether she's started on the mutations too soon. Oh, it has nothing to do with the classes, they say, just the location. She looks around her room. They're right, it could be neater. But they elaborate. It has nothing to do with the room, everything to do with the hall. Each week, on the way through the hall to her room, they've had to endure shouts and insults because they're overheard speaking English. She almost suggests that perhaps they shouldn't say anything between the front entrance and her dormitory door, but realises how ludicrous this sounds.

'Didn't you tell them you were here to learn Welsh?'

Their faces make it clear they didn't get a chance.

They have turned up for the last time, and when they go, a small part of their tutor's idealism goes with them. Surely it must be possible to stand up for something good (a Welsh-speaking hall of residence) without simultaneously doing harm (losing potential Welsh speakers)?

Let us return to the first few diary entries of 1978. She writes an extraordinary list of the things she would like to achieve. Amongst them:

Go to University

Get a degree

Become a Welsh teacher

Work for the BBC

Have a child and make sure they speak Welsh

Write a book

It is rather spooky in the sense that, without referring back to the list in the intervening years, she achieves it all. Despite the challenges, and much disillusionment at times, she never loses her desire to 'do something good for the language, do something good for Wales'.

Re-reading the diaries for the first time in years, it seems to me (that teenager, if you haven't already guessed) that journeying with the language has been a bit like travelling on the old school bus. It's a little battered but more than serviceable. Now and again, people come along and try to tart it up with gaudy stickers, but they soon fall off. On a good day, the bus isn't choosy – it picks up everyone along its route, the farmer's daughter and her siblings, the garage owner's sons, the old post office's children, the kids from the council houses, the teacher's daughter, the descendants of wartime refugees. It waits patiently at the end of the lane for the ones who got up late, who are still struggling to get into their jumpers as they sprint to catch up. The passengers don't always get along. Pencil cases are often tossed around, and there is guaranteed to be someone smoking at the back. But no matter how noisy they are, there is always a hush when they round the headland above the sea and everyone stops nattering for a moment to thank their lucky stars that they, of all people, have been fortunate enough to be born in such a special place, travelling a route together, towards a view like that.

DON'T ASK FOR THE MOON

Liz Jones

That summer it rained for weeks. Susie, Gary, Carl* and I spent most of it huddled around a Formica-topped table in the Cosy Café. We sat at the far end of the long aisle, secreted away in a private, windowless alcove. There we would chain smoke, nurse tepid cups of rust-coloured tea and ponder over books, politics and films.

I felt comfortable there, comfortable with these, my new friends. With them I could be myself, or at least, I could explore what 'being myself' meant. It was a question that in our different ways all four of us were pondering. The Cosy became our academy – a place we went to pool our knowledge and try to make sense of a perplexing world. It also came with its own juke box, its records frozen twelve years ago in 1965. With no David Bowie, Roxy Music or Elton John, we played early Beatles singles (the B-sides, we all agreed, were the best), Elvis (again, the B-sides were the best) and half-forgotten groups of our early childhood: the Dave Clark Five, the Animals and, a throwback to an earlier time still, Glen Miller's wartime swing, 'In the Mood'. That was the one we liked the best; the older the better.

We preferred to live in the past. The present was complicated and confusing; it demanded decisions. It insisted we think about careers, what to do for the rest of our lives; decisions we did not feel ready to face. To paraphrase the Sex Pistols' still-banned single 'Anarchy in the UK' (which I discovered later that summer), we didn't know what we wanted, but we knew how to find it.

There, above the beat of an old record, we would attempt discussions on literature, arguing who was the best – Kafka, Camus,

111

Dostoevsky or Tolstoy. (I spent most of that summer reading *War and Peace*, skipping over the war bits, which I found boring.) We argued over politics, too, with Susie and Carl making the case for liberalism, while Gary and I invoked Marx and Lenin with all the binary certainty of youth.

The one thing we always agreed on was our love of old black and white films (the term 'classic cinema' did not exist yet). *Casablanca*, *The Big Sleep*, *Double Indemnity*: we loved them all. The high point of all our Sundays was the TV matinee slot when, as the rest of the house slept off their roast dinners, we would be studying every look, every gesture, the angle of every hat worn by Bogart, Bacall, or Bette Davis. Those films transported us into the past, or at least a glossy, expressionist version of a past imbued with glamour and romance where, like Bogart, the hero would wear a white tuxedo and, like Ingrid Bergman, the heroine's beauty in soft focus, would espouse love and high ideals.

Carl was obsessed with Bette Davis, her film *Now, Voyager* in particular, where she played Charlotte Vale who, while recovering from a nervous breakdown, embarks on a passionate affair with a man she meets on a South American cruise (played by a smouldering Paul Henreid). I can see Carl now, throwing back his head, drawing on his imaginary cigarette (he was the only one of us who didn't smoke) and becoming Bette Davis: 'Dahlin, don't let's ask for the moon, we have the stars'.

As naive as I was, even I could not fail to see that Carl was gay. He could not be anything else. Everyone, it seemed, knew that Carl was gay, except for Carl himself. In our town – a town of ex-miners, foundry workers and boxers – being 'queer' was weird and dangerous. Diminutive and bookish, Carl already made an easy target. If it weren't for his brothers, things would have been even worse for him. He came from an old traveller family, whose reputation for being 'rough' was passed down from generation to generation long after it was justified. Still, his two older brothers looked the part: square and muscular, with what looked like a permanent snarl on their faces. They were also ferociously protective of their little brother. Yet even their watchfulness would not have been enough to save him if he had come out. The prospect was unthinkable.

Carl, like the rest of our little group, was searching for something else. I was searching for something else. I had just left school knowing I had messed up my A-levels and would not be going to university. It seemed my mother, who had always told me I wasn't 'brainy' enough for university, had been right all along. Even though I was now happily settled with my grandparents, her dire predictions never left me. If only I could be better, cleverer, perhaps she would want me.

With university no longer an option, I was left with a limited set of choices: a job in Hoovers, the bra factory, or Woolworths, or if I was lucky, a 'nice little job in an office' – the pinnacle of my well-meaning gran's ambitions for me.

I had already had a taste of working in an office during a week's work experience at the classified adverts department of the local paper. I loathed it. My main duty was to deliver typewritten advertising copy to the print room – a dingy, dungeon-like basement, dominated by the roar of the press reels and the stench of wet ink. Before entering, I would hover at the door, bracing myself for the inevitable whistles and catcalls that would greet me. It was the same for the other 'girls' in the office, from teens to grand-mothers, few escaped. 'You've got to give as good as you get,' advised Maureen, the motherly woman on the next desk. 'You just look down at their willies and say, "Is that all you've got to offer? I'd save your breath if I were you." That usually shuts them up.' I wish I could have been like Maureen – able to laugh it off and give as good as I got. I wished I could have controlled the tightness I felt in my belly as I entered the room. I wish I could have stopped my cheeks and neck from flushing bright crimson as the catcalls started up.

At the end of the placement, my boss – a rotund, rosy-cheeked man with a plentiful supply of 'blue' jokes – gave me some career advice. 'You should wear more make-up,' he said, 'to help you get a good job.' I think he meant well.

But I had plans of my own and they did not involve wearing more make-up or getting a job. They were not so much plans as non-plans. After leaving school I had secretly decided not to look for a job. Not just yet. The future was abstract and unsettling; it could wait for a while. Instead, I signed on the dole. With youth unemployment at an all-time high, I reckoned the DHSS would not notice one more jobless school leaver. My non-plans were vague, as non-plans would be. They involved lolling around the local library and working my way through the Russian literature section. After meeting Susie, Carl and Gary, I had a new non-plan to add to the list: to spend as much time as possible with them, my intriguing new friends.

Yet only a few months before, I had had plans – real plans. The problem was that none of them were mine and as a result, I had sleepwalked into getting engaged. Richard had been in the class above me in school. With his long hair and round 'granny' glasses, I thought he looked like the young John Lennon; I was smitten. When he came up to me after assembly and asked me if I wanted to come to the Scala to see *Cabaret*, I almost fainted. On our first date, he told me that he had just landed an engineering apprenticeship at Hoovers. It was – as my gran was quick to inform me – a good job with promising prospects.

After his first pay packet, Richard took me out for steak and chips at the new Berni Inn. We ate by candlelight, sharing a bottle of Blue Nun. It was my first ever glass of wine and of course it went straight to my head. We held hands across the table and, by the time our Black Forest gateaux had arrived, he had asked me to get engaged.

114

That getting engaged was anything more than a sweet, romantic thing to do, that it was a prequel to marriage, had only occurred to me in the most abstract sense. It was only when his mother asked what I wanted for an engagement present, and I replied 'David Bowie's new album' (the first thing that entered my head), that I felt the full weight of the commitment I had made. The icy silence that followed was mortifying. 'I was thinking more of a tea set,' his mother said at last. I turned to Richard for help, but he was studying the swirls on the carpet. The tea set was my department and I was letting him down.

After the inevitable break-up, Richard got engaged to Tina, a girl who had been in the same class as me. They were married a year later. Looking for something different, I found an advert for a local am dram group in the library and decided to go along. It was there I met Susie, Carl and Gary.

At five foot, Susie was even shorter than me, but her confident, outrageous glamour made her appear much taller. With her off-the-shoulder dress, her gold high-heeled sandals (an outfit she wore in the middle of day), and her prop of a pink Sobranie cigarette perched at the end of a long holder, she was guaranteed to turn heads. Unlike me, she had no fear of attention.

Gary, two years my senior, had dropped out of art school. This impressed me; to be at art school was romantic enough, but to drop out was downright Bohemian. He had just come back from Brecon, where he had been making Welsh dragon ashtrays for local souvenir shops. With a premature stoop and an almost-emaciated body, he was not good looking, yet with his crumpled linen jacket and collection of silver bangles that jangled from each wrist, he exuded a style of his own.

Carl, a year younger than me, looked even younger than his years. With his tweed jacket and and tie – all of them gleaned from church jumble sales – his taste in clothes, music and, most of all, film, was set firmly in the 1940s.

As for me, with my round face, bobbed hair and smart baggy trousers, I looked like any other eighteen-year girl in my town. Yet I never quite fitted in with other girls like me. Now, among this little group of outsiders, I had found somewhere to belong. When I 'confessed' to them my engagement present humiliation, they exploded into laughter. It was not mockery, but a laughter that said 'Don't worry, it's fine'; it was a laughter that brushed off my shame and embarrassment. In their company, I felt expansive and life felt full of possibilities, even though none of us seemed to know what they were.

In the drama group, we were reading a play called *Hans, The Witch and the Gobbin* (sic). It was a peculiar tale – a light, fairytale comedy. No one seemed to know whose idea it had been to perform it. I was cast as the witch and threw myself into the hammiest of cackles and hisses. Gary, a more sensitive actor, played the Gobbin (a kind of goblin-but-not goblin figure), injecting the role with subtlety and genuine pathos. Carl and Susie played a brother and sister who, like Hansel and Gretel, got lost in the woods and stumbled into the witch's house. They were chosen for their impressive ability to emulate received pronunciation. (I hadn't yet realised it, but this was convent-educated Susie's natural accent.)

When the director, an aspiring actor not long out of drama school, decided to pull the production less than a month before opening night, we were baffled. Perhaps he had decided that directing low-budget amateur dramatics would do his career no good at all. Perhaps he had found himself out of his depth and was suffering an attack of cold feet.

It was after the show was cancelled that the four of us drifted into the Cosy. There we soon developed an unspoken rule that the future was never to be discussed; we were never to ponder over what we wanted to do for a living, or where we wanted to go. Instead, we rattled around together, like a tin of misshapes from the chocolate factory. We were ridiculous, of course, a bunch of misfit fantasists, young poseurs, edging further and further away from reality. Yet we gave each other the courage to be ourselves, to be as individual as we dared. In our secluded corner alcove, we were shielded from the world and the decisions we knew we would have to make one day, but wanted to postpone for as long as possible. We were all teetering on the riverbank, afraid to jump in, fearing the shock of the cold water. Yet gradually, almost imperceptibly, one by one, we were dipping our toes in the river.

It was Carl, the youngest, who was the first to leave. He had found a job in the Tax Office in Cardiff, he announced. He promised to meet up with us, evenings and weekends, but we all knew it wouldn't be the same.

Then Gary left; he just disappeared without saying goodbye. We searched for him around town, but no one seemed to know where he had gone. He had probably gone back to Brecon to make more ashtrays, we agreed. None of us really believed it. I decided to call on his house; I hadn't been there, but as I knew which street he lived in, it wasn't difficult to find. A woman answered the door with the same shy smile and slight stoop as Gary. She blinked when I told her I was looking for her son, although she seemed quite pleased. 'He's fine,' she said. 'He should be back in a month or so,' she added vaguely.

A few days later, when Susie told me she was leaving, I was not surprised. An exotic butterfly like her was destined to fly away. She was going to London to study French, she said, a language she had learned to near-fluency in convent school. She would be staying with a relative in Archway and was leaving on Friday.

And so I was alone. My three best friends, the foundation of my tentative new life, all gone. Now our friendship felt like a mirage, a strange midsummer dream. It was too late, as well, to reconnect with my old schoolfriends. Having all achieved their ambition to get engaged, they were now preoccupied with savings accounts and interest rates – ways they might most quickly accumulate funds to get married and buy a house. They all had nice jobs in offices too: in a building society, the library and the manager's suite of the bra factory.

There was no route back for me – I had wandered too far away. Lacking any better ideas, I decided to look for a job. I even managed to find one, although it was only temporary – a government-funded job creation scheme to help alleviate youth unemployment, based in the local hospital. I was one of three on the scheme: two girls and a boy. They placed us in a windowless basement where the medical records were kept. Our job was to sort through the hundreds of buff-coloured folders and look through the patients' records inside. If a patient was over 70, and no contact had been recorded for the past ten years, it was assumed (presumptuously, looking at it through the eyes of my much older self) that they had died. In those cases, we would throw the folder, as ostentatiously as possible, into the growing pile in the corner, watching the dust motes dance in the air. We were dead record clerks: three Bartlebys sifting through the past ailments of the missing presumed dead.

This job was more cheerful than it sounded. With no one to supervise us (we never even knew who our boss was), the boy would bring his cassette player in and play his recording of the John Peel show the night before. It was in that fluorescent-lit basement with its dust-filled air that I heard punk rock for the first time. The raw, angry energy of bands like the Sex Pistols and X-Ray Spex was a revelation. The world was changing, they were saying, and if you don't like it, you can just fuck off.

Punk taught me that I was angry. It propelled me along the long journey to discover the source of that anger, rooted as it was in parental abandonment. Poly Styrene's high octane, operatic, punk feminist anthem, 'Oh Bondage, Up Yours', became my battle cry.

Yes, up yours! Up yours, sleazy men who wolf-whistled and leered when I had only been trying to do my job. Up yours, mam and dad, for making me feel I was never good enough. Up yours, engagement rings and all the paraphernalia of 'bottom drawers'. Up yours! was my liberation. I was angry and there were others out there just as angry as me. I was not alone.

It was the day of my A-level results and I had woken up to a bad attack of stomach cramps. I had worked hard all summer to avoid thinking about them. Now, the all-or-nothing, make-or-break decisiveness of the moment filled me with dread. My English teacher, Mr. Rees, frowned as he handed me the brown envelope. I knew he had already seen my results. I opened the envelope and yelped. The results were mixed, but at the top of the typewritten page, imprinted into the thin sheet of A4 paper, was a shining A for English.

Mr. Powell told me I should apply through clearing. I had no idea what 'clearing' was. When he explained it meant that I might find a place at university, not next year but next month, I couldn't believe it. This September, I could be at university. Me. At university.

In less than six weeks, I was at Aberystwyth studying English. It was the only university I knew of. I had been there once before to visit a friend. It had been snowing and Penglais, the long, steep hill that runs from the hilltop campus down to the town below, was iced over. Students were sledging down it, on trays they had 'borrowed' from the campus cafeteria. Living in a place that was relaxed enough to tolerate this mass theft of trays appealed to me greatly. It all looked so carefree, so studentish.

During my first term, Gary turned up. His impromptu visit was the first time I had seen him since his disappearance. At first I didn't recognise him; he had filled out, yet his face looked more drawn somehow. He sat in on the semi-easy chair in my student room, eating a boil-in-the-bag chicken chow mein – all I had to offer him.

I sat on the bed besides Tim, my boyfriend of a few weeks, watching Gary pick at his food.

'Is this Vesta?' he asked, referring to the brand of chow mein. I nodded. It was his most coherent moment during the visit. I asked if he wanted to stay, but he said he had to get to Wrexham to see a friend. He didn't have a car and there were no buses at that time on a Saturday. But he insisted, saying he would hitch a lift.

I walked out with him, keen for us to spend some time alone together.

'Where have you been?' I asked.

'Bridgend,' he replied. 'I checked myself in.'

I didn't know what to say. Bridgend was our local code for the nearby Penyfai Mental Hospital. 'They'll drive me to Bridgend' you would say about someone who was getting on your nerves. We would laugh at it; laugh away our fear.

As I watched Gary go down the hill, his stoop more marked than ever, I wished I had not been so shocked when he told me.

'You have some weird friends,' said Tim, on my return. We were not together long.

That was the last time I saw Gary. I still think of him from time to time, have Googled him, searched for him on social media, but nothing. I fear the worst, but I hope I am wrong.

A few months after Gary's visit, I received a letter from Carl. Would I come to his baptism, it said. He had recently converted to the Mormon faith and was inviting me to be his 'chief witness'.

There, in the brand-new concrete and steel Church of the Latter-Day Saints, the congregation gathered in the lobby, just below an elevated glass-lined pool. It was a perfect vantage point to watch the baptism. Carl appeared in a long white robe, towered over by the preacher, an American wearing a sharp-looking business suit and clutching a Bible to his chest.

'Thank you, God, for this fine young man,' he said.

Carl was a fine young man: a sensitive, kind, clever young man. But he was not the young man those words were intended for.

He was strapped into a hydraulic chair that whirred and lowered him into the tank. Underwater, Carl's gown opened up like a white sea anemone. More whirrs and Carl emerged, wet and beaming.

Despite the impressive chair, the ceremony felt sad, lacklustre; even the preacher looked uncomfortable, as if he knew this new member of the flock was trying to be something he could never be. I wondered if Carl had hoped that being submerged in that gleaming, glass tank might somehow wash away his sexuality.

For my part, I never challenged his sexuality; I never dared. If I had, I reasoned, he would be affronted.

Later that summer, I went to visit Susie in Archway, where she was still comfortably set up in her friend's cottage. Her friend had gone home to Hong Kong for six months and had left Susie in charge of the house.

That night, she cooked tofu and vegetables and taught me how to eat with chopsticks. Afterwards, she told me she never wanted to go back home again, that her father used to climb into her bed at night and 'grope' her. She said it as casually as if she was telling me she preferred Darjeeling to Earl Grey.

'What do you mean?' It was all I could think of saying. It was the densest of questions.

'He would come into my bed. Often.'

I'm not sure what I said next. I can only remember feeling a strange, shivery incredulity. It was so ugly and incomprehensible, so beyond my scope. And this was Susie telling me this: glamorous, self-assured Susie. No, I couldn't make sense of it. I said nothing. I didn't have the vocabulary.

Since then, Susie and I have only seen each other a handful of times. Beyond an exchange of Christmas cards, we have had little contact for decades. I had always intended to raise the subject again;

to apologise for my ineptitude, to ask if she was okay, if she wanted to talk about it. But we had drifted so far apart, it would have felt like asking someone I hardly know to tell me their darkest secret.

Years later, I saw Carl again, but not in person. He was on TV, where he had turned up as a contestant on *Mastermind*. His specialist subject, Bette Davis. What else? He gave his vocation as a civil servant and his home as Cardiff. He wore an immaculate, expensive-looking tailored tweed jacket. His features had thickened and his hair was grey, but he was unmistakably Carl. He sat on the black leather chair, swinging his hands ostentatiously as he answered question after question correctly. His body was twisted to one side, as if sitting side-saddle on a horse. No longer attempting received pronunciation, his sing-songy valleys accent was tuned to perfection.

Then came the question he would have been hoping for: In the film, *Now, Voyager*, what was the famous closing line that Bette Davis said to her co-star, Paul Henreid?

Carl took a theatrical pause, before throwing his head back and replying, 'Dahlin, don't let's ask for the moon, we have the stars.'

It was the campest of performances and Carl was having the time of his life.

I pictured him in Cardiff (in arty Canton, perhaps), in some Edwardian bay-fronted house, which he shared with his husband. Their home would be stuffed with Clarice Cliff pottery (his favourite). They would be living just round the corner from Chapter Arts Centre, where Carl is running a classic cinema night with an upcoming season of, yes, Bette Davis films.

I hope I am right.

* Names of people and places have been changed to protect confidentiality.

CH-CH-CHANGES

Carolyn Thomas

The decade that started with the deaths of Hendrix and Joplin didn't bode well, but we were still flushed with a kind of hippie idealism and fired by the publication of *The Female Eunuch*. All ready for the excitement of university, a few of us were probably too naive to realise how close we were, but it was the case that boyfriends were mere accessories, to be uninvited when we were together, singing songs from *After the Gold Rush* and *Tapestry* round my mother's untuned piano, drinking cider in the Cross Keys or, late at night, listening to Zappa, Curved Air and Leonard Cohen. There were, of course, boys in our midst but they were part of the gang, didn't count as potential beaus. Looking back, the truth is we weren't really interested in relationships – our friendship was much more important – and, with typical teenage arrogance, we tended to scorn those at school who were preoccupied by the kind of wedding, house, carpets etc. they'd have.

Leaving Wales for Newcastle was like entering another universe, let alone another planet. The journey north was disconcerting. To the east, bare flat plains stretched out unremittingly and I was used to the lush Neath valley, where the river lazily snakes its way between the mountains. Turning away from the alien, monotonous scene outside, I began to conjure them: luxuriant in woodland, Craig Gwladys, with bald Marchywel looming behind it; the bulk of Drummau, guarded all year round by the giant monolith, Carreg Bica, except on Easter Sunday when it goes to bathe in the River Neath; Cefn Morfydd, with its prehistoric earthworks, Bronze Age ring cairn, Roman marching fort and ubiquitous sheep. While moving away from it, I was attempting to capture a landscape steeped in history, myth and legend.

The new landscape I witnessed on my train journey made me feel strangely exposed but, as we approached Newcastle, I was dazzled by the huge, skeletal bridges. The pattern of arches, repeated in the massive Tyne Bridge, the double-decker High Level Bridge and, between them, the Swing Bridge, continued in the gigantic portico of Central Station. I was well used to rail travel in Wales but the magnificence of this enormous structure dwarfed Neath General, Swansea High Street and Cardiff Central.

Everything was different: the accent, the colour of the buses, and the city itself where the medieval castle rubbed shoulders with brutalist office blocks; where a strange grotesque, the Vampire Rabbit, adorned an elaborate pink building rich in columns and pilasters and balconies; where the cathedral with its lantern tower was unlike anything I had ever seen. Street names like Gallowgate, High Bridge, Pudding Chare, Low Friar Street were totally unfamiliar, resonant of a history very different from that of Neath, where Duck Street, Cow Lane, Orchard Street and Cattle Street suited the old market town. Wales is not short on castles but the imposing stern edifice, the 'new' castle which gives the city its name, was very different from the unassuming Norman ruins in Neath and Swansea or the fantastical hodgepodge in Cardiff. This castle was a symbol of merciless English power, slightly unnerving.

But I soon grew acclimatised to my new surroundings and, at university, it didn't take long to discover like-minded arty hedonists, left-wing feminists, revellers in the joys of being young, free, uninhibited. It was 'Maggie May' and 'Brown Sugar', 'Layla' and 'Lady Marmalade'. We thought we'd be 'Forever Young'. There was much to-ing and fro-ing, attractions based on personality rather than gender and, in a word, promiscuity. I found myself enamoured of a beautiful, clever blonde keen to share her ideas, her records and her bed. During vacations that year, we exchanged highly charged letters mixing ardour with theories about books and politics, probably uninformed and pretentious, since we took ourselves far too seriously.

It was fleeting – we both had other irons in the fire – but she was the first and when I think of her now it is with fondness. Actually, I smile when I think of some of the others. We were excited. Discussions about politics, music and literature went on into the early hours as we were 'Blue' with Joni, took a 'Walk on the Wild Side' with Lou. For us, like Bowie, life was 'Hunky Dory'. Flushed by a night's drinking in the noisy, smoke-filled Union bar, with its taps for Tartan and Federation ales, its rows of Newcastle Brown and Amber bottles, we were elated. We favoured the anachronistically named – and long-since restyled – Men's Bar, where the jukebox seemed always to be alternating between 'Whiskey in the Jar' and 'Life on Mars'. Little wonder, then, with so much euphoria, that we were frequently likely to wake up in a bed other than our own. It was a time unmarked by possessiveness or jealousy or exclusivity, when friendship and exuberance were the drivers on a madcap journey of pleasure and delight. Nilsson's 'Without You' and Andy Williams' 'Solitaire' were reserved for enthusiastically rowdy choruses to the bar's jukebox, not solitary and gloomy introspection about failed 'relationships'.

Everything was changing.

Unaware of our middle-class privilege, we went on demos, wrote atrocious verses to each other, occasionally swore undying love and rudely dismissed the more conservative behaviour of our peers. Already louche, I was having a fine time, several people remarking that 'You're So Vain' might have been penned for me...

Going home was a shock to the system...

Nothing had changed.

The schoolmates who had anguished over furnishings for their future ideal homes were mainly at Teacher Training Colleges in Swansea or Carmarthen or Barry or Cardiff – some brave souls made it as far as Bangor – and most were reuniting with their boyfriends or, rather, future husbands. In some cases, they were already affianced. Others had met new young men but the pattern of ambition was the same – there would be a wedding, a house, a career and, eventually, children. My own circle of intimates picked up where we'd left off, smoking the odd joint and listening to Bob Marley on long lazy summer afternoons in Aberavon or Porthcawl when we weren't working holiday jobs. Their amorous adventures, though, were strictly heterosexual. I felt a bit isolated – not depressed because we were still having too much fun, but unable to participate in their banter, adopting an enigmatic attitude to avoid revealing too much. I don't think I was alarmed that their reaction would be anything other than accepting, but somehow it didn't feel right.

I was restless, too. While university pals lived in places like London and Manchester where there was plenty of action, I was in lovely south Wales. I say that with no irony, because it is beautiful, peaceful, with a deep sense of community, and I was blessed with a liberal family. During my school years, friends were always welcomed at my house and we could smoke, drink and have the kind of high jinks their own stricter parents, among whom were numbered deacons, would have blanched at. Anyway, I had no idea where I could go to encounter the ladies and, besides, had I known, I doubt I would have had the confidence – or courage – to walk into a bar full of strangers, risk getting recognised. Instead, aware that 'Love is the Drug' unobtainable, I lapped up the summer sun with 'Dragonfly' and wrote letters.

My mother's cousin was, reputedly, 'one of those' and, if the subject were ever indelicately raised, my mother's response was always 'that's a horrible thing to say'. Consequently, it was never broached at home and if there were any intimation of gay activity in a television programme, the channel was swiftly changed. There was known to be a lesbian (hushed tones always accompanied the word) in town but she was considered eccentric, slightly mad. To this day, I don't know who she was, but when her name was mentioned, knowing looks would be exchanged.

I think, at that time, most people's idea of a lesbian relationship was based on the butch/femme stereotype invariably invoked on the rare occasions it was represented in the media or alluded to in smutty adolescent jokes. That's really what the word symbolised for me: I couldn't make a connection between what I was up to in Newcastle and the word 'lesbian'. While at school, everyone had flocked to the Windsor Cinema (a Friday night ritual) to see *The Killing of Sister George* which most of my mates found repellent. Certainly, I felt no affinity with the characters, rather a slight shudder of disgust. Thinking about it, this may have had more to do with the fact I found Beryl Reid, Coral Browne and even Susannah York, in that ridiculous baby doll nightie, totally unappetising. The evident superficiality of my response is compounded by a very different reaction to Ingrid Pitt in *The Vampire Lovers*, which gave me a distinct thrill.

I knew, though, that my parents wouldn't want to know. I didn't want to upset them and, besides, they didn't need to know. After all, it's a long way between the respectability of the Neath Valley and the fleshpots of north-east England.

So, throughout my undergraduate days, I lived a double life. I certainly wasn't unhappy. I found I could easily compartmentalise things, and none of my liaisons was serious enough to cause complications in that strict division. My parents always welcomed friends to stay but rarely were they those with whom I'd engaged in any libidinous activity. If they were, sex was off the menu, the walls in our family home being notoriously thin.

My social life began to change after I'd completed my degree. I stayed in Newcastle to begin my postgraduate work but most of my fellow hedonists moved on to study or work elsewhere. I moved in a circle of mainly gay friends but there was an unspoken understanding between us that we were off limits to each other. There were tensions: some embraced consciousness-raising and began to prefer women-only events; the Radical Feminists were distinctly anti-men, something I was never comfortable with; and some, myself among them, were happily irresponsible, content with having a good time. I was quite happy to invite any new acquaintance to 'Touch Me in the Morning'. I should probably be ashamed to admit I remember more about the Social at the end of the National WLM Conference in Newcastle than the event itself.

As a political animal, I was firmly in the camp of Socialist Feminists, having stood alongside both women and men from my undergraduate days when unity against the Bloody Sunday outrage was more important than raising my consciousness. At home in Wales among the family, I was considered to be, at best, going through an eccentric if naive ultra-leftist phase and, at worst, to be dangerously radical. Some took to whistling 'Part of the Union' when I appeared; my response to them was a friendly grimace. *Panorama* footage of a National Abortion Campaign demo briefly focused on me in close up, yelling beneath a red banner. It proved to be of much more concern – and alarm, lest the neighbours should see – to my family than any doubts that may have been growing about my sexuality.

Newcastle didn't have many gay venues and the Eldon was largely the preserve of men, but the 1970s saw the opening of the Senate Bar and the Casablanca Club. It wasn't that we were uncomfortable in the bars we frequented, but here, suddenly, we had a place of our own to drink and somewhere to dance to the latest disco sounds and 'Feel Love' with Donna Summer. It felt like a community. Everything was changing.

I never had to come out in Newcastle. In my circles knowing looks weren't needed, but in Wales, I remained firmly, safely, frustratingly in the closet. Nothing had changed.

My romantic life was never discussed, though it was clear that a few of my old close friends were beginning to draw their own conclusions. A couple I was quite open with, but in other cases the issue – and it was an issue – was never raised, probably because they felt they didn't want to intrude, and I didn't feel I could just blurt it out. We were all easy with each other so what was the harm in remaining silent? Of course, I know now that I should have trusted them – and myself – more at the time but we all live with the benefit of hindsight.

My parents, meanwhile, remained oblivious. At least that's how it appeared. I doubt it ever crossed my father's mind – if anything, I think he was quite relieved I wasn't bringing home unsuitable young men, or those he deemed unsuitable since, in my teens, there had been no shortage of candidates. My mother I'm not so sure about. Once or twice, there was a passing word or a fleeting expression that suggested she was more clued in than I gave her credit for. She was a bit of an enigma when it came to anything gay. As a hairdresser she knew a lot of gay men and her speech was littered with Polari: she never 'went' into town, always trolled, wore slap and, after standing or dancing for a long time, complained about aching in her lallies. She numbered a couple of local fellows, who were well known to be gay, among her friends but at the same time voiced ludicrous stereotypes – gay men, 'queers', were 'lovely dancers' but also 'vicious when they fight'. She'd have been as unconscious of the homophobia implicit in these observations as she was of using gay slang and remained blissfully unaware of any contradiction between adoring the gay men she knew and her views on gay men in general. As for gay women, the topic was closed.

Then, in the cold winter of '76, I met someone and it was serious. We moved in together and I was entirely committed. With Dylan,

I was filled with *Desire*; there'd be no more running around for me! Instead, it was exclusivity and Joan Armatrading's 'Show Some Emotion' rather than libertinism and Iggy Pop's 'Lust for Life'.

The first time I took her to Wales, my parents greeted her as they'd previously greeted all my friends and we had a blast. Proudly, I introduced her to the rugged grandeur of Worm's Head and we sat in Mumbles, eating ice cream, looking across the bay to where Mynydd Dinas and Foel Fynyddau tower scornfully above the industrial sprawl of Port Talbot. We could have been any 'normal' couple but I knew the looks that would be exchanged by passers-by had I taken her hand. I took her to see the waterfalls at Pont Nedd Fechan, told her about the flying viper of Blaen Hepste and the Ceffyl Dŵr. My parents drove us to explore the caves at Dan yr Ogof and afterwards, over a drink in Tafarn y Garreg, my father recounted the story of the Lady of the Lake. I was full of joy to be able to share my Wales with her and she seemed enchanted. But my Wales in the Seventies would not have accepted us and something in my mother's attitude towards her changed during the course of our visit.

It was almost imperceptible and she remained warm, civil and hospitable, but I knew that something was nagging away at her. Before we returned to Newcastle, she took me aside and said 'Don't let her spoil you'. I'm still unclear exactly what she meant – was 'spoil' a belated synonym for initiation into the rites of sapphism or did she just mean 'hurt'? It was a kind of code: she clearly didn't want to say more and I feigned ignorance, so still the unspoken remained just that, although part of me knew that, whatever it meant, it was said with love.

When my parents came to stay with us, we slept in separate beds. A friend from London, who came from a super-trendy family, berated me and threatened to out me if I didn't do it myself. I was appalled. It was not because I was fearful: by this time everyone at work had made up their minds and, if anyone felt moved to ask, I was open – you could say I was completely out (less difficult when you're a lecturer than it would have been in some occupations). Rather, it was because I knew, or thought I did, how my mother felt about her cousin and I didn't want to hurt her. Self-deception? Cowardice? Perhaps. But I make no excuse. It's how I felt at the time. Nothing had changed.

By the late 1970s things were getting nasty. The National Front was making its pernicious presence felt and I found myself standing shoulder to shoulder with fellow members of the Anti-Nazi League in the fight against racism. Things were serious, threatening, and, although I still danced to disco and listened to the albums from sunnier years, the new sounds from the bands who formed Rock Against Racism were capturing the spirit of a frightening time when we had to stand up and be counted. In 1978, 'Glad to Be Gay' instilled in me a sense of pride, despite the fact that some of those I knew scorned it as a 'male thing'. The following year's 'We Are Family' became an anthem for that pride, that defiance, that solidarity, that part of me that remains unchanged.

The 1970s was a conflicted decade for me in many ways. Not an unhappy time – my life in Newcastle was wonderful and I enjoyed being 'home' in Wales with family and friends, though the two felt worlds apart in the way I was living and the opportunities they had to offer. However, I was dishonest with myself and others. Of course, I did actually come out to a few more close friends when I 'fell in love' and, since my partner of the time accompanied me to Wales every summer to the end of the decade, others worked it out without any judgement whatever. Yet it remained a taboo subject with my parents. Nothing had changed.

Could I have acted differently? Of course. Would it have been easier? I doubt it. My mother was right, though. She might almost have been familiar with 'Rumours' (she quite liked Fleetwood Mac and I sometimes caught her humming away to 'Rhiannon'). Things didn't work out in my relationship and we had our own Winter of Discontent, but that's another story.

Years later I met my long-term partner, over whom there was no pretence from the start. Just as the decade had been important for my political education, I had learned my lesson in matters of the heart: I was never going to be dishonest about our relationship. There was no grand announcement. We made no attempt to hide the nature of our feelings for each other and it was actually my mother who came out. Having indulged in a few too many gins one Christmas, she told Sue, 'Carolyn doesn't think I know but I know what she doesn't think I know and I'm happy you'll make her happy.'

Everything changed. Wales was Newcastle; Newcastle was Wales. Both my parents loved her and when my father died, the only person my mother asked for was Sue.

Perhaps I'd grown up (though those closest to me would say that's never likely to happen), and, certainly, during the 1980s, we had different battles to fight. The decade that started with the deaths of Hendrix and Joplin ended with the election of Thatcher.

The Seventies were a weird time in many respects and, depending where you were, what you were doing and what your life was like, they may have been a time of discovery or celebration or hiding of sexual identity. For me, they were all those things and it could sometimes be challenging to reconcile them. Social 'norms' were pretty well entrenched but, in a volatile political climate, they were being challenged. And I was lucky: I was privileged in my university education, my friends, my job and my parents, not necessarily in that order. I don't doubt it was much harder for many people, but I can speak only from my own experience.

Looking back, I fully accept I made mistakes, but I learned from them and I go on learning. Having said that, I still have no clue about the whereabouts of gay bars in Swansea or Cardiff and I rather suspect no such thing exists in Neath...

RICE PUDDING AT
THE ENDS OF THE EARTH
1977

Rona Laycock

We pause at the top, as on the best roller coaster, and then we're off. The death trap, rattle-box taxi takes the bends wide, a wheel is airborne, hovering above a rusting hulk that did not make the corner last year.

Fear is a metallic tang at the back of the tongue. Another bend, another prayer to whomever may be listening. We are at the mercy of a maniac who puts the car into neutral and switches off the engine for the downhill run.

> everlasting journey
> promised by each hairpin
> to the careless traveller

Peter loses his nerve and screams at the driver who rolls his eyes and asks, 'Why engine? No need, this way cheaper!'

> dust covered Death
> scythes through time
> driving a taxi

Images flash by: burqa-clad women, children playing with chicken heads, fat-tailed sheep, Lee-Enfield rifles carried with enviable nonchalance and a Liverpool Football Club shirt.

We reach Kabul. A line of hippies waits outside a bank to cable Mom and Dad back home to send more money. Their speech is slurred and dotted with 'Cool, man,' 'That's radical, man,' and 'He sells the best shit this side of 'Nam, man'.

We head away from Chicken Street to find a cheap hotel where we revel in being the only non-Afghanis in the place. A welcoming pot of jasmine tea and the journey is forgotten for a while.

'Sigi's Restaurant:
Good Food and Rice Pudding'
surprise in Kabul

A German, old enough to have fought in the war, runs one of the restaurants. We discuss this in muted voices. Someone says it is quite possible; the *Abwehr* had units in Afghanistan during the war to keep an eye on the British in India. We're intrigued but not confident enough to ask the proprietor about his origins. He looks like a Hollywood version of Rommel – white hair and piercing blue eyes.

It takes a few days to organise transport to visit the Buddhas of Bamiyan. A slow process but our patience pays off. We find a driver, Jahid, a tall good-looking man with a noble nose and green eyes. Green and blue eyes are said to be the legacy of Alexander the Great's army as it swept through.

Alexander the Great to the western world but known here as Iskander Gujaste, Alexander the Accursed or the Two-Horned One. Mothers still threaten their children with a visit from The Two-Horned One if they misbehave.

We are, clichéd as it sounds, following in his footsteps. We see the same mountains, feel the same earth under our feet, walk under the same skies and breathe the same air as he did. We do not feel the same urge to conquer this land-locked jumble of deserts and mountains.

into the homeland
of master horsemen
the golden boy

Jahid speaks no English and our Pushtu is scant but we settle into a companionable relationship. He loves his country and wants us to understand and appreciate how important his culture and heritage is to him. All along the route he points out important historical sites, especially places where battles were fought.

When Alexander strode across the land he was only twenty-nine but already he had fought his way across an empire and proved his old tutor, Aristotle, wrong. He could not see the ends of the Earth from the top of the Hindu Kush. That view was tantalising him from further East, or so he thought. I am twenty-six, time yet to conquer an empire, but which one?

After a rough journey along dirt tracks leading through the mountains, we stop for a moment on a small plateau. We can see the snowy summit of Koh-i-Baba to the north; the bone-dry air crackles with static as we wash the dust out of our mouths with bottled water. Nomads' tents are pitched a mile or so distant and from those black tents tiny dots speed towards us. As they grow closer we see they are children, so out come the sweets and pencils we carry for just such occasions. When they reach us they stop, chests heaving in the thin air and make a request we cannot understand until, eventually, one of them takes grease from the vehicle's axle and rubs it on his arm. Grease – that's what they want. We rummage in backpacks and dig out suntan lotions and hand creams and the children are delighted.

rationing oxygen
on ancient trade routes
cobalt skies

The air is so dry that their skin becomes parched and shrivelled in no time; then we realise that many of the elderly people we marvel at, toiling on the terraced fields and running sure-footedly up and down steps hewn into rock faces, are probably no older than us.

Boys play us a farewell tune in thanks and send us on our way.

> mountain air —
> boys' flutes
> answer a nightingale

The only other life we meet on the journey is a flock of sheep guarded by the biggest dogs I've ever seen. They hurl themselves at our vehicle and we cower inside as they slaver at the windows without even having to jump on to their hind legs. They do an efficient job of keeping the flock safe from wolves but the sheep have a very nervous air about them.

> guarded by carnivores
> on a dust blown road
> fat-tailed sheep

Not far from here Alexander found a village that claimed kinship with Greeks. The inhabitants believed they were the descendants of Dionysus. The invaders saw ivy for the first time since leaving home and were happy to drink the offered wine. They stayed long enough to enjoy the Bacchanalian hospitality, apparently dancing naked in the mountains before moving on. Not a popular pastime in the country today.

We have to part company with Alexander; his story continues elsewhere. It is a strange feeling, almost as if we were saying goodbye to someone we have grown to know on a short journey. Like those people you befriend on holiday, exchange addresses with, and promise to meet up again. You never do and that is usually for the best. However, I have a feeling we will find Alexander's footprints a little further on in our journey. Paths fork so many times in life that, eventually, they will cross again.

We continue on to Bamiyan where we find a small group of yurts available to visitors. Dinner, served in the largest yurt, consists of fish we have to catch ourselves from a murky pond that is reluctant to give up its wildlife. Although it takes us an hour to catch enough fish for the five of us, Jahid has no problems and catches a sizable fish in five minutes and disappears with his booty.

I am exhausted and my head feels as if it is going to burst; the guidebook describes this as mild altitude sickness. I sleep well but not long enough. A hand shakes me just before dawn; I am forced from my bed and search, stumbling and grumbling, around the freezing yurt until I find warm clothes.

Then outside, catching my breath in the sharp, thin air.

It's gloomy, but as we stand on a high bluff the sun climbs slowly into the sky and reveals in the distance ice-covered mountains glowing pink; nearby the fat-tailed sheep baa and birds of prey wheel above us, their cries echo around the rocks.

> eagles rise on
> a shiver of thin air
> Buddha smiles

The broad valley is perfect; smoke lies across the fields like early morning mist. I think of our warm bed lying empty in the yurt; the indentations we moulded in the night are still witnesses to our sleep.

The sun rises through the crags and *they* are drawn into its light and warmth. How to describe them? Vast, silent – of course, and grown out of the rock face.

Serene, unaffected by the years that have passed since their creation and since Genghis Khan's hordes defaced them, the Buddhas of Bamiyan. Their presence is palpable even at that distance and we stand in silence.

> frostbitten houses
> in the shadow of holy men
> morning voices crackle

When Genghis came this way he slaughtered anything that moved, even the mice, in revenge for the death of his grandson. (In March 2001 the Taliban completed the job he had begun. By destroying the Buddha statues they kept up the tradition of victors attempting to wipe out all evidence of previous cultures.)

Hazaras with their Mongol features remind us of the thousand men Genghis left behind to seed the valley. Even as they work the fields of wheat and barley their eyes draw us into history. I read somewhere that almost 17 million people worldwide are direct descendants of Genghis Khan. Seems he was quite the ladies' man!

> on dun coloured hills
> black goats cry for their kids
> the goatherd sleeps
> only tells them in his dreams
> the hour of their deaths

Animal dung pats are laid out on the roofs of houses, drying in the sun, fuel for the winter. Long irrigation channels cling to the hillsides, mile after mile, bringing water to the fields and trees of the valley. They are small miracles of engineering and a triumph of determination over adversity.

dung on his hands
the young boy laughs
thinking of winter

Push on. Breathe the dust through freeze-dried nostrils until we reach the lakes. Sapphire, lapis, cobalt and turquoise hurt eyes accustomed to forty shades of beige. Band-e Amir, given brilliance by a sun that is marking time.

Tea at the *chaikhana* and we are the centre of attention. Music blares from a tinny transistor and the talk is of Russians. We reassure them we're British and things look up; God knows why, given our mutual histories. The Russians are on our heels, though, and these hills, gorges and caves will soon be home to the mujahideen, armed by the West and hailed as heroes. Like all heroes they will fall and become the hated Taliban and, eventually, demonised. But for now all is calm. The tea is sweet and hot, served from a samovar. Soup is offered. It bubbles and steams so it is probably safe. We eat, even the blobs of fat that float in the tawny mixture. The dryness of the air means we crave oil, grease and fat.

under corrugated iron
at the ends of the Earth
goat tastes good

Let me tell you about the toilets, bane of the fastidious Western traveller. The hole in the floor stinking and rustling with vermin, the bush you think is safe but is in full view of mountain men standing just within the maw of a cave, the hurriedly constructed sarong loo-wall that flaps in the breeze. We tried them all. Clasping each other's hands to prevent a fall into the lowest circle of hell that must lurk under the hole, trying to distract those who may be watching and then weighting the sarong with stones. We learn just how capacious a bladder can be. We also risk dehydration by not drinking enough.

A young girl passes with a herd of goats; when they pause she pelts them with clods of earth or stings one on the back with her stick. She is tiny but they obey her without hesitation – until they find sweet new shoots in a crevice in one of the travertine dams that hold back the lakes. Now they are oblivious to her tantrums and she gives in and squats in the shade of a thorny bush, one eye on them and the other on us.

Discussion turns to the colour of the waters. A beige lizard scurries past our feet – barely perceptible, so clever is his camouflage. His tiny limbs are a blur as he makes his way from cover to cover. We are distracted by his presence and the little girl has started singing to gain our attention. The water is such striking blues because of the mineral content.

A few weeks before our arrival, a European woman was shot dead by local men scandalised by her wanton behaviour and dress as she sunbathed and swam in the lake, too scantily clad for their sensibilities. It's hard to understand how they could be offended by her life but not by her death. We are as far from understanding this mindset as we are from flying to the moon. There's an echo to be heard in our own society whenever we hear the phrase – *She was asking for it*. From where did this judgemental attitude spring? And will it ever be tempered with reasoned argument?

someone's daughter
fair hair billowing in blue water
beyond our reach

The hills and lakes lull me into believing we are timeless. A million sparks flit around my brain as I contemplate my place in this relentless cycle of being. The Buddhas seem completely at ease with the cosmic scale of things. But then again, they're just statues. How to cope with eternity, infinity, the way that everything is rushing to an end, however distant, and then what? A new beginning?

The little girl and her goats are moving on; we are moving on. Sometimes I just want to sit still and listen. You can't listen in the past or the future, I like that. I hear a cicada buzz, the scrape and stumble of the herd of goats or, with eyes closed, those unidentifiable sounds that lurk just on the edge of hearing.

It is a moment when I am present ... I have presence of mind.

There's a phenomenon known as the Reminiscence Bump where older adults have strong memories of what happened to them during their late teens and early twenties. It is believed that this happens because that period is full of new experiences that shape our lives. For me, the Seventies was that time. My first job, getting married, and moving away from the UK to live in a series of very different cultures.

After qualifying as a teacher I left home in Llanelli and found work in a school in west London. I lived in a bedsit and had all the freedoms I could wish for.

When David and I married he was already working in North Africa, so that was our first home together and from there we moved to Pakistan. It came as something of a shock to live in such conservative cultures where women had little or no control over their lives; indeed, most of them were essentially owned by their fathers, brothers or husbands.

It brought home to me how lucky I had been to have had working-class parents who saw no reason why I should not become an engineer, nurse, teacher or train driver! They believed Britain was changing and the chance to enter further education, a chance neither of them had had, meant better life chances for me.

141

To be able to live work and travel to so many amazing places at that time was an opportunity I have never taken for granted, and those experiences form the biggest part of my Reminiscence Bump.

SPIRITS HAVING FLOWN

Sue Davies

In 1978, I ran away to sea.

Impetuous young men often do. They get restless and go off in search of adventure, gold doubloons and exotic maidens in faraway lands. This, however, was the 1970s, a time when even the WRENs didn't go to sea and I was in the middle of my A-levels at a very nice grammar school for girls.

So it came as a bit of a surprise.

It was Jacques Cousteau's fault. My dad watched all his programmes on the TV and I had one of his big glossy books full of amazing photos. In the 1970s scuba diving was a daring new pursuit exclusive to scientists and explorers in places with coral reefs, palm trees and turquoise water, unlike anything we could see at home. The people I knew generally ventured no further than Blackpool or Pwllheli, and apart from one or two young ladies in my class whose mummy and daddy took them skiing or to 'Fraance', the only understanding most of us had of 'abroad' came from Judith Chalmers or *Whicker's World* on a recently rented colour telly.

I was 17 and under pressure to decide what I was going to do with my life. The girls in my class were destined for university or motherhood but both seemed like prison sentences to me. The trouble was, my way ahead was far from clear. All I had was a sneaking secret vision of myself saving whales and befriending dolphins like Jacques Cousteau, so I thought I would do Marine Biology.

I started my A levels with good intentions but insufficient application. I was always in trouble, whether it was for exotic adaptations to my school uniform or for lighting a fag off a Bunsen burner. I yawned in despair through the stupefying sagas of Jane Austen's women in English Lit; the only Lit I engaged with being an entertaining exchange of love poetry with the maths teacher in the back of my homework book. I was also the biology student who ran weeping out of class when they put a small dead rat in front of me and told me to cut it up.

I appreciate that none of these were my finest hours but I just didn't seem to be a good fit for anything. I remember staring out of the windows of too many dreary 1960s classrooms on too many bright, beckoning sunny days and just longing to be out there, wherever there might be.

Then a careers master appeared in school one day and asked me if I had ever considered going to sea in ships.

Wow...

I didn't even know you could do that. There were no ancient mariners in my family. We lived inland. The seaside was my uncle's house on Anglesey. My grandad had been in the navy during the war, apparently. But he wasn't a seaman; he was a printer.

Nevertheless, there was something about the career master's question that day that exploded like a star in my imagination and blew apart the classroom walls for ever.

The impetus sent me fearlessly fibbing my way out of school and onto a train to the Shipping Office on Salford Docks. The man there, with remarkable calm when you think about it, asked if I wanted to be on deck or in the engine room. I had no idea, but happily, swiftly thought the view would be better from the deck so chose that. He told me I had to get myself into Nautical College and get accepted onto a Deck Cadetship by a Shipping Company who would agree to pay for it.

So I did.

My younger self amazes me now: how I found out what to do

and where to go, then just did it, armed with nothing but the reckless optimism of youth. I had no idea what lay ahead, just an exhilarating sense of imminent escape into a big wide amazing world. So it was, that somehow, in secret and without satnav, I engineered my presence at job interviews in Liverpool and London and still got home in time for tea in my school uniform.

I discovered I needed physics O-level to get into college, so I borrowed my best friend's books and crammed it that summer, with the dog, in the field at the back of our house. In September, I passed the entrance exam for Fleetwood Nautical College.

At the job interview that got me into a well-known (at that time) shipping company, I found myself perched on the edge of a chair in front of yet another board of stern-looking men, but this time, my main interrogator, with his eyes half-closed against the smoke from his pipe, was nodding slowly.

"You have all the qualifications. I suppose we'll have to let you in," he said.

And that was that.

I remember walking up to the Nautical College for the first time and stopping to gaze up at the blue sky, at all the aerials, the radar scanners gently turning on the roof. The moment felt absolutely loaded with possibilities.

I felt myself to be a courageous pioneering creature, indestructible and independent, but found out years later that my father had had to sign a letter allowing me to go. My mother, I also found out later, had been devastated by my career choice and by my secrecy. Nevertheless, and without telling my father, she repeatedly sent me money 'just in case' and hers were the only letters I received in the early years. How precious they became as they followed and found me all over a world without mobiles or emails, or Zoom.

I was the only female pupil in the Deck Cadet class of '78 and the most poorly prepared. To equip girls for the careers and the lives we were expected to follow in the 1970s, we were taught such things as probability and matrices (and love poetry) in maths. Sadly, on the very first step of my brilliant career as a celestial navigator, I was confronted by spherical trigonometry in a class of young men who already knew what that was.

It didn't help that we were all terrified of the navigation teacher. He was a former sea captain of the 'old school' and no one dared stand up in his class and ask him to explain anything. His scorn was excruciating, but I had no choice. At night the boys could go back to the college hostel where they were staying with the Mates and Masters and ask for their help but I, as a girl, wasn't allowed to be with any of them. I was put in a B&B in Blackpool ten miles away and although my landlady was lovely, her spherical trigonometry was not top of the class!

I was to meet several men like Captain Horrible in those early days: men for whom the idea of women at sea was genuinely incomprehensible and outrageous. The final time I stood up to him, the boys were behind me as usual, keeping their heads down but with their pens out ready to capture the answers. The Captain didn't even start to explain anything. He just roared at me like Mr Bumble, yelling that I was a Split-Arsed Mechanic and shouldn't be allowed at sea. The room went silent. So did I. What could I say? I quietly packed up my books and walked out. I carried on walking through the college gates and got on the tram and would not cry until it set off.

It was two weeks before our final exams.

The boys told the Head of Year what had happened. He came himself to my digs and coaxed me out and persuaded me to return to the college. He made the Captain apologise to me in the corridor where everyone could see him and hear my response. He apologised quietly. I responded quite loudly with a very seaman-like phrase and what a joyful experience that was! Then the Head of Year taught me himself every day in the library, and because of him I passed my 2nd Mates' Certificate.

When I joined my first ship at midnight in Gijon, northern Spain, I was with three engineers and a sparky I had met on the plane. It had been my first flight and also for the first time, I was drunk. The ship – my first view of an LPG tanker – resembled a giant plateful of spaghetti and I was led through a maze of steel alleyways to the crew bar. Sadly, in the British Merchant Navy in the 1970s, officers did not go to the crew bar. In fact, officers and crew did not fraternise at all. We ate in the Officers' Saloon. They ate in the Crew's Mess. Our cabins were on different decks. I was joining this ship as an Officer Cadet and I had no idea. I just thought everyone was very friendly and I smiled politely when the Bosun showed off the hunting-scene tattoo on his back and with a flourish whipped down his jeans to reveal where the fox disappeared.

I also had no idea how, several hours later, a very large and angry First Mate found me lying hideously hung-over in my cabin. This was not a brilliant start to my first day at sea. I was, however, still fully clothed – which apparently, for a first trip cadet, was quite something.

I had been led to believe that there would be other women on the ship. There weren't. It turned out there were only four of us in a company of over two thousand men so we were thinly spread through the fleet and very much a novelty. Men at sea had not yet had time to get used to women being there. A question at my job interview should have served as a warning:

"What would you do if a crewman knocked on your cabin door at night?" Mr Pipe Smoke had asked with a grave expression. (Would they even be allowed to ask that now?)

"I would call for a responsible officer," I'd spouted.

I could see he knew my answer was both ridiculous and what was expected of me. He had spent his life at sea. He knew it was just as likely to be the responsible officer who knocked on my door at night.

I was to sail with all sorts of characters over the coming years. There were men on every ship and throughout the ranks who were great fun, honest and kind, and some have remained the bedrock of my odd band of friends to this day. But I found myself surrounded by a whole range of behaviours and emotions: resentment, protectiveness, lust, derision, drunkenness, even infatuation sometimes. I was aware that the attention I received – good or bad – was not because I was something special. It was simply because I was the only female there.

Occasionally one of the men would even say as much to me or reproach me for being in a boilersuit, getting dirty, getting drunk, (just like them). Some reckoned I should have been at home, wearing a dress, cooking dinner, producing a man's heirs.

I remember one young man sneeringly showing me a photo of his pretty wife with her clean shiny hair, in her nice dress, holding her baby. He told me she was lovely and I was unnatural. I silently envied her. Then, not very long after, her lovely man knocked at my cabin door.

One or two of my shipmates were proper, certifiable, lecherous creeps. A 2nd Engineer springs to the front of the queue. At midnight each night as I came off watch, he would be lying in wait on the deck above my cabin. He made two Junior Engineers hold his ankles so he could dangle over the ship's side and watch through my window as I got undressed for bed.

There were some nasty characters too; again, one particular piece of work springs to mind, but I refuse to give him headspace even now. These were people who abused their power over others and they were able to do so because there was no sexism or bullying legislation then and no HR Department or police force at sea.

Sometimes a sort of rough justice was the best one could hope for.

I hear that it is different for the women who go to sea nowadays. There are lots of them and they have much more of a sense of their own empowerment and the accountability of others. One told me recently, with a sort of arrogant confidence we just didn't have back then, "I wouldn't have stood for any of that."

Well, we didn't have that choice, so we stood for it and we dealt with things as best we could. When men in higher ranks said you could lose your job if you disobeyed, you just believed them. You had no reason not to.

'Mental Health' was not something I remember noticing in the Ship's Master's Medical Book.

(The pictures showing the effects of 'tropical' diseases on seafarers' private parts, however, were frequently pointed out to me, along with the extraordinary messages one could send to describe them to the doctors ashore, entirely by the use of flags!)

In total contrast, however, throughout my memories and popping like spangles on a moonlit ocean, were moments of extraordinary tenderness:

There was one Easter Sunday in Port de Bouc when I was missing my family and came off watch to find beautifully decorated chocolate eggs arranged on my bunk, without a word from whoever had put them there.

And the washerwoman in Kingston, Jamaica, who reached into her bag and produced a mango for me, the first I had ever seen. She stroked my face and told me I reminded her of her daughter.

The dockers in New York in minus 25 degrees who gave me a warm woolly hat that I've worn every winter to this day and the dockers in Birkenhead who searched the second-hand shops around the docks for my cassette player. Some local ladies had taken it from my cabin the night before.

And smiling Pepe the Peruvian docker in Matarani, who opened

Brazil nuts for me with his forklift truck down in the bottom of Number Three hold.

There was a pilot in the Suez Canal who came up onto the bridge with a sweet lemon from his garden for me, and another who had sailed with me before and offered his compliments over the VHF from the Russian ship behind us.

And there was Yanbu in the Red Sea and a photograph I treasure, of me radiant on the bridge wing of my favourite ship and beaming up at my favourite 2nd Mate with a big bunch of beautiful flowers in my arms. They had just been presented to me for being the first female officer into the new port in a mad ceremony involving white doves and temperatures of 50 degrees where we had to keep moving to stop our shoes melting on the deck!

Then there was the Captain who wept beside me on the bridge, one night as we sailed from Livorno. He had been in the Deck Boy's cabin and seen the presents he had bought for his mother and sisters. It was the boy's first trip to sea and he was due to pay off the next day. He'd been out celebrating and no one had been able to find him. We left his body trapped and drowned in the cold dark water under the jetty.

I was at sea at a time of momentous change in British Shipping, at the cusp between the old ways and the new. I was there when it could take six weeks to cross the Pacific Ocean and you could spend several days in port because you had to stop cargo whenever it rained. I was there when we had duty-free alcohol and cigarettes onboard and we all drank the bars dry on ship and onshore and smoked endlessly. There were some extraordinary characters and mad runs ashore all over the world from the Straits of Magellan to the South China Sea. We enjoyed so many unspoilt tropical beaches and infamous seafarers' playgrounds that since have been sanitised or lost under high-rise buildings.

These were the early days of containerisation and ships that still had derricks and 'tween decks rapidly adapted to cope. Without any kind of automatic locking systems, we cadets would climb like monkeys on top of the boxes, two or three high, leaning over precariously in an attempt to secure the lock fasteners with long forked poles.

And I remember a man from Marconi sailing with us on a trip from Avonmouth to South America. We were still position-fixing by dead reckoning and sights of the sun and stars but he was there to test some new equipment, which he said would help us find our way by the use of satellites.

We called him Howard Hughes, enjoyed ourselves getting him drunk ashore and mocked the unreliability of his modern technology compared to our sextants and nautical tables. We had no idea that this 'sat-nav' was to totally revolutionise centuries of worldwide navigation by sea and air and land – even finding its way into every housewife's pocket.

For me, however, more than anything else, when I look back at my 1970s, I see personal moments that remain unsurpassed, experiences that left so profound an impression that I can almost see and hear and breathe them now, after forty years.

I remember my first watch alone on the bridge. I was 19 and entrusted with the care of a large LPG tanker and the lives of thirty sleeping men. It was night time in the Red Sea with the flames from the well heads and the jewelled lights of other ships moving as gracefully as ballerinas on the black glossy swell.

I remember the sea as a perfect disc around us in the Tropics and at sunset, how the fiery light would glow on decks made opalescent by the humid air. I see myself playing my harmonica, swaying on a bridge wing under the constellations, with the faint fragrance of warm spice on the breeze from some distant land, thinking of the words of Omar Khayyam and his 'great inverted bowl' of a sky.

I remember dolphins leaping over the bulbous bow, flying fish landing on the main deck and scooping them back into the sea, and unknown little birds that would rest awhile on their amazing journeys and be given scraps by the cook.

I remember the minarets of the Bosphorus and the snowy peaks of Tierra del Fuego, the seas and straits whose names and legends had enchanted my childhood: the Sargasso Sea, the Sea of Marmara, the Straits of Magellan, Messina, Malacca, the Bermuda Triangle, the Gates of Hell.

I remember dry dock in Naples, Capri and a bearded man in a wheelchair softly singing 'Luna Caprese' in the Villa Comunale.

I remember the fun of calling up the pilots on the VHF as we waited in the shimmering anchorage at Port Said for a place in the convoy for the Suez Canal and the responses from the other ships when my voice entered the babel.

And outrageous watches ashore with my shipmates in Valparaiso, Cristobal, Pascagoula, Cartagena, the coconut-dotted beaches of Maceio and Recife, the Missions to Seamen and the bars, all the bars!

And stepping onto a quayside in Callao in Peru and suddenly realising where I was and that my friends were still in school.

Then there was that night high above the clouds at the top of the World, wide-eyed at the window of a Boeing 747 while Japanese people slept cocooned all around me. It was Christmas Eve, I was in my teens and on my way home after six months on a much-loved ship, with so many tales to tell my mother of wonderful things she had never seen. As we quietly slipped through the Arctic night I replayed over and over the in-flight music on my earphones. To this day, when I hear it, I have to stop and breathe deeply as it carries me back.

It was the Bee Gees, 'Spirits (Having Flown)'.

TRY HARDER

Sheila Kitrick

When we remember the past, it's usually a selective process dependent upon the extent to which we have consciously or unconsciously repressed fragments of experience. Thus, my superficial recollection of the 1970s might bring to mind youthful vitality, music and dance – a perfect antidote to living through Covid-19, economic dearth and civil unrest.

It's tempting to seek relief from the reality of now by remembering the good times, but in so doing you run the risk of spraying paint stripper over a bodged wall. Old layers of repressed truths reveal themselves. A decades-old refuse tip of ill-judged actions and mistakes won't stay put in its home decade. It becomes harder to counterbalance the dead weight of remembered failings with memories of happiness and self-worth.

'You were a terrible mother.'

'We never lived anywhere for long enough to make friends.'

'You only thought about yourself and what you wanted.'

'You took us from a nice girls' school in Dorset and dumped us in a naff school on a sink estate in Tottenham.'

'You are a bad mummy.'

Imagine yourself in the dock searching for words with which to defend yourself against the accusations of your fifty-plus daughter, in the cultural climate of 2021? Your awkwardly-spoken rhetoric about getting by fifty years ago fails to make a case. The increasingly lame delivery is seen as evasive and probably playing for time in which to spin historic events to justify irresponsible actions. Any attempt to elaborate and cite original sources will certainly be countered with a sneering cry of 'don't blame the times'. I don't, but the culture existed, and I was part of it, and I need to give this more thought.

Were we more or less enlightened in the Seventies by accommodating the good and evil dichotomy that is human nature? Back then, post puberty, the compelling need to clasp friends, acquaintances and strangers to our collective bosoms, did not exist. A smile, handshake or word or two seemed to suffice. 'Love-ins' were not the norm, or if they were, I was elsewhere. We did not emote on demand, having been told by wartime parents that crocodile tears 'cut no ice'. By the same token, everyone under the age of thirty was not infantilised.

I think these observations are fair, but would I describe them thus if I were twenty-something rather than seventy-something? It's a tricky question to answer because the perception of the twenty-something I once was changed radically between 1970 and 1980. A contextual understanding of my experience of the decade might be improved by providing a brief historical background.

I entered 1970 in Dorset, as an uneducated and poor twenty-seven-year-old single mother of two. I'd left my London school in 1957, aged fifteen, and apart from work experience had no further education. Shortly after my twentieth birthday, I married Roger, a twenty-one-year-old submariner (now deceased) and accompanied him on a two-year overseas posting to Malta. I found married life in a hard-drinking naval community difficult to adapt to and Roger proved to be unstable and physically abusive.

I learned, from other wives – especially Sherry, the wife of a Chief Petty Officer – that Roger's behaviour was not uncommon in overseas communities like ours and you lived with it.

We returned to the UK at the end of 1964 with our eleven-month-old daughter and the marriage limped on until 1967 and a second pregnancy. Roger was posted to Portland where we bought a small house but, following the baby's birth, I found proof of my husband's infidelity before and during my hospital stay. Our relationship fragmented and one awful night, without preparation, I ran. We were broke and homeless until Sherry, who lived locally, took us into her home. My divorce was finalised in May 1969 and a maintenance order, which subsequently proved to be unenforceable, was granted: I was also awarded sole custody of the children. By Christmas 1970 we had moved into a council flat and my solicitor later advised me that Roger had auctioned off the entire contents of our Portland house including my personal possessions. With the proceeds, he'd bought himself out of the Navy and left the country. I sued him under The Married Women's Property Act, but in his absence I received no compensation. Likewise, the DHSS failed to prosecute him for fraudulently claiming benefits as a married man. As a result, we were awarded a DHSS benefit pending his return to the UK. We never saw Roger again.

I met Ash, a self-employed carpenter, at a music venue in 1968 and became very fond of him. He'd been living in his car and it was agreed that he could stay at our flat over the weekends when he was working away.

In the meantime, I needed a supplementary income.

Sherry's parents, Sam and May, owned a busy pub and B&B in town and they offered me a cleaning job. Sam had a second job with the County Council and this fact along with his guidance was to have a major effect on my future.

During the Seventies, Dorchester was a popular tourist destination, famous for its Iron Age and Roman history and the literature of Thomas Hardy. Busloads of tourists, including Americans, would pull up at the Antelope Coaching Inn for refreshments. I was employed to work on buffet lunches served in the 'Oak Room', an upper chamber that had once enjoyed notoriety as Judge Jeffreys' courtroom during the Bloody Assizes in 1685. He had been known as the 'hanging judge' and was said to haunt the courtyard of the inn. I became the purveyor of its history and, positioned in front of an area of oak panelling, I'd explain that due to Judge Jeffrey's unpopularity with the mob, he'd exit through a false panel onto a flight of steps leading down to a tunnel running under the streets, to his lodgings in High West Street.

During 1971, an ex-Yorkshire miner and his wife asked Sam's advice about their plan to open a nightclub in Dorchester featuring a weekly 'Striperama' night. There was an established nightclub in town, The Steering Wheel, that had featured headline performers of the times such as Billy Fury, and although I don't think the Stones ever appeared there, they did stay down the road at the Kings Arms Hotel – but as far as I know, no strip shows.

The Town House, with its London skyline décor, duly opened and Sherry was recruited to manage the bar. I would occasionally help out on the eight-hour shifts, paid at 25p per hour. The performers were bussed in from London and the shows proved to be massively popular, with a mainly male audience packing the club to capacity.

I'd never met a professional stripper before, nor seen a performance. My scant prior knowledge had been derived from photographs hanging outside Soho strip clubs showing very posed and, to my teenage eyes, old and artificial-looking women. The ladies who came to perform at the Town House looked very different. They were all accomplished dancers with choreographed acts and, in combination with great rock and roll music and flashing lights, their dynamism served to plug our flagging energy.

My life changed again around my thirtieth birthday when an anonymous 'neighbour' informed the DHSS that I was cohabiting with a man. An officer from the department duly turned up and confronted me. I explained that my boyfriend stayed with us at weekends but was living elsewhere during the week. I added that I received no money from him and argued that the benefits had been awarded in place of an unenforceable Maintenance Order. He was however adamant that Ash should pay or go, so I handed him the benefit book saying I wanted nothing to which I wasn't entitled. He accepted it, leaving us without a regular income, but no further action was taken.

When Ash came home the following weekend, I told him what had happened and he said I'd been a fool to cave in and that I should fight for my rights.

I was humiliated, I cried, and made to feel like a criminal. The argument raged on until he lost his temper and walked out. I was disappointed by his reaction, but thought he'd come back – which he didn't. My female friends condemned him but the men were ambivalent. My two girls, now aged eight and four, were used to him working away but as the weeks passed, they began to miss him and so did I.

One morning after my cleaning shift, Sam took me aside and declared:

'You're getting everyone down with all this moping around.'

'I try to hide it,' I said.

'Well, try harder,' he replied. 'If you are unhappy, start thinking of a way forward and I'll see if I can help – give me a week or so to ask around.'

In the meantime, I had other concerns.

My eight-year-old was due to transfer to middle school in the autumn and was struggling to read basic texts. My fear was that she'd fall even further behind in a bigger school. Sherry's daughter was in the same class and doing well but it wasn't working for my daughter. Sherry thought I was overreacting. I wasn't so sure.

There was a well-regarded private convent school in Dorchester and I made an appointment to see the Mother Superior and told her my story. On the grounds that my father was Catholic, she decided to regard my girls as Catholics who were deserving of an education.

She offered to take both girls, free of charge but with one proviso. I had to buy a full summer and winter uniform for each girl. Only one store stocked the uniform at a cost of over fifty pounds, plus shoes and I had six weeks to find the money. I met with the owners of the Town House and told them that I needed more than just the odd night's work. The result was a regular weekly shift, assisting Sherry, on the lucrative Striperama night. A dressmaking friend, who'd acquired some velvet cloth, made a couple of outfits for me comprising hot pants with matching long waistcoats. I lived in hopes of attracting tips from customers whose attention was usually elsewhere. In the event, my efforts didn't go unnoticed as the performers, on their visits to the bar, all of whom knew what I was saving for, made loud and favourable comments about my new look.

During the week Sam had been discussing my situation with colleagues in the education department at County Hall and, as a result, they interviewed me with a view to assessing my potential for further education. They offered me a place on a full-time A-level course at the South Dorset Technical College in Weymouth. The subjects chosen were English literature, economic history and sociology. Importantly, I was to receive a full discretionary maintenance grant, to be reviewed at the end of each term, based on tutor assessment and attendance. I signed up without hesitation.

At the end of six weeks, I'd earned my girls' uniform money. When my eight- and four-year-old entered St. Genevieve's in September 1972, they looked like all the other girls streaming through the gates.

I felt proud of all three of us as I took the train to Weymouth to begin the next chapter of my life. Fifteen years after leaving school, I entered the 'Tech' as a student, owing a great debt of gratitude to

Sam and Dorset County Council who didn't care who I lived with and said so.

I joined a group of around a dozen long-haired male and female students aged sixteen to twenty-one, most of whom wore skinny tops and bell-bottom jeans. How different from the uniformed fifteen-year-old classmates I'd parted from in 1957. There was initial embarrassment during roll call, when we called out our names and ages. My classmates fell silent when I whispered 'thirty'. Our class tutor, an economic historian dressed in denim who looked about the same age as me, moved on quickly. Afterwards he apologised for putting me on the spot, having no idea how old I was.

An unforgettable lecture during that first day opened up the world of poetry to me. 'Thrushes' by Ted Hughes exposed me to contemporary poetry and its dark analytic tone has stayed with me ever since.

The initial awkwardness that had existed around my age was quickly forgotten and I made friends who helped me through my early struggles with academic subject matter.

My daughters settled into the convent school despite having to adjust to a much stricter regime, and subsequently my elder girl's reading improved to such an extent that she began to read for pleasure.

Having not seen Ash for three months, I met him in town one day and he asked if he could visit the girls. Sherry and other friends thought I was doing just fine on my own and that I'd be a fool to let Ash back into my life but the girls were so happy to see him and I did let him back in. He was ambivalent towards my college work, considering it a waste of time, except for the grant. He equated my ambition to pass exams and progress to higher education with him aspiring to become an architect.

The results of the first in-house exams were OK and fulfilled the conditions of the grant and I began to wonder how and where I might study beyond A levels. The economic history tutor believed

I could take his subject to degree level but, knowing that I needed extra income to support my family, said I'd be better off returning to London with its wide choice of H.E. institutions and employment opportunities.

In March 1973, I put my name down on a nationwide list for a 'mutual exchange'. This system enabled council tenants to move around the UK. I was surprised to receive a response within days from two elderly sisters who'd been living in their Tottenham council house since childhood and dreamed of retiring to Dorset. I liked their house and they in turn liked my flat so the move was on and Ash hired a van.

The stops along the pre-motorway route must have presented quite a spectacle to onlookers when two adults, Sherry's thirteen-year-old son, a German Shepherd dog and two children carrying caged budgies tumbled out of the cab.

For the first time in many years I was living closer to my parents, and they helped out during the first few days. The sisters had recommended the local school that they attended as children and its similarity to my own primary school served to reassure me. We went along to meet the head and a couple of class teachers who spoke well of their school but obviously, from their smiles, thought I was exaggerating the academic potential of my five-year-old. Places for September were offered to both girls and next on my list was a visit to Haringey Borough Council's Department of Education, to see if I might complete my A-levels locally. The officer I spoke to seemed sympathetic but didn't think an offer of a discretionary grant was likely. He did however encourage me to explore the possibility of enrolling on an A-level course offered by Tottenham College of Technology.

I was duly interviewed by an A-level tutor, a formally dressed economic historian who resembled, as I remember, today's Doctor David Starkey. He read the testimonials from the Dorset lecturers but doubted my ability to pass exams in all three subjects as the London University Board syllabus was different in all three subjects to that of the Associated Examinations Board, and marked to a higher standard. He did however offer me the chance to try, subject to funding.

I wrote to Dorset County Council and, within the week, they agreed to fund me. I took the written offer to the education department at Haringey and was advised that they could now offer me a grant as some of their university applicants had withdrawn. The grant was enhanced by London weighting so I was better off. I notified Dorset County Council of Haringey's offer and thanked them for their past support. The grant was not payable until September so in order to cover the rent, summer activities were arranged for my daughters whilst I found temporary work.

I began my second year of A-level studies at Tottenham Tech. by joining the most diverse, multiracial population I'd ever been part of. My class group comprised Greek and Turkish Cypriots, African, Indian, Spanish and a minority of indigenous white students with varying religious beliefs. The age range was wider and another first for me was the exposure to a politically charged atmosphere. The second miners' strike of the Seventies began in the autumn of 1973 and it seemed that the majority of the students in my group supported them. There were regular political seminars attended by some high-profile left-wing activists and politicians. Apart from some theoretical knowledge picked up from first-year sociology I was, at thirty-one, largely ignorant of grass roots politics. I learned however that my acceptance into this group was dependent upon my catching up fast, and I did.

Not so easily resolved were problems that arose for my daughters at school. My elder girl was viewed as intelligent but too shy and well mannered, and the younger, something of a child phenomenon with a reading age well in advance of her five years.

A few weeks into the term, I was called to the school after my younger daughter had been attacked on a flight of internal stairs and her glasses broken. I took her to the North Middlesex Hospital and apart from bruises the X-rays showed no head injuries. I attended a meeting at the school the following day and, receiving no satisfactory assurances for the safety of the girls, I took them with me to the Department of Education at the Borough Council Offices and refused to leave until they came up with a solution. They gave me the pick of any school in Haringey, with the freedom to visit as many schools as I wished. I chose a new primary school close to Wood Green, where the girls settled and made friends.

I didn't do well in the mock A-level exams in January 1974, having focused too much on becoming part of the culture. Following serious discussions with my subject tutors, I re-focused on the academic work and when advised that I needed an O-level in addition to three A-levels to meet minimum university entry requirements, the college arranged for me to sit an English language O-level exam. Upon passing the exams, I was offered places at two London polytechnics to read for Bachelor of Arts degrees in history but chose to accept a place at The City University in London to read for a Bachelor of Science degree in psychology.

On reflection, the ultimate success of three years at university as measured by passing the final exams was derived from a combination of brinkmanship and luck. I was handicapped from the outset by a total knowledge void in arithmetic and maths – unhelpful in the pursuit of a science degree. Thus I was always searching for the means to compensate and catch up.

Arriving for the first lecture or exam of the day in Clerkenwell and food shopping at the end of the day in Tottenham depended entirely on London Transport and a bus turning up on time.

In the spring of 1975, a fellow student invited me to spend part of the summer in his cousin's Greenwich Village loft and sculpture workshop. I hoped to fund the trip by using my J4 student visa to work in the US. My girls were to spend the summer with Sherry in Dorchester and I invited Sherry's daughter, Patti, to accompany me. Following our arrival in New York at close to midnight we couldn't gain access to the loft and I prevailed upon some New York policemen to find us a hotel for the night. Next morning, we met our host, the sculptor, his ballerina girlfriend and Mario the lodger. I left Patti with them and went out to find a job.

I was hired by a Danny de Vito lookalike who ran an advertising agency on Broadway. The staff dreaded his caustic sarcasm but he could be generous and would help out 'resting' actors with temporary employment. He also provided Patti with some 'off the books' home work. Out of hours, we tagged along with some of the actors who showed us around Manhattan, and one great night they took us to see an off-Broadway production starring Rita Moreno, where we got to meet Telly Savalas – unforgettable.

Having saved enough for our fare and travel, we took a Greyhound bus to Los Angeles, via New Orleans, and during 100 hours of travel and stopovers we had many positive experiences with the exception of one: a bus driver's failure to empty the lavatory tank. We found out later that this route out of Atlanta was well used by poor families, black and white, as it was on the day in question. Foul fumes built up and circulated, causing distress to young babies, nursing mothers and the rest of us. At the next stop when the driver still refused to empty the tank, we sat on the steps of the bus, refusing to move until, with ill grace, he did.

Befriending a distressed fifteen-year-old boy en route to visit his estranged father in Houston gave us wonderful insight into his life with his mother in the Bayou; we reluctantly declined his invitation to visit him on our way back. We listened through one long night to the woes of a thirty-something cocaine addict with a missing septum, who invited us to visit a nightclub she part owned in L.A.

Many hours were well spent persuading a young deserter from the military to stay on the bus and give himself up when we got to San Diego and a military base.

We stayed at the L.A. home of my cousins who fed and entertained us before we departed to visit Tijuana, Mexico, for a day. We took our next Greyhound across the desert to visit Las Vegas and onwards to stay in San Francisco. We'd met a rock musician in New York and accepted his invite to stay at his house should we travel back via Cincinnati – we made the detour. It was a magical stay during which he took us over the border into Kentucky for a night to listen to bluegrass music before we boarded our final Greyhound to New York.

We were running late for our flight home and had no subway tickets with which to pass through barriers at Kennedy. A bunch of young black guys, seeing that we were in trouble, lifted us and our luggage over the barriers.

Following graduation in 1977, I accepted a post as a clinical research associate in pharmaceuticals based in Dagenham. Having no car, another move and change of schools were necessitated, and I was offered the tenancy of a local council house. My science grade entitled me to spend one day a week setting up and running a study based at St. Clements Hospital, the psychiatric wing of the London Hospital. It generated a publication as did a second study at the Institute of Psychiatry. The second publication resulted in a job offer from Rhone Poulenc Industries in Paris. The contract included private education for my girls, now aged sixteen and twelve, and, in August 1980, we three left to start a new life in Paris.

SEEKING REFUGE IN
SEVENTIES CARDIFF
Personal Reflections

Sue Harding Sky

It was 1974 and nearly everyone smoked then. We met in a stuffy back room in a Cardiff pub – the Women's Action Group. I was one of the younger women in the group and had recently moved down to Cardiff from Leeds Poly. I was a student, midway through a social work course. My feminism was thriving, fed by my casework experiences of visiting families in Barry, and – thanks to my being a subscriber to *Spare Rib* since its early days – my awareness of women's movement activities elsewhere in the UK and the rest of the world.

One Monday night the discussion topic was domestic violence, the prevalence of 'battered wives' (in the language of the Seventies) across all sectors of society, and the news of the setting up of a women's refuge in Chiswick, led by Erin Pizzey. The women in the Cardiff Women's Action Group were a mix of middle-class academics who were starting promising careers and women with a more alternative or political activist stance. Some women had a mortgage and there was even the odd husband, so I felt I was at a very different stage in my life. I was 24 years old, living on my own in a bedsit in Roath, Cardiff, with my women's liberation ideals and motivations strong and growing stronger.

Everyone acknowledged the importance of 'doing something about domestic violence', but that's as far as it seemed to be going. Through my social work placement, I was meeting plenty of women who were suffering abuse and here we were, from our comfortable, safe positions, theorising and sharing shocking anecdotes we'd read or heard. It felt as though the group was completely separate from the lives of the women we were discussing, and that the pioneering work in establishing a refuge in London was out of reach to Cardiff feminists. For me it seemed an irresistible combination of providing practical support, within the framework of my feminism. 'But why can't we have a refuge in Cardiff, there's so much need for one?' I challenged. 'Surely if we're motivated enough then we should be able to make it happen.' I remember how quickly the responses came in: we would love for that to happen but we're too busy; we haven't got the funds; it's too much for the group to attempt.

Deep breath and, without really considering the implications of what I was saying, I began to express my outrage and frustration. I declared that, as I was finishing my social work qualification course in the next two months, I was prepared to give a year to attempt to set up a Women's Aid refuge in Cardiff. The implication being, 'how hard can it be?'

I have since been told that some of those at the meeting didn't really know if I was seriously intending to turn my back on the opportunity to take up a post as a social worker once I had qualified. Of course I was serious. And of course, once they realised that, the women in the group were prepared to support me.

What followed over the next two years was the most intense, exciting, innovative, challenging, intimidatingly high profile and, frankly, frightening time of my life.

Youthful determination, clear-sighted targets, a powerful sense of the right direction, outrage at the lack of provision, all riding on the wave of the Women's Movement. The time was right to put into action our politics of socialism and feminism to meet such an indisputably important practical need. We were going to be providing a safe refuge for women and children who were being physically abused by the men in their families.

In July 1974, having qualified, I began a full-time post as a social worker in Barry Social Services. I made sure that my sympathetic managers were well aware of my intention to resign once the Women's Aid Group had made sufficient progress for the project to seem viable.

In the meantime, we began to gain expertise in raising awareness of the project amongst those with access to money and amongst the media for the publicity that was so vital to us.

We knew that we needed to build up funds for the group while at the same time trying to navigate our way around the bureaucratic hurdles that were in the way of setting up the refuge itself.

Without the immediacy of the internet, making an impact and challenging social attitudes was a much slower undertaking in the 1970s. It involved writing articles and press releases for local newspapers, hoping they would be accepted, then waiting for responses. It also meant arranging talks at the meetings of a diverse range of organisations – Townswomen's Guilds, Soroptomists, Ladies' Circle, Women's Institutes, University Wives Group, National Housewives Register, Church Groups like the Mothers' Union and the Young Wives Groups.

Never having spoken in public before, I needed to learn the skill of clearly presenting the facts as well as tempering my fierce deter-mination and political belief that refuges were vital to saving the lives of women and children. I didn't want to frighten the gathering with my strong feminist ideology that they didn't necessarily share. These talks would focus on raising the awareness of the audience as much as fundraising because we felt it was important for them to realise that 'wife battering' was not restricted to ill-educated or working-class men, but that professionals such as doctors, teachers, judges, and police officers were also likely to undertake the practice of abusing their partners. Many an eyebrow was raised at this piece of information.

Often, the talks would be followed by cheques in the post and letters of appreciation and support. One memorable occasion was the AGM of the Barry Ladies' Circle when a group of us had to turn up looking smart to receive a donation of £100. I only had my Laura Ashley maxi dress but it seemed to meet the requirement. We were thrilled with such a large addition to our funds and we used it to install a payphone in the refuge. We turned down the suggestion of a plaque. The small group of us who attended that meeting were certainly bemused by our foray into the unaccustomed world of Ladies' Circles.

The tougher end of the campaign involved letters to Cardiff City and South Glamorgan County Councillors for support and to my amazement this resulted in an invitation to have tea in the Lord Mayor's Parlour with Councillor Albert Huish. He believed in the need for the refuge and was very enthusiastic on our behalf, naming Cardiff Women's Aid as the chosen charitable group for his year of tenure, 1974-5. He was the Labour Councillor for Rumney in the city and was particularly well aware of the powerless position of women living in housing estates, with no escape options. Coincidentally, the first woman to come to the refuge was from his own constituency.

As our confidence in making the Refuge into a viable proposition grew, we turned our attention to obtaining a council house for the purpose. Several meetings with Cardiff City Housing Department ensued and eventually a three-bedroomed terraced house in Adamsdown was offered to the group for nominal rent. It was in a poor decorative state but that was hardly a deterrent for us. Along with furnishing the place for women and children, we needed to ensure the residents would be able to continue to have access to local services. By now I had resigned from my full-time professional social worker post and was signing on as unemployed at the dole office every Tuesday morning. I spent all my time meeting with officials from various statutory authorities, such as the Department of Health and Social Security, where I was able to arrange for future residents to receive financial support whilst living at the refuge without disclosing the actual address to the DHSS clerks. This was crucial to ensure there would be no slip-ups in telling husbands where their wives were living. At the same time, I reached an 'understanding' with the senior DHSS official that I would not be pressurised into taking another job whilst I was involved in setting up Cardiff Women's Aid. This was an informal arrangement, very much of the time, and could never happen now, I'm sure.

In addition, I met with local GPs, health visitors, head teachers, solicitors and the police. All these professionals needed to be persuaded, to varying degrees, of the importance of their being flexible and of their accepting that they needed to take great care when recording the address of the secret refuge, to ensure the safety of the women and their children.

The meetings of Cardiff Women's Aid had by now transferred to the Friends' Meeting House in Charles Street, and we began discussing how to go about actually running a refuge. I was convinced that the refuge should be self-help, run by the women themselves, no warden required. After all, they had all run homes of their own and would be able to organise the refuge with the support of myself as full-time volunteer and other group members when available. This approach was a bit of a leap for some in the group, who had experience of more conventional hostel set-ups.

Another principle that I held firmly was that we should always speak to the woman herself before she came to the refuge. No more calls from professionals that began 'I have a woman here who...' That sentence would be cut short by my saying, 'Please can I speak with her?'

As news of our campaign began to spread, through articles in the *South Wales Echo* and the *Western Mail,* the BBC Wales broadcaster, Vincent Kane, invited us to take part in *Wales Today* and *Week In, Week Out*. He was a high-profile journalist and after we convinced him of the seriousness of the project, he supported us to such an extent that he attended as host at an early fundraising disco held in the Electricity Club in Llandaff, Cardiff.

This was an example of the rather incongruous range of activities involved in establishing an innovative project like Cardiff Women's Aid in the mid-1970s: from presenting evidence to the Parliamentary Select Committee on Violence against Women (1974) and negotiating Urban Aid applications with civil servants from the Welsh Office, to organising rock 'n' roll concerts in the Commodore Club on Penarth Pier or fundraising discos at Club Mont Merence (Monty's) in Charles Street. These discos took place every Wednesday night and were collaborative fundraising events between three cooperative groups: Cardiff Women's Aid, 108 Community Bookshop and *Cardiff People's Paper*.

Even before the refuge had opened, I was asked to provide professional supervision to a Probation Service student who was keen to explore the innovative ways of working within Cardiff Women's Aid. I think her placement comprised rather more practical work (decorating bedrooms, for example) than her tutors might have intended. This student has recently told me that the experience with Women's Aid had a significant effect on her subsequent career in social work.

In the summer of 1975, we had the house, fairly fully furnished with donated beds, wardrobes, chests of drawers, sheets, towels, clothing and kitchen appliances; we were nearly ready. Then we had our first referral and the first woman came to the refuge one morning in July. I have a lasting memory of her, on that first afternoon, in the garden with a bandage on her head and a paintbrush in her hand, giving a coat of white gloss to the donated wooden ironing board. She was determined to help. At that moment I knew Cardiff Women's Aid was going to be here to stay and I have never stopped being in awe of the resilience and practicality of women in the face of the greatest of challenges.

We established an evening on-call rota amongst volunteers, so that we could take turns in collecting women who needed to come to the refuge. This could be quite a frightening experience at times, when called upon to go to pick up a woman at night. It could involve driving alone to unfamiliar areas in Cardiff to collect a terrified mother with her children, hoping that the violent father would not suddenly reappear. This did happen sometimes and could involve a confrontation and fast getaway in a volunteer's (usually rather old) car.

At this time, we could not guarantee that the police would intervene on behalf of the woman, especially if her partner had not actually hit her on the night that she was trying to make her escape. There have been some changes in the law and in attitudes since then, but there is still a long way to go.

Some of the volunteers would regularly visit the refuge in the evening for informal sessions to provide additional emotional support for the women.

Cardiff's was the first Women's Aid refuge in Wales and I am proud to have played a role in leading the way for other refuges to be set up, initially in south Wales but spreading rapidly. The growth in numbers of Women's Aid groups prompted the establishment in 1978 of Welsh Women's Aid, to coordinate and spearhead campaigns to challenge the legislation and to provide funding for paid staff to run refuges and give specific support for the children.

Women's Aid refuges are now integrated into the support provision for women and children across the UK, though still insufficient in number. The 1976 Select Committee recommended one refuge place per 10,000 in the population; this figure is now adopted by the Council of Europe. It represents a requirement for

300 places in Wales. Here we can claim 38 Welsh refuges with 383 bed spaces in total, but even so, every year many families have to be turned away due to lack of provision. There is a continuing requirement for more housing options, for vital support services for children and young people who have experienced abuse, and for specialist services for diverse groups in the community.

We've come a long way from those early challenges faced by a small group of women activists in Wales in the 1970s, but it's clear that the need for campaigning is not over yet.

'IF I STRIP, HE'S GOT TO STRIP!'

Sue Jones-Davies

Actor and singer Sue Jones-Davies, famous for appearing nude in the film Life of Brian, *tells Lindsay Ashford about getting into show business in the Seventies.*

On the set of Life of Brian

I never thought about acting as a career when I was at university. I was going to be a social worker or a writer. But in the summer of 1971, after graduating from Bristol, I went with a group of musicians and actors up to the Edinburgh Festival. The revue we were in was transferred to the Hampstead Theatre in London. I hadn't intended to go to London – I'd intended to go with a friend from Bristol who was a composer, who'd said: 'Why don't we get on a boat and go to Brazil?' But anyway, we all went to London and ended up living there.

It was great, because in those days you could get gorgeous flats, or a squat. Some areas were quite grotty, but we were lucky: we lived in a fabulous place at Clapham Common – a listed building – for a year. It only cost about two quid a week – you could live very cheaply in London then.

When the revue finished its run, I needed to get work. There was a job going on the reception desk at a theatre in Leicester Square – but I was so hopeless at it that they put me downstairs, doing cataloguing. Someone else down there was also trying to get acting work and he was going for an audition for *Jesus Christ Superstar*. I didn't have an Equity card, which proved you were a member of the Actors Union, but I went for the audition anyway. In the 1970s it was much more free and easy. Quite a few of us got into the show who didn't have a card – which of course wouldn't happen now.

It was exciting to be part of *Jesus Christ Superstar*. I was in the Chorus. You got invited to receptions and events. In the first month we had nuns picketing at the stage door, telling us we'd all go to hell.

Everyone else in the cast had come from a very theatrical background – they'd been to the Italia Conti School or they'd been to drama school, so I felt quite out of my depth, really, because they had so much experience. Even though most were younger than me, they'd come up through that trajectory of stage school. Growing up in Fishguard, there was nothing like that. There were good piano teachers and ballet classes to a certain level, but no drama lessons.

My parents were quite relaxed about me being in the show, despite the controversy it caused. They weren't particularly religious. Mum was Church, Dad was Methodist, but after the war I don't think he ever went again. He was a maths teacher and Mum was a housewife. They were very supportive – they never said, 'Why are you doing this?' or 'Why don't you get a proper job?' Maybe they were anxious, but they never expressed it.

The next big thing in my career was landing a part in the TV series *Rock Follies*. I was pregnant with my eldest son, Siencyn. I found out I was pregnant having just been told I'd got the job. I went back and said, 'I've got to tell you, I'm pregnant', and they just said, 'Okay – we'll cope.' Towards the end of that first series they were having to shoot me at an angle to hide the size of my tum. Then we were recording the album that came from the series, and I was only a couple of weeks from going into labour. I had no role model for how to conduct a pregnancy. I felt fine so I carried on until a fortnight before Siencs was born. He came early and we had nothing ready: no clothes; no cot; just an enormous old pram with wonderful suspension. The pressure that social media has brought, with its emphasis on perfection in all departments, didn't exist. There was a much more laissez-faire attitude to childbirth, which had its good points, although it didn't work for everyone.

Chris and I were never married. We debated it, but I couldn't accept any of the ceremonies. They all asked you for conditions I couldn't agree with. I was strongly feminist, and I thought: I just can't go along with it. My feminism went back to before university. I remember, at the age of fourteen, being absolutely horrified to discover that a woman couldn't become a priest or a bishop. Up till then I'd gone to the little church where we lived I enjoyed it – you sang in the choir, that sort of thing. I mean, I was never going to want to be a bishop, but, to find out that your sex cut you off from some jobs – that shocked me. And as time went on, I became more deeply aware of inequality everywhere.

I was working at the Chichester Theatre before my eldest son was born and I remember there was a petition going around about abortion. Naively, I was going up to everyone, asking them to sign it, and I was absolutely flummoxed when one man I went up to refused. He wasn't rude to me, but he was angry because he was a staunch Catholic. I just assumed everybody felt like me: that everybody should have a choice and that abortions should be freely available, so that women weren't dying in the streets. I think he was as confused that I thought he'd sign it as I was that he wouldn't. Experiences like that, they mould you.

I was just as naive about the Pythons. I hadn't watched much telly at Bristol, when *Monty Python* first became popular – and we didn't have a TV for a while after that. So, I wasn't a fan, particularly, and going for the part of Judith Iscariot in *Life of Brian* was just a job initially. I got it because the girl they'd originally cast had dropped out. She said she didn't want to strip. Well, having come from a background of shows like *Hair* – not actually having been in it, but knowing people who had – nudity didn't really bother me. The issue for me was if it had been salacious. So, I said: 'Well, if I strip, he's got to strip.' – which he did. It wasn't *sexy*, so I didn't feel I'd compromised myself.

The filming was in Tunisia, over nine weeks. Siencyn, my son, was only seven months old, so he came too. I had a very nice woman, Rowena, to look after him. Chris came out, too, for some of the time. He ended up being given a part: he played the centurion who can't stop laughing at the name 'Biggus Dickus'. Practically everyone there got roped in for one scene or another. It was crazy, really. Of course, no one knew, at that time, what a huge success it was going to be.

I didn't even attempt to get to know the Pythons because they were this tight little circle who were so well used to each other. I didn't feel I got to know them as people, the way I got to know others in the cast. At the time, Graham Chapman had just come out as being gay. I didn't feel very comfortable around him. In the bed scene, I was very conscious of him recoiling if we touched, which was difficult to avoid as we were lying naked next to each other!

Michael Palin and Terry Jones were quite easy to get on with. John Cleese was very distant – totally wrapped up with the writing – and Terry Gilliam was just buzzing with ideas for the set. You felt he was up there, inside his own head most of the time. Eric Idle had just split up from his wife – who was quite a feminist – and he was there with somebody else, who was very beautiful.

Chris and I used to go to a local café outside the hotel compound where they served the most amazing fish soup – hot, hot – and I remember dancing on the table: it was great. The whole nine weeks was like a holiday, really.

I don't recall much about the time the film came out. I do remember that one of the places they banned it was Fishguard, so my mam and dad couldn't go to see it – and I was quite pleased about that. Some people said it was blasphemous, but no one ever challenged me. Having done *Jesus Christ Superstar*, with the nuns picketing the show, it wasn't completely strange for me to hear these things being said. To me, *Life of Brian* just poked at the anomalies in religion.

Later in my life, when I started doing yoga, I learnt about Buddhism – but I don't call myself a Buddhist. I suppose the attitude I have is just be kind, compassionate. Be kind to others and to yourself – and do as little damage to the world as possible while you're here.

Looking back to the person I was in the Seventies, I was very idealistic. Well, not even idealistic, really: I just couldn't understand why other people had a different point of view. The Vietnam war, for example: I couldn't understand why everyone wasn't writing letters about it. I've learnt to accept that each person has a viewpoint and if you get too worked up you become strident.

Of course, *Life of Brian* is something that's stuck with me from the Seventies – but one good thing, now I'm older, is that people don't recognise me anymore. I used to get irritated when men would call out things like: 'Brian! Put that Welsh tart down!' or quote lines from the film and expect me to know the next line: that kind of nerdish behaviour. It's very nice to have a claim to fame – I'm not going to knock it – though I hope that if people got to know me, they'd realise there's a lot more to me than just stripping off!

I moved back to Wales in my late thirties to do a teaching diploma in Drama and English at Aberystwyth University. I became part of a Welsh singing duo Cusan Tan. We sang folk songs and original compositions and with two other musicians toured the States for a few years. Later again, I trained as a yoga teacher. And I am still teaching to this day. Alongside these jobs I became an Aberystwyth town councillor for Plaid Cymru and even became Mayor for a year.

However, if it's the stripping off that people remember ... if that's the legacy ... well, that's fine.

FROM PSYCHEDELIA TO REALITY

Rose Simpson

Clinging to a rock face in Snowdonia, looking across the mountains and valleys of Wales, I learned to love the lie of the land. That was during my time in York University Mountaineering Club. A couple of years later, in 1968, when I first tried to live in Pembrokeshire, it was as an alien in a strange country and I couldn't acclimatise. My next attempt, in the early 1970s, was more determined and better planned. Fifty years later I am still here.

From 1967–1971, I was a member of the Incredible String Band. 'Psychedelic Folk' they called us in the press or 'The UK's answer to San Francisco Flower Power'. True to our fairy-tale image, we moved to Wales and lived for some time in an old farmhouse called Penwern, not far from the Pentre Ifan Cromlech. The age-old landscape and its myths and legends blended for a while into an equally fantastical life of music. We soon found out that our countryside retreat was not a practical base for a band which spent most of the year travelling or in studios.

At first, the band had been a group of romantic dreamers. We floated through the theatres of the world and each stage became a new encampment for us gipsy players. In a haze of incense, and often marijuana, we invited large audiences into our small world of songs and fun. We thought that music and poetry could change the world, making it a better and more beautiful place. As we sat on the main stage of the Woodstock Festival of Peace and Love in August 1969, Welsh folk harp on the floor beside us, we were seen as visitors from the Celtic Twilight, inhabitants of an imagined land beyond the sea.

But life at Penwern was far from idyllic, however it appeared to the fans. The band found itself there as a result of a chance meeting in the lift of the Chelsea Hotel in New York. Two 'multi-media performance artists' were, they told us, thinking of a forming an artistic commune. They were drawn to Pembrokeshire as much by its low rents as the chance to live close to a landscape steeped in music and history. We were initially doubtful, but the glamour of Welsh bardic culture and its ancient language were sufficient to convince us.

The house the performance artists had found for themselves, and which we shared during 1968-9, was remote, dilapidated and virtually abandoned by the farmer. He must have been delighted to find someone willing to pay rent and warm it through to prevent further decay. Down the local pub, or so it was said, he talked about his strange tenants and his grandiose plans for the future of the property as a country club. After a few months of living there, we could see little likelihood of that happening. Who would want to drive down a maze of tiny roads, trees forming a dripping canopy overhead, to finally arrive in that bleak landscape? We were comparing the grey seas of the Pembrokeshire coast with the bright sun and sparkling surf of California.

The Pentre Ifan Cromlech looked appropriately strange and visionary in the film *Be Glad for the Song has no Ending* that Peter Neal made of us. We draped ourselves around the landscape, dressed as Fates or Gods or Voices from Beyond, but it was cold, wet, and miserable up there on the hillside. There wasn't a decent restaurant for miles and the local shop hadn't heard of aubergines or tahini, never mind the soy or fish sauces that made a macrobiotic diet almost tolerable.

Robin was perfectly happy sitting on an upturned bucket in the former farmyard watching the life that ebbed and flowed with the agricultural seasons. The main farm buildings were elsewhere but some old barns and sheds remained, used as overflow during lambing-time or other busy periods. The working farmhouse was also somewhere else: a big modern bungalow on a more convenient corner of the land, probably with a fitted kitchen and a three-piece suite, in a lounge with patterned wallpaper and coordinating curtains. We were never invited to visit and had no inclination to step into that less visionary world.

If we heard Welsh spoken as someone passed through the yard, we listened in awe and respect, but we didn't meet the locals and they kept well out of our way. They probably thought us drug-crazed freaks who would corrupt the children.

We were sufficiently remote from their lives to be unaware of such criticism. Our rural Wales was an imaginary place, even if my belief in such fantasies was already waning. In the evenings, we sat round the farmhouse fireplace, like the peasants had always done. We sang together, read poetry, and told each other interesting tales of Druids or obscure facts of Welsh history.

With no television or newspapers, we saw little of what was going on in the real-life Wales of Cardiff or Bangor. I was willing to see the farmer as descendant of the ancient Demetae and imagine the wild red tresses of a Celtic Boudicca tamed by his wife's permanent wave. Rural life, however, forced harsher realities upon us. Big Ted the pig was no Falstaff character – a jovial beast to write songs about. He was a smelly predator who forced his way into the kitchen and ate the few fresh vegetables we had.

The old house, with its slate-slab floor laid directly onto the wet earth beneath, always felt damp. Mats grew a faint sheen of mould, first grey-white then green. Since we all spent a lot of time sitting on the floor this felt unhealthy. Grubby armchairs that the farmer's wife wouldn't allow through her new front door exhaled the dust of the dead horses whose hair crept through tears in their covers. Shabby old cushions were stuffed by feathers plucked from the Christmas geese of many yesteryears. The cheap cooker in the kitchen had been bought specially for us, as the farmer proudly pointed out, but the old sideboard alongside it looked like a plywood coffin on legs. A greasy pine table scored by the knives of long-gone farmhands was the only other work surface.

As we came and went, according to tour schedules, we brought back with us the food and the comforts that might make it feel like home, but to no avail. Someone always ate the last biscuit or forgot to bring stock cubes. The open fires, on which we depended for all warmth and hot water, would never light easily and went out overnight. Then there was no newspaper or sticks to relight them. We were constantly arguing over the single bathroom. Tempers flared over who should get the hot bathwater and who should be first in the queue to reuse it while still lukewarm.

As the band became more successful and the inevitable frictions arose between us, the musical life became a pain for me, not a pleasure. One day, in late December 1970, I suddenly decided to leave. With no prior discussions on the practicalities of finance or futures, this was a rash move.

A week or two later, living in a bedsit in London and with no obvious way of making a living, I was still happy with my decision. Going to the supermarket, counting pennies, paying rent, felt like real life, more manageable than walking over the abysses of the music business. But Camden High Street in rush hour was also aggressive, and inhuman, not a place in which to build a life. I remembered the peace of Welsh landscapes and thought of being part of a small community, where people knew each other and worked together for shared futures. That looked like a realisable dream.

By Christmas 1971, I was the mother of a young baby and accompanied by Paul, her radical pacifist father, then working for subsistence-wages at *Peace News*. I had managed to get some money from the last tour with the band. We had both done all the casual work that we could find and saved hard for some months. It was the same factor of cheap property that brought me, the baby, and her father to Powys.

We wanted our own home in the clean air of the countryside, where the child could grow in peace and security. A simple life, in tune with new definitions of environmental responsibility and personal freedom, looked possible in Wales. 'Small is beautiful', Schumacher told us and this was the smallest country we could think of where we might find work and make our own way. While I was reading the *Mabinogion*, listening to Welsh folk music and learning Welsh verbs, Paul was investigating Welsh Nationalism and Cymdeithas yr Iaith.

Looking in Welsh newspapers, bought by post, we found two possibilities. I got a coach from Victoria to Wrexham and looked at a depressing semi-detached on the edge of the town, then found my way down to Machynlleth.

On one of the back roads around the town there was a large old farmhouse, with an elderly tenant in the basement, and it was for sale at a cheap price. It was unattractive to locals who didn't want to upset the lady downstairs or argue with a difficult neighbour. A wall would have to be built to separate the properties but that might not settle all disputes. For us – with more rooms than we could use, a smallish garden, and a front door opening onto a quiet road and wild hillside – the house was ideal. Paul could hope to set up study weekends for non-violent activists and offer Cymdeithas yr Iaith free office space, while they sorted out their finances to secure a more central location.

I had cut off all connections with my previous life. Robert Plant of Led Zeppelin was now just a neighbourly old acquaintance, someone from whom I could borrow a car and learn to drive. The hippy pop musician in trailing skirts, snakeskin slippers, ribbons and beads was now the young mother in jeans and stout shoes to keep out the rain, child comfortably perched on one hip as we walked down the path into town.

There was an old barn at the back of the house with a loft caked in chicken manure. We dug up the lawn and used the manure to turn it into a vegetable garden. Our chickens were kept in a little shed near the house, more convenient and safer from foxes. We found that the rabbits we bought as pets bred far quicker than we could ever have imagined. Neither of us could bear to kill them so we had to give them away, despite the child's distress. I picked blackberries on the hillside, gratefully accepted windfall apples in autumn and filled cupboards with neat rows of jam. I found old Kilner jars in a box sold for 50p at the local auction and learned to bottle and pickle as my mother had done in the post-war years of rationing. We grew vegetables and stored our eggs in old sweet jars full of isinglass. We baked our own bread and bought the rest of our few necessities in the local shop. The grocer, universally known as Nigel, had just taken over a small supermarket and his overnight trips to Liverpool markets kept the town stocked up at a reasonable price.

Work was more of a problem than we had envisaged. Paul helped at the Wednesday market and that small income was paid in kind rather than cash. Unemployment Benefit was another method of redistribution of wealth, we decided, so that justified our dependence on it for a while. We started a bric-a-brac stall on the market and acquired a pair of enormous wooden cartwheels in exchange for a tea set. Using his very limited carpentry skills, Paul made a rough axle for the wooden wheels and we lashed planks over it to construct a sort of cart. Having only one axle, it had to be balanced at each end by the tea chests full of books which were our main stock-in-trade. Other boxes were piled on top and, with the child perched happily on the highest point, we wheeled it down to the High Street every Wednesday. Wearing straw hats in summer, we looked like refugees fleeing the Vietnam war as we wobbled along the road, veering from side to side. Occasionally a box shifted, the balance was lost and one end ground into the dust. Then all had to be re-packed but luckily the child never fell off. Once we arrived at our pitch on the street, boxes went underneath the contraption and the cart turned into a table.

Soon there were other stalls selling antiques, Indian imports and various tools, all run by young incomers escaping, as we were, from the cities. Our children played under the tables, sat on the pavement, and ate chips or went down to the park together, when there was one old enough to supervise.

The bookstall turned out to be a successful venture, enough to justify Paul leasing, then finally buying, one of the High Street shops. He painted it all white, scavenged wood to make shelves and set up a second-hand bookshop, with a bric-a-brac section and some antiques. He put out small chairs and toys to amuse the children while the parents talked. There were home-made posters pinned to the wall – 'Guitar lessons, all styles', 'Cot and baby clothes, free to good home', 'Tantric Yoga for all. Wednesday 7 p.m.'. It was a meeting centre, not just for incomers but interested locals too.

Paul's experience in radical politics was useful when nuclear dumping in the nearby hills was proposed. Madryn was a grass-roots protest movement. Techniques learned in US anti-war protests were passed on to the burgers of Machynlleth and they made the most of their new skills. Their water was never polluted or their roads blocked by the transport of nuclear waste.

The Centre for Alternative Technology opened about a year after we arrived and its founder members soon discovered Paul's shop, but they had wealthier backers and a clearer plan for the future than us. My personal contact with them was limited. In my years with the band, I had met too many people who shouted the slogans but disliked their inconveniences.

Despite loud statements on universal freedom and liberation, many a young male Radical had been brought up in a home where Mother was effectively a domestic servant with occasional holidays. They expected their own female companions to do the same tasks, while also being freethinkers who would not ask inconvenient questions about unexplained nights away from home. They were pleased that their liberated wives intended to work, but not necessarily willing to take on the household tasks or childcare which would enable them to succeed. Saving the planet, the workers, or the peace, was more important than earning a living or taking the children to school.

The same old diversionary tales were told, to make us young women feel better about our impoverished lives. Heavenly glories took on the new forms of Universal Peace and Harmony. A paternal God was replaced by Hindu deities with blue faces and many arms, a smiling Buddha or Gaia and the Creator Goddesses of primeval time. This was us, the men told us, linked through our bare female feet to the rhythms of the universe, in tune with the Moon and guided by the stars. The instinctive creativity of women, they said, was better than dominance in intellectual or public roles. That message was also more subtly passed on through album covers, advertisements and the rambling philosophies of long-haired gurus.

There were few attractive options available anyway, stuck far from centres of population and with incomes so low that a healthy diet of brown rice, lentils and vegetables was inevitable. Even the bus fare to Aberystwyth had to be scrimped from the housekeeping, while buying a large toy for the child was only achieved by asking Aunty for an early Christmas present. Most women I knew didn't complain, not even to each other. Whatever ideology had landed us in that place we still believed in it, most of the time anyway. Nevertheless, the daily oppression of housework and children, with no help from automatic washing machines or efficient household equipment, undermined both health and spirits.

We stuck it out because Machynlleth and its surrounding villages had many charms for us city girls. Walking our babes the miles from one old house to another, tying them insecurely into old bicycle seats for longer trips, we could spend long hours surrounded by beauties. I had never seen so many wild flowers as when the primroses and bluebells came out every year. We climbed the hills and made little picnics of heavy home-made brown bread and jam, sitting up there with the children, and looking down on the valleys and lakes below. I learned the smell of foxes, saw squirrels in the trees and rabbits in the fields, and it felt like a Victorian children's book come to life.

The ancient houses were inconvenient but they were beautiful, as was the old oak furniture that landlords sometimes left in them. The simple design of a sycamore dairy bowl or the huge earthenware crocks lined with creamy glaze were as good as anything in London's Design Centre. Their attraction was not so obvious to those who remembered getting up at dawn to milk the cows and standing on icy stone flags making butter. To us, these remnants of the rural past were a joy and we piled up our apples or potatoes in them, despising the plastic conveniences of modern kitchens.

Improving the house was a major occupation for most of us who had moved down from the conveniences of cities. Once it was watertight and vaguely functional, we wanted it to look good too. I gazed enviously at oak dressers, tridarns, shepherd chairs and cricket tables, but I was always outbid at the Machynlleth auction. Antique dealers formed rings to exclude outsiders. Some, mostly based in the Borders, were already exporting containers of Welsh oak to the USA every month or two. Furniture shipped direct from the 'Hen Wlad' of their forefathers was precious to those who had made homes across the Atlantic.

Smaller auctions and Farm Sales were our best hope, if we could borrow a car to get there. If the fine antiques were beyond our means, there was usually some old painted furniture which could be stripped off to show the wood beneath. I became a dab hand with wire wool and caustic soda, the cheapest paint stripper. My fingernails turned orange, even under the rubber gloves, but the soft glow of polished pine in candlelight, and the smell of beeswax when finished, was worth the effort.

Antony Sheppard opened a shop on the High Street and sold expensive Liberty linen at knock-down prices in his January sales. Gloriously patterned curtains soon framed our old windows. Worn chairs were covered in patchworks of William Morris prints and his Hera peacock feather cushions were ubiquitous in the homes of us incomers. By the mid-1970s, there were quite a few families in Machynlleth and the surrounding villages who had left England and chosen to settle in Wales.

Laura Ashley employed local outworkers and her fabrics too appeared in every jumble sale. Like many of my friends, I sewed dresses copying those that Laura Ashley sold in her London shop. They lacked a certain finesse but that didn't matter. We all appeared at local barn dances in our floral prints, pin-tucked bodices with long sleeves, high frilled collars and floor-length skirts. We looked very Victorian, and modest, belying any reputation for lax moralities. Most local girls were then wearing low-necked, tight-ribbed jumpers, and miniskirts, which revealed coloured knickers under their 'American Tan' tights as the evening progressed and dancing got wilder.

When Antony Sheppard opened another shop on Penrallt Street, selling clothes and Anello & Davide shoes, in soft leather and bright colours, our city tastes had come home. Then he had the brilliant idea that 'Fishermen's smocks' in soft brushed denim with stand-up collars and pockets all across the front would be quick and easy to manufacture and useful casual wear for a wide market. Their international success ensured years of local employment and put the name of Machynlleth on the fashion map.

As time went by and children grew up, most of us incomer women found some kind of work and widened our horizons. We returned to education and got professional jobs, or learned new skills and started up small businesses from home. We found our different places in the local community and the children benefited, as we had hoped, in small schools, knowing all the neighbours and being as safe as they could be on their independent trips into town.

Many of our children rejoiced in Welsh names which the grandparents struggled to spell on parcels sent down for birthdays or Christmas. Angharad and Eilir mixed with Saffron, Rainbow, and Roshana on school registers and accepted each other's difference with no questions. When I asked my six-year-old daughter which of the angels in the Nativity Play had won in the local Eisteddfod, she found it hard to describe her to me. She used every feature she could think of – her clothes, her mum, where she lived – missing out the most visually obvious identifier of ethnicity. She just didn't notice, as further delicate questioning established.

The school Eisteddfod, then the Urdd, then the National Eisteddfod, formed a hierarchy of performance and skill which most of us incomers supported wholeheartedly. We were delighted that music, art and drama were considered essential education and pleased that everyone got a chance to be onstage, even if it was in the back row of the choir. Some of our children did win prizes at the National Eisteddfod for recitation in Welsh or singing, others were encouraged to play instruments and all grew up thinking these were valuable skills.

My daughter went first to the local Welsh-medium playgroup then into the Welsh-medium school system, like many others from English homes. I was proud when she came home to tell us the names of colours and numbers in Welsh and sing her little songs. It was usually the mothers who tried to learn some Welsh themselves and I had an English friend who refused to speak her mother tongue at home, to prevent the children lapsing back into English at the school gates. Most of us tried to help the children to reach a level of proficiency that surpassed our own.

It took great determination to develop a fluency in Welsh. I did Open University courses and learned to read and write reasonably well but my contacts with native Welsh speakers had already been established through English. Changing to slow and formal Welsh just inhibited daily conversation. My daughter learned to cope in school although she never seemed to speak Welsh willingly. However, thirty years later in the London Welsh Club bar, she sounded unmistakeably local when she replied in kind, quite automatically, to a 'Bore da'.

One summer, Paul decided that our house was an ideal base for a group of deprived inner-city children to enjoy a country holiday. We cleared out the two rooms of the attic, scrubbed the wood floor and dragged a job lot of foam mattresses up three flights of stairs. The mattresses had been acquired when an activities centre closed down, which is probably when the idea originated.

We thought it looked very clean and functional. There was only one bathroom in the house and no central heating, but then it was summer and a campsite on a farm would offer no more facilities. Paul spoke to the group leaders and they assured him that our house was fine and they were grateful for any free accommodation in Wales. They would organise all catering and entertainment for the children, who would be out all day, so all they needed was somewhere to sleep.

Their arrival by minibus, windows open and all shouting at each other, set the tone for the visit. The people next-door, already unhappy at their unconventional neighbours, were horrified by the arrival of a vanload full of noisy children. Bursting out of their travel confinement, all the children wanted the bathroom instantly, or said they did, and those who couldn't wait decided the hillside was a reasonable alternative. There were few passers-by but, nevertheless, it didn't generate goodwill from any observers, or from me. I seized my girl and hid with her in a ground-floor room, where I spent the rest of the evening. I couldn't cope with the noise and bad language of the group. I succeeded in contacting a friend, packed up my girl and we left home for a few days.

Apparently, the children were not impressed by their holiday accommodation. They had expected Butlins, or at least the basic facilities of a proper campsite with showers, toilets and a play area. An old enamel bath with stains, an ancient WC and a vegetable garden they weren't allowed to play in were no acceptable substitute. Mattresses on the floor just meant a free-for-all of bouncing, tumbling and fights. At night they were cold and when it rained, as it always did at some time, then there was only a washing line strung across the room on which to dry the endless anoraks and socks. They took out their irritation on each other but also on the town. Fights broke out down the park and I heard rumours of shoplifting and unpleasant behaviour on the beach at Aberdovey. It was an ill-conceived venture from the start, probably fuelled by misunderstandings on all sides, and we never discussed it afterwards. Certainly, the idea of a Peace Centre receded into the background of our lives after this first experiment.

I regarded this as a gain rather than a loss. All I had wanted was a home in a landscape I enjoyed and a certain freedom to pursue my own interests and raise a child safely. Wales gave me all of those things, despite its long rainy days and lack of work opportunities.

There were occasional irritations caused by repressive remnants of a chapel culture. The elderly lady downstairs insisted that even my daughter's doll wore proper underwear when it went out and we had to be careful not to offend her. But she also knitted dolly a cardigan and made us a cake, so the relationship was positive from the child's viewpoint.

For me, at that time, the social life of the small Welsh town was never impossibly limited. There were houses to visit and gatherings to go to, even the very occasional trip away. I found a greater diversity of wildly unconventional people in mid Wales than I could ever have expected to meet in central London. In that small world, I met names from academia, politics, music and art that I would not have encountered elsewhere. They were mostly chance meetings, friends of friends looking for local knowledge as they passed through for a concert, a lecture, or a rally. The understood formalities of privacy, discretion and keeping distance which would be observed in the city didn't count, when there were few others who would recognise, notice, or even care who was visiting.

My life was busy enough at first with home and child and, when the novelty of it all wore off, there was always another challenge: a new language, a teaching qualification, shorthand and typing – something else from which I hoped to earn a living. The disillusions of my first stay in Wales stood in the way of further such mistakes. I never expected to find a new utopia. I knew that the locals were quite happy without the benefit of any Enlightenment that my friends and I might bring and that our guides and gurus were no better than they should be. This time, I made unlikely friends in strange places, saw my daughter's schoolfriends grow up, get jobs, and create their own families. Some left Wales but many stayed, and when Wales celebrated the turn of a new century, they were the locals watching the fireworks, with children who couldn't imagine a life anywhere else.

In the late 1960s I had arrived, more or less by accident, in what then felt like a different world, whose language, customs and history were alien to me. On that occasion, the dissonance arising from a clash of cultures was so great that I, along with my friends, abandoned the experiment. The next time I went to Wales, in the early 1970s, I had chosen to be there, along with others like me, leaving behind English cities to make a better life. Over the next decades, most of us settled. Even if we ourselves have never felt Welsh, many of our children identify with a country whose native language they speak well and whose culture they share.

CAT

Christine McLennan

Christine McLennan, sustainability educator and pioneer, tells Rebecca F. John about life at the Centre for Alternative Technology.

We were at the beginning of our life. Looking for adventure, I suppose. We were always into alternatives, my husband Roger and I – especially alternative energy. We both had that passion and that was what we wanted to base our lives around, really. Then we saw this advert for a smallholder at the Centre for Alternative Technology.

At that time, right at the beginning, it was a community of people. They wanted engineers, gardeners, biologists – all with the same aim of exploring future options that were going to be helpful to the environment. We experimented early with solar panels, wind power. It was very basic, you know. We had a milking cow, goats, chickens, pigs. All on a small scale.

Every time a pig got mature enough, we would discuss what to do with it. Through the winter we wouldn't have enough food to keep them, because we used to feed them with our compost, the food waste, so when the time came for them to move on, it was either, 'Do we kill them and keep their meat?' or 'Do we sell them to someone else to be a live pig?' We did sometimes kill them, and they ended up being salted and hung up off a beam in our community kitchen. But there were a lot of discussions first, because some of us didn't eat meat, and those of us who did thought you might as well know the meat you're eating, that it's had a good life, not been pumped full of antibiotics. We were all feeling our way, trying to do our best for the environment as earnestly as we could.

Since we weren't professional farmers, we used to rely on our neighbouring farming community to help us out with advice. People were curious and happy to help.

It's a very tight-knit Welsh community around here, in Machynlleth, and when we first arrived at the Centre, some locals thought, 'Who do they think they are – a load of English, mainly middle-class, people coming in and taking over this old quarry?' Some believed we were hippies. I've never been a hippy in my life, but because we lived in this place, this community – the 'shit and wind centre', they dubbed it – that established the image.

The local farmers would say, 'We've been using water power since the 1900s; there's nothing new about that!'

Our kids went to the local school and we used the local doctor's surgery, so we really integrated into the local community in the end. It was a challenge, though.

When I first came to Wales, I didn't even know there was a different language, I was so ignorant. I found out after going into a local shop for a newspaper in Machynlleth, and they were speaking this strange language. I was around twenty-three at that point, and I should have known. I learnt Welsh consequently. It's a continuing process. I went to university at Aberystwyth during my time at CAT and got a teaching qualification and you had to be able to speak Welsh to teach in the area, so that was an added incentive.

I was one of the only ones with a working-class accent at CAT, and so I felt a little bit of an outsider there, too, at first. Other people had the means to leave their other jobs and lifestyles and support themselves. A lot of people had left respectable scientific careers with a mission to see if they could create energy that wasn't going to harm the planet.

At the time, there was the energy crisis, power cuts, the miners' strikes. It was just dawning on people – the impact that our use of fossil fuels was having on the environment, in terms of pollution and the excess CO_2 in the atmosphere, and weather changes. There was a seed of that happening then.

Meeting Roger determined my future role in life. I was at school when we met, and we had this shared interest which perhaps led me further down the alternative route than I would have ventured on my own.

I arrived at CAT with my twins and a tiny three-week-old baby. I had my fourth child in 1980 while we were at CAT. So we raised our family there for 13 years.

The Centre was a great place for kids growing up, because it was so safe. It's based in an old slate quarry, which had been abandoned for thirty or forty years at that point, so it was just a collection of ruined engine sheds and slate-cutting machinery. Nature had already reclaimed much of it. Oak, birch, and ash grew all around, and the native wildlife made a home there, too. It was beautiful. The site was the ideal place to launch our projects and experiments dedicated to developing cleaner technologies for the future.

We rebuilt the old miners' cottages so we could live in them. We didn't have much money, so we became a charity, and we were donated odd buildings which were turned into communal kitchens and offices. We had very little electricity because we generated our own. I had the biggest family so I had a washing machine. We had an intercom system and I used to have to ask all my neighbours, 'Can you turn all your electric off so that I can run the washing machine, please?' So you became very aware of energy use and how to be frugal with it.

We were like pioneers. It was a big adventure. We were all on a mission. And it was great for the children, because they spent their formative years surrounded by a diverse community of energised and committed people

When we first got the job, we were contracted to remain living on site for two years, so that visitors could see people truly were living this renewable lifestyle. We were all paid the same wage in the beginning. There wasn't a differentiation between men and women's wages, which is still a factor in life now, isn't it, so that was good. There were also various add-on benefits. If you had children, for instance, you were given a little bit more of a wage to help with that. If you lived off-site and were trying to pay a mortgage, you got a little more. It was done in a very fair way.

We had a weekly 'Monday Meeting' where we discussed all our plans and concerns, and there was a rota for everything. In fact, we used to have an allocated 'ogre' – a role which would be taken over by someone different each week – to ensure we were all pulling our weight. We used to share the cooking. There was one particular gardener who was interested in pushing that aspect of life at CAT, and I've heard reports of slugs once being served up in an omelette, but I never ate slugs. Or not knowingly anyway!

Some people couldn't get along with a non-hierarchical system, and left fairly swiftly, but Roger and I stayed a lot longer than our initial two-year commitment.

That's not to say it wasn't difficult at times. We were surrounded by a lot of different adults, with different opinions on how to bring up children, so that would be a challenge – people saying 'You shouldn't let them do this or that'. We had our own house, but there was a lot more mixing with people than you would experience in your ordinary life.

We lived in a row of cottages. Because it's a display Centre, there was a route that visitors had to follow, and our living quarters were supposed to be off limits, but one day I came home and my living room was full of boy scouts. They were in the bedroom, everywhere. Seventeen boy scouts roaming around the house! They just thought it was part of the circuit.

It was quite hard being a mother and a nappy washer in the early days. I used to hang the nappies on the line in front of our cottage, and some members of our staff would say, 'You can't let people see nappies on the washing line.' But I would say, 'Well, hang on. It's the best way of drying – out in the open air rather than using electricity. People want to know we're living a normal life.'

We were in the spotlight quite a lot, which is another reason why some people left. They didn't like being on show. Visitors would look over the fence at you. There were issues like that which were a bit of a downside, but there was a peak visiting season in July and August, and outward of that it was fine. We got our privacy when all the visitors went home.

There were more upsides than downsides, I would say.

We arrived just after the cottages had been renovated, so the weather wasn't really an issue for us, whereas it had been much more primitive for the very first people to arrive: at one time they had tarpaulin acting as a barrier from the rain when the roofs were still being reconstructed!

It was a little bit isolated from town, and I couldn't drive, so I did learn to drive a petrol-fuelled car. We were advocating moving away from fossil fuels, so I only drove my car – guiltily – when it was a necessity. We did have an electric truck at CAT. It came from a factory floor. It wasn't really suitable for the rough, hilly terrain the quarry was on, so it didn't last very long, but it could do six miles quite easily.

They're saying that there's a pledge now to move all vehicles away from petrol or diesel by 2030, so it's kind of come to fruition, what we were talking about all those years ago, I suppose.

Roger and I lived very happily at the Centre. And then we decided to leave because Timmy, my son, has Down's syndrome, and there weren't many boundaries there for him. It was an opportunity, too, to give someone else a chance to live on site. We moved just three miles away, and we're still here, in the same house. Roger and

I are semi-retired, but we're still very much linked to CAT. Roger gardens there two days a week, and I am a part-time tutor. After I got my teaching certificate, I ran a small environmental theatre company at the Centre, and then, as times changed and the last of the residents left, the accommodation was opened up for university students, school groups, and self-catering holidays. My job was to educate young people in sustainability – particularly using our Eco Cabins as residential units. The Eco Cabins had their own unique renewable energy systems, which groups could monitor in order to work out their own energy use day by day. The Centre was like an outdoor classroom that offered great practical teaching opportunities.

Almost everything changed in the end. It had to. We were into self-sufficiency and being off-grid, but as we attracted increasing numbers of visitors, which helped with our income, we didn't have enough power to provide for everybody, so we went onto the grid. Any excess power we harnessed we would sell to the National Grid and if we had a shortage we would buy it back in. Also, as the mainstream took on all those ideas we started out with, so the Centre had to adapt and change into a learning centre.

Teaching by doing – that was the thing. I think that has stayed all the way through.

It's amazing that CAT is still going after forty-five years or more, considering all the traumas that society has gone through: recessions and things like that. I think if we'd come now to the Centre, it wouldn't have had the same appeal as it had then. The adventure, the pioneering spirit. We all had this fire in our bellies and we were allowed to do it. We were young and had a passion for our common aim, despite disputes and arguments and differences of opinion. Yes, it was a bit idealistic, and as the years went by, those ideals got rubbed off a bit. We stopped being a cooperative. We started being a hierarchy. We became a PLC, and so worked with the banks a lot more, and they wanted a more hierarchical system in place. That did change things a lot.

But you can't escape the fact that it was a unique place, with a lot of good results. And Roger and I still feel very connected to the Centre and its message. As much as we can, we live a sustainable life. We're human: we do have a car, but we do a lot of biking. Our children, too, have taken a lot of what they learnt at CAT into their adult lives. My daughter works for Dulas Engineering, producing solar fridges for Third World countries to keep their medicines and vaccines cool. My son is a gardener. My daughter is a teacher of drama and English in Northumberland. They did rebel, in quite a lot of ways – most of them eat meat now, which we still don't – but they came out of their unusual upbringing as very well-rounded human beings.

I suppose the greatest success CAT could hope for would be to shut. We've evolved into being an education centre, and most of our activity now is based around running distance learning courses for postgraduate students. But if all our ideas were taken into the mainstream, there would no longer be any need for CAT.

And people are adapting – it just takes time. Wales was the first country to start charging for plastic bags and the number of plastic bags now in circulation has gone down by 90%, so they tell me.

Quite often I say, 'Well, what are you going to do when the oil and the coal run out?' People don't want to be inconvenienced, unless it hits them in the face, and of course anything new is strange. But climate change is increasingly impacting on people's lives, now, so they have to change because they can see it in front of their own eyes. And Britain is such a good location for wind and water and wave power. It's an island with much potential for renewable energy – so much to benefit from. It's just a question of trying to change people's attitudes.

I had a great opportunity. I was privileged to have that opportunity.

TWO LIVES
From Wool to Water

Virginia Isaac

Life was certainly smaller, slower, and simpler then. Whether this was on account of it being the 1970s, our part of Wales, the peace of rural life, or the naivety of youth, it is hard to say. Whatever, it was an extraordinarily formative time and I look back with enormous affection and gratitude.

I was just 22 when I arrived in Wales from an upbringing in suburban Surrey and three years as a typical student at the University of East Anglia, in Norwich. I followed my boyfriend (as many of us did in those days!), who had studied philosophy and economics but had a hankering to do something more practical. His parents were brought up in the Amman Valley and had just bought a farm (even though they knew nothing about farming) in the midst of the Brecon Beacons, so we headed there for a short break.

In some ways, it was an accident that we ended up living on the 200-acre hill farm in Trap, directly beneath the stunning Carreg Cennen Castle on the Black Mountain.

"Can you hear anything?" my boyfriend, Phil, asked me as we lay in bed, enjoying doing nothing, one glorious morning in August. "No," I said lazily, luxuriating in the peace. "Isn't it wonderful?" At which Phil leapt up. "That's the point; we should be hearing something. It's a beautiful day and someone should be out there cutting the hay – why aren't we hearing the tractor?"

Thus, in 1975, began the first day of the next thirteen years that I was to spend in the tiny village of Trap (inhabitants *c.* 80). The farm manager had upped sticks and left, in the middle of haymaking, and there was no one to take over. Phil agreed to give it a go while his parents sorted things out and we agreed to stay on for a week or so. We didn't have to stay, but somehow weeks turned into months and there was always a reason to stay on a little longer. I had never lived in Wales, had never farmed, and did not have a practical bone in my body.

Phil's parents were tolerant of me living with their son and under their own roof. They had spent most of their time in London and they were reasonably worldly wise. I was not aware, however, that as far as the locals in the close-knit village knew, we had separate bedrooms! Apart from frequently referring to me as their 'daughter outlaw', my future in-laws did not make their concerns apparent. Only much later did I realise how uncomfortable my presence had made them. There was a reputation to think about.

Luckily, we got married and had two children in quick succession. We bought the land and stock off Phil's parents and we lived in a caravan while we started to build our own house on the farm. At the same time, we taught ourselves how to look after a flock of 400 Welsh Mountain sheep, manage a suckler herd of twenty, and raise calves. *Black's Veterinary Dictionary* was Phil's 'go-to' book, as we soon learned that if an animal got sick, it often died. We could not afford to call the vet. Life was hard but we did not see it that way. We lived in a kind of bubble and did not know any different.

Phil and I were keen not to be seen as outsiders. Phil's Welsh heritage helped, and I made it known that I was, in fact, born of German parentage. Somehow, not being labelled as English made us feel more at home and more confident. We were never treated with anything other than the utmost friendliness and kindness and our agricultural neighbours gave us much support and advice as we tried to get to grips with farming life. I suspect that there was a certain amount of amusement behind our backs – as we would buy pretty Ayrshire calves (that would never fatten), or try to pick up piglets at the Mart, promptly dropping them as they squealed blue murder – but they saw that, young and inexperienced as we were, we were trying to farm seriously and it felt as though they tolerated and respected us for that.

We also resolved to master the Welsh language! Our initial enthusiasm was dampened by our attempts to practise what we had learned in the Cennen Arms after our weekly lesson. "Helo, sut ydych chi?" I would say, proudly, as I entered the pub, only to be told that in that part of Carmarthenshire, they did not speak formal Welsh and used the more familiar, "Helo, shw mae?". Also, it was tempting not to learn the language when everyone spoke English anyhow. When my son was born and we had no babysitter, it was a good excuse to give up. We tried a couple of times after that, but it was never very successful.

I soon felt very comfortable, though, with the other mothers. On social occasions there was generally strict segregation of the sexes. Women would instinctively gather on one side of the room or table and the men on the other. Women talked about children and schools, forthcoming events and (inevitably) the challenges of living with their husbands; while no doubt the men talked about farming and machinery, rugby, and politics. Although I found this strange at first, it came to feel quite natural. I soon realised that in no way did the women feel subservient. On the contrary, we knew we were the bedrock of the village society and tolerated the men for their foibles! We just found each other more interesting. We were all fairly isolated on our individual farms; there was often no one else to talk to except for our menfolk and children. The women enjoyed being in each other's company and were keen to get together. I felt that it was a compliment that when I walked into the bar, people would look up and greet me with a smile and carry on speaking Welsh. Eventually, they would translate here and there but I liked the fact they did not feel they had to make any exceptions for me. I was increasingly one of them.

Nowhere were the gender roles more distinct than on the farm. As a wife and mother, my work was predominantly in the farmhouse while Phil laboured outside. There were exceptions to this, of course. For most of the time when we were farming, we had our own Jersey house cow which was my responsibility, hand milking morning and evening. I was also in charge of the chickens and the regularly escaping pigs, and often would help with feeding the calves. Most of the time I would go out, in all weathers, with one child on my back and dragging the other, complaining, by the hand. The fact remained that there was real equality and equal respect. No job – whether inside or outside – was more important than the other. Reflecting on this fifty years later, it may be because no monetary value was put on our respective contributions. There was no sense that looking after children and housework was unimportant because it was not paid. Phil was not paid, either, for harrowing the fields or injecting the sheep. In the early days, our main income came from selling our lambs at the Mart and that was a joint endeavour.

Life was not easy. We had spent all our resources on purchasing the farm and animals and buying materials to build our own house. But when it came down to it, we did not need much money. I was much influenced by John Seymour's Book, *The Complete Book of Self-Sufficiency*, published in the second half of the 1970s, which meant that we had a flourishing vegetable garden. Some of my happiest moments were when the children were asleep and I could snatch an hour or so weeding, planting and sowing. On top of that we had the milk from the cow, eggs from the hens, and plenty of our own lamb and beef in the freezer. My weekly expedition to 'Fine Fare' in Ammanford was a pretty spartan affair.

We prided ourselves on trying to be as self-sufficient as possible. With pails of Jersey cream all over the kitchen, churning butter was a must – time-consuming but generally successful. Making cheese – and finding rennet – was not so successful and my attempt at curing a sheepskin was pretty disastrous. We dutifully ate our way through our home-smoked bacon, but we did not repeat the exercise! Looking back, I can understand why people simply go out and buy butter, cheese, and rugs – but at the time, it felt exciting and creative to be able to make these things, however badly. It gave one a sense of agency that you do not get from simply purchasing from the shops. It also introduced us to the vital importance of fresh, organically reared meat and vegetables and the importance of nutrition for good health. The children were only allowed 20 pence worth of sweets on a Sunday and we avoided all processed food. This was also something that I had learned from my father – E.F. Schumacher (author of the hugely influential, *Small is Beautiful*) – as he had also been President of the Soil Association for many years. Although I suspect that he was slightly alarmed to see his Surrey-bred daughter decamp to the Welsh hills to live the simple life, I did feel that deep down I had his tacit approval.

We were not unusual though in our attempts at generally fending for ourselves. Living in the depths of the country, miles away from a town, it made sense not to have to rely on buying everything in. Most of the farmers had their own meat and vegetables. Many had eggs and chickens (as long as they escaped the fox) and our local dairy farmer – Eddie Llaeth – delivered milk to all who needed it. Using the *Complete Guide* as our bible, perhaps we did try to go further than most but, after a while, and as other activities kicked in, the novelty soon wore off.

One major advantage of living where we did – and one that we only really fully appreciate now – was the total lack of what would today be referred to as 'status anxiety'. Perhaps as an outsider, I could not read the signs but there seemed to be no 'keeping up with the Joneses'. The farming folk, generally went around in old clothes, driving battered cars. It was simply not practical to dress up or spend money on status symbols and foreign holidays were seldom spoken about. Phil and I had no idea who might be rich or poor and the wonderful thing for us was that it did not matter. There was no feeling of inferiority; everyone had an air of independence and a sense of themselves and their place in the community. It was an equal society and looking back, I am sure that this was a major contributor to the overall lack of stress. No, we did not have much money. Yes, we had to borrow from the bank. But the daily quality of life was not affected.

When the children were very little there was not much opportunity to go out anywhere. Our main social interactions were either through the Cennen Arms or when selling lambs at the mart. As a young 'English' girl, I did find the latter rather daunting. Usually, Phil oversaw all of this but on occasions when he was away, it was left to me. However hard I tried, I felt that I stuck out like a sore thumb! The sympathetic haulier helped me shoo the animals into the pen prior to the sale but when it came to the auction, I was on my own. On the whole, I did not have a clue what the lambs were being sold for – the breakneck speed of the Welsh auctioneer's patter was impossible to understand – and I simply agreed to whatever price was concluded. I was clearly out of my comfort zone but proud that I had managed it all the same.

Life got into a much easier rhythm once the children were old enough to go to school. Christopher, our elder, started at Ysgol Trap when he was four. There was the grand total of fourteen pupils in the whole school, split between two classes, overseen by the redoubtable and talented head teacher, Mrs Davies. Education was through the medium of Welsh but that was not an issue as classes were so small that each child had individual attention. Christopher quickly understood that he spoke Welsh at school with his friends and English at home.

With Joanna, his younger sister by seventeen months, stuck on her own on the farm, it seemed that the time was right to explore the possibility of setting up a nursery or playgroup in Trap. There had been a mini population explosion in the village, and I wondered if other parents might welcome the idea. I talked to Mrs Davies, who agreed to call a meeting in the school. Thus, Trap Ysgol Feithrin was born, with eight two- and three-year-olds its first pupils. It just showed what a small community could do. One parent offered her converted outhouse for premises; another offered to become the lead childminder/teacher (assisted by one of the children's grandmother). There were no regulations (that I was aware of) that had to be adhered to, no inspections or checks or health and safety measures that got in the way. Instead, it was a wonderful community effort where we all pulled together very quickly for the benefit of our children. Many of those friendships between the toddlers are still active today. Somehow, helping to set up the playgroup made me feel that I had 'arrived'.

Being elected to go onto Ysgol Trap's PTA and then chairing it, becoming a school governor of four local primary schools and then being elected nationally to be an officer of the Welsh Confederation of PTAs – all followed on from that initial suggestion of a playgroup. It also meant that when we did eventually move back to England, I was ready to take up a succession of roles in education on the national stage.

At the same time, Phil was persuaded to join the 'Trap Show Committee' which, conveniently, seemed to entail regular planning meetings in the local pub. Often the wives would go along as well (with children in tow or playing outside). It all felt so safe – a small community where everyone knew each other and looked out for each other's children. The annual show was not the most exciting event in the calendar, but it was an important one for which the whole village turned out. The men would sort out all the logistics and the women would organise the produce tent and the catering. My job was usually to make about twenty pounds of potato salad!

My life was full. With plenty of purposeful work, two small children and feeling integrated into the community, I did not need anything more. The wider world passed us by. We weathered the exceptionally hot summer of 1976 – bringing in the bales of hay and stacking them on the hayrick in the barn – and also the big freeze in 1979 when it was so cold that the diesel in our little Zetor tractor froze. Without a television, the trials and tribulations of the Winter of Discontent was just a distant echo. Our concerns were focussed on ensuring that the sheep had enough to eat, keeping ourselves warm and the children entertained. What was happening 'out there' seemed very far away indeed.

Like most farms in the area we had access to plenty of wood. This was used, not only to fuel our equivalent of a Rayburn and to heat the house (we had no central heating) but also to help in the construction of the house, which gradually grew in size when we found time to build it. Of particular pride was the purchase of a large bench saw which meant that we could cut all our own beams for the kitchen. I was Phil's labourer (and still am, come to think of it), helping to heave recently cut down trees onto the bench and pushing them through the massive saw. Goodness knows how much money we saved, doing so much ourselves, but building the house and running around the sheep as an extra sheepdog, meant that I was fitter and slimmer than I have ever been since. I can still hear Phil shout "Ginny, get round! ... NO, not that way!" I understood then why some of our sheepdogs would abruptly return to the farmhouse in a sulk when they had had enough.

As well as the wood, we also had our own water. This was not unusual and most farms in the vicinity had their own springs. What was different (and what we did not know when we bought the farm) was that our spring was an offshoot from what was probably the largest natural source of spring water in Wales – the source of the Loughor, or the Llygad Llwchwr. Water was pumped half a mile up the hill to the house by an old hydraulic ram pump which used the water to power itself. The water was pure and unfiltered and in plentiful supply, except, when at critical moments – usually when the house was full of visitors – the pump decided that it needed 'bleeding' and ground to a halt. It was only when the header tank was empty, and the taps ran dry that we would realise that someone needed to trail the half mile down to the spring and reset the pump.

The water, though, was also responsible for our next venture. On a wet and windy Welsh afternoon, we were sitting in our small farmhouse kitchen when a relative suggested that we should bottle our water and sell it. At first, we thought he was joking. After all, this was in 1978, long before sales of bottled water became a 'thing'. But we were up against it financially and needed to find other sources of revenue, so we decided to give it a go. If we had known then what we know now about how extraordinarily difficult it is to bottle pure water and then to sell it, we probably would not have done it. But, in the naivety of youth, we hardly gave it a second thought, and that was when Brecon Waters (later Brecon Carreg) was born.

While the locals had been tolerant of our efforts at farming and self-sufficiency, it was clear that they thought that we had completely lost it when we announced that we were going to try bottling Welsh water! We were the first to do so. There is a whole book in the development and growth of the water bottling enterprise, but for me, at the time, it was an opportunity to start flexing my muscles in a different direction. Phil and I knew little about business and certainly nothing about business planning; we simply found out what was needed and got on with it. We set up a very simple manual bottling line in a converted cowshed, put out the word that we needed some help and recruited a couple of mothers of children at Trap School. Phil took on the role of 'Factory Manager' and I helped with PAYE, recruitment and cooking the lunch for Sarah, Jackie, Betty, and Yvonne, on the two days a week that we got the line going. Very little was automated so one of us put the bottles on the start of the production line, another put the caps on and then two more would pack the bottles into boxes and take them away at the end.

Everyone respected that Phil, as Factory Manager, was the Boss. But we knew how to get round him and much merriment was had by all. Phil never understood how Betty and Yvonne – either side of the bottling line – could keep chatting ALL DAY, and if they ran out of conversation, they sang. It was beyond him, but so long as the work was done (and my goodness, the ladies were fast) he turned a blind eye. I was worried that they would get bored and suggested that they moved into different jobs. They tried it for a day, but they missed the camaraderie and asked to go back to their old positions.

You would think that this was boring and tedious work, and of course, in some ways it was. But the whole experience was generally fun with lots of chat and gossip and regular bursts of raucous – but melodious – Welsh singing. I doubt we could have got away with that today! (I visited the factory a couple of years ago – to find three separate highly automated bottling lines, with just one engineer in a glass fronted cabin watching and ensuring that everything ran smoothly. No singing there.)

Setting up the bottling factory, however, introduced us to the corporate world that had, until then, entirely passed us by. For three years we had hardly gone further than the nearest towns of Llandeilo and Ammanford. Suddenly we were parachuted into a world of selling to national brands, (Waitrose was our first customer) and having to deal with a succession of partners and funders once we realised that perhaps we had bitten off more than we could chew. We certainly did not have the resources to grow the enterprise on our own. Bottling water is not a cottage industry. Suddenly the slower, simpler life became less so and started to take on an entirely new dimension.

When Spadel of Belgium – that of the 'Spa' Water fame, who saw what was happening to sales of water and wanted a base in the UK – became involved, things quickly went up a gear. The large company – one of the largest bottlers of water in Europe – wanted to be sure that the spring would not run dry and that there was a plentiful supply of water before they made a final commitment. We started to lead a double life – farming some of the week and bottling the rest. We accepted that ultimately the two would not be compatible as you could not really have animals wondering all over the spring catchment area, but until something definitive happened we had no option but to carry on balancing the activities. An anxious year then passed for Phil and me. We were running out of money and while we knew that there was plenty of water, we did not know if it would be enough for Spadel's purposes. Suddenly, everything became a lot more serious. Phil and I had to go for training in Spa – he for production management and I to learn how to oversee quality control and microbiological testing of the water. This was all in French, to boot! A very different world.

It was also a life full of contrasts. One moment I was racing around after small children, milking the cow or bottle-feeding baby lambs; the next, trying to look calm and collected, entertaining half the Board of Spadel S.A., who had flown over in their private jet to see how things were getting on. It helped, though, that the owner – a large, charismatic and forceful character, who seemed to terrify his staff, was a farmer at heart. He saw that we were naive but seemed to relate to the fact that we had a farm to run as well as the bottling plant to manage.

While it may well be that we ultimately sold the business – and the farm 'lock, stock and bottle' as we would say – too cheaply, we were happy and we learnt a lot. The Company treated us kindly and we stayed to run the business for a further two years until we felt that it was time to move on.

What marked our time on the farm in Wales was the autonomy, the independence, the freedom. While financially we were constantly up against it, we did not lack for much. The friendship and supportiveness of the community – especially, for me, from the women – meant that even living in the depths of the countryside, one never felt isolated. Of course, there were challenges and the odd falling out but the bonds that I formed there have lasted until today. Our children, who live in England, have gone on to be highly successful in their careers, and I am confident that the down-to-earth, grounded upbringing that they had in the 1970s in Wales has contributed to the confident and resilient individuals they are today.

Phil and I moved back to England in 1988 to take on new challenges and to give the children a wider education. But we always intended to come back and re-embrace a more sustainable lifestyle. We bought a farm again in 2006 and settled in Carmarthenshire for good in 2020. Once more, we are surrounded by hills and pigs and cows and chickens and have invested in a large polytunnel. Fifty years may have gone by, but much feels just the same. We are older and wiser and, of course, couldn't live without the internet. But the community and friendship are still there and Phil's appetite for new projects is unabated.

'A vineyard perhaps?'

NOTE: The house that we built on the farm (Llwyndewi) is now used as the Headquarters for the multi-million enterprise that is Brecon Carreg (see https://www.breconwater.co.uk/)

TORN DRESSES AND REBEL RULES

Nic Hafren

It was the hot summer of 1976. I was thirteen years old. This was my induction into snogging, excitement, power, fantasy, music and feeling that I belonged. We were a gang.

The six eternal weeks of school holidays was spent in the little seaside town of Broad Haven with my best friend Chrissi and her sister Carys, who was five years older than us.

I had one tiny cassette of the Beachboys' twenty golden greats. On the cover a sun-bleached surfer coasted a rolling aqua wave and in Pembrokeshire we imbibed all the glamour of California in one soundtrack. This was our theme tune as we played pinball in the Galleon Inn.

After a nervous start, I confidently ordered lager and black from the bar and we chatted to Nigel, Sean and Andy from London. By 10.30, I would be moved on by a policeman for snogging Sean, who wore a stars and stripes tee shirt and bagged jeans. I would later lose him to the more mature Carys, and would have to make do with Nigel. We would swap boyfriends with casual ease that summer. It was a glorious heat haze of discovery and how the mere act of kissing could send a boy into tortuous bodily changes and us into spasms of giggles.

When my mother left me in the care of 'Auntie' Marilyn, I took full advantage and disappeared with a twenty-one-year-old to the neighbouring beach of Little Haven for my first official date.

I had no idea what to say and once he realised how young I actually was, I was speedily returned to the safety of the gang, who were busy throwing each other into the hotel pool, fully clothed.

I didn't want the summer to end and when the house next door to Chrissi came up for sale my mother was persuaded that it might be a good idea to buy it.

We moved from the lovely village of Wenvoe to an enclave of houses at the edge of a vast sprawling estate in the east of Cardiff. During my first day at school, the silver Parker pen ceremoniously presented to me by Dad for starting at this new institution, was 'borrowed' by Tania Hallicott, who indicated that 'no' wasn't an option, and I was initiated into what was actually and statistically the worst performing school in Wales.

Within a year I had become a punk, dyed my hair orange and acquired a twenty-one-year-old boyfriend for real.

I had been a good girl up until then, a girl who did well in almost everything and who loved poetry. In this school however, art was graffiti, poetry was a football chant and hockey sticks were definitely weapons. I quickly learned that the only way to survive was to be a rebel.

Angie Jenkins looked to be a good candidate for a friend, having five older sisters, each one taller than the next, until Hazel topped them all at six foot. Every one of them was good at sport. The Jenkins sisters could keep me from being a victim – that and the boys from the basketball team and the fact that I was going to get edgy.

I remember the day when I walked past the hairdressers in the Edwardian Arcade in town. Glancing in at the music and impossibly fashionable staff of Jingles, I hoped that perhaps if I could get a job there I could find my edge.

I lied, telling them I was sixteen, and by the next Saturday I was washing hair. The other hairdressers were impossibly trendy compared to my fourteen-year-old self. I needed to quickly acquire some straight leg jeans and plastic sandals. My mother was set the task of knitting several mohair jumpers in baby pinks and blues.

The way to the heart of Janet, the scary receptionist, was offering to do her shopping in Cardiff Market. I would return from there impressively armed with fresh lobster and acres of vegetables for her as well as change from a tenner.

The accompanying soundtrack was never the Beachboys but Blondie, The Cars, Talking Heads and always David Bowie.

These hairdressers were funny and had a disdain for the customers that bordered on rude but it never stopped repeat custom. A mouse could step in and emerge in the cascaded glory of a crazy coloured peacock. On a hot summer day, we would entertain ourselves by lounging on the upstairs chaise longue and firing spray guns of water onto the shoppers walking through the arcade, who would wonder why it seemed to be raining.

I became their little mascot who would be sent on errands to buy ice-cream. Carrying two cones in each hand and wearing a boob tube was a perilous task as inevitably one hairdresser would run out and pull the stretchy, strapless top down, knowing that I would walk bare-breasted rather than drop a precious ice-cream. I learnt exhibitionism and the art of swagger.

We would buy our clothes from Gentlefolk Jeans across the arcade or Paradise Garage on St Mary's Street. The clothes were alternative and glamorous: a mixture of Vivienne Westwood and slinky catwalk. Skintight Lycra with the material slashed to reveal flesh. They embraced me into their fold and before long I was modelling hair with vermillion and fuchsia streaks.

Some of the staff were employed for their style as opposed to any apparent ability with a scissors. Electra, of Anglo-Indian heritage, was glamorous and I looked up to her as my style icon. She wore leopard print shorts with black leather tops and satin scarves: bondage with a twist.

The salon was a hangout for photographers and film-makers and a huge photograph of Electra lounging across an American car, hung in the window, which accompanied another of her being ogled by a cop on the Jingles business cards.

Electra was a terrible stylist. She was in fact so bad that she was consigned to only cutting the men's hair, since they didn't seem to complain. The inherent sexism of the 1970s was utilised with pragmatism. Societal norms were being challenged in a hairdressers; the rule book ripped up and thrown like confetti on the salon floor. The attitude was, yes, you can be a sexist wanker, but we're going to take your money and give you a crap hairstyle as revenge. Perhaps you'll think twice or maybe even stop being a wanker. Whether they were gay men or from minority backgrounds, the stylists all shared a common understanding of living with prejudice.

Outside the haven of the hairdressers and gay clubs my group had to build their armour. Misunderstood by straight members of a society who were still watching *Love thy Neighbour* or *Terry and June* on the three channels available, our answer to ridiculous chat-up lines was mockery. We were merciless but this could have the peril of the spurned turning nasty.

The talk was blunt and sometimes, especially for the boys, there was violence. There was little societal understanding in Wales in the Seventies of tolerance and acceptance of diversity. It felt like sometimes the only option was to say, 'Fuck You'.

After being screamed at by Janet for the cardinal sin of leaving conditioner in a customer's hair, I was given a slip of paper informing me that I was on a warning. As soon as she turned her back, Electra smiled at me and deftly ripped it into pieces before dropping it into the bin that the receptionist was carrying. Janet, uncertain, paused but carried on walking not quite believing that anyone would challenge her authority so openly.

At lock-up, Electra invited me to join a chosen few who were attending a small gig in Tiger Bay and it was there that I saw a band whose lead singers were two girls with enormous beehive hairstyles screaming and seriously performing 'Rock Lobster'. They had come all the way from California. The B-52's were electric and I was hooked! From then on, we would travel to Newport or to the Top Rank in Cardiff every weekend to see a different punk band performing in the infancy of their gigging life.

Siouxsie and the Banshees, The Police, Adam and the Ants, Iggy Pop, The Stranglers – every week would be a different outing and the gap between the old Seventies, where I was a child, enveloped in the safety of my parents and laughing at *Carry on* films, suddenly became a world away.

Our parents were from a generation that we wanted to challenge. Their responses felt so out of touch and the sitcoms tinged with casual racism just felt wrong. My friends were suddenly from different ethnic minorities and we would end up in the Casablanca Club or in a shebeen in Cardiff Docklands after a gig in a throbbing atmosphere with the most amazing music.

Being one of the youngest, I was in awe of the group that I hung around with, but I could also suddenly see that there were choices. My comprehensive was trapped, a dreadful 1970s block of concrete, with staff holding on to wild-eyed frightened charges on the verge of stampede. Inspiration or learning was an occasional, incidental occurrence.

There was dreadful deprivation that was not addressed. Tania (she of the Parker pen theft) would regularly expose herself to whoever was teaching. Her aim was to get attention and disrupt the class and it was a plus if she was thrown out.

Today I would hope that this might be a red flag for revealing some abuse at home and would not go un-investigated.

The sixteen-year-old me just wanted her to get on with it so that I could get a few O levels and leave.

Outside school, I was having sex with Peter, a punk. He was charming, but was in the habit of picking fights when drunk and was eventually sent to prison for GBH. I remember turning up at Newport Magistrates Court for the sentencing along with other punks. He was made an example of and given a longer sentence, but danger was written onto his face. Whether I fell for the romance of a rebel or the motorbike without a helmet, I couldn't really tell you. At the time the violence seemed unreal, as though I was in a film rather than in the cold reality of a grinding life.

He wrote long love letters from his cell, which I think I still possess somewhere in the attic. I visited him once in Cardiff Prison and not really knowing what to bring I went shopping in Marks and Spencer's and stocked up on my personal favourite – their individual trifles! When I was finally let through security he was fuming – apparently, I should have brought a lump of hash hidden in a crisp packet. I never went again.

There was a cloud of tension hovering over a lot of concerts. I remember seeing The Clash and knowing that there was going to be a problem; I could usually spot it and would make my way away from the front of the crowd. I was a soft punk really. I wanted to be glamorous with a punky edge – never a hard core.

One evening the Cardiff band Rudi and the Russians were playing and afterwards the guitarist came over and introduced himself as Lars. He was strikingly dissimilar to the boys at school. Tall, finely chiselled and intense, but with a deep laugh when I teased him. There were no cheesy chat-ups. His mother was Norwegian and a painter. What would follow was my introduction to literature and art.

I went to life-drawing classes at Llanover Hall, where the young girl in me felt uncomfortable but nevertheless continued to sit and draw and then read the Somerset Maugham book that he handed to me. It told the tale of the artist Gauguin and his escape to Tahiti. We grabbed every bit of art from Warhol to the work of Frida Kahlo and the photographer Lee Miller. I was whisked to an exhibition of

Modigliani in Paris and bought a giant-sized poster which would decorate every student flat in which I ever lived (and there were many) for the next ten years.

I wish that I had been brave enough to sing in one of the bands. It was what I yearned to do with all my heart but I felt too small, too young and never good enough.

It would take me years to shed the shackles of my upbringing and forge my own values.

My parents were not unkind – I always felt loved – but there is no doubt that they were of their time. Born in 1930, my father was sexist in a gentle sort of way; a gentleman sexist which is perhaps the most difficult to identify and the hardest to combat. I accused them of racism and I accused them of sexism.

Claudette was of Somali heritage but had been adopted by a white family from Ely, never knowing until many years later that she had a biological brother and sister who had also been adopted by different families. There was Martim, who was Portuguese and Afro-Caribbean. We had Marco Spanish and Marco Italian. Meanwhile Audrey was Afro-Caribbean, Tim was of mixed heritage, partly Chinese, and Panos was from a Greek background. Sam was trans and lots of our gang were bisexual or gay. Why do I mention this? Because it matters and because it opened my world and because this fed into an openness and tolerance and a desire to embrace excitement and newness. It matters because my friends experienced prejudice, but we were about inclusion and sometimes we needed to be sharp-tongued to stop the name-calling dead in its tracks. Our clothes made us different but we saw ourselves as ahead of the curve in a town that was sometimes behind the times. Society couldn't understand us and actually we didn't need its approval.

I came from valleys parents, born and bred, who thought it was funny to say that the first black person they had seen was a miner.

They denied being racist and actually tried hard to be fair and to embrace difference, but they found this difficult. They are both dead now and perhaps I am doing them both a disservice, but I feel that my father would have struggled with my child's gender identity, sexuality and their preferred pronouns.

Today, I work with women to try and help them with issues of confidence and I identify a theme. Perhaps I am trying to right the wrongs of the underachieving female, to make life a little bit easier for the next generation.

My parents wanted so much for me to be a teacher in a secure job and actually my mother wanted me as her best friend. I could never be that. I loved her but the gulf was too wide.

Punk music was a catalyst for change. We rebelled against the status quo. My parents doffed their caps to authority, which is why they never questioned the school being absolute shite.

I remember my father putting on his tie to go and see the completely crap head because I had been sent home from my geography O level for not wearing a bra. Apparently, it was putting the boys off their exams. I missed half an hour of the exam and got a D. Dale the gym (as he was known) said, 'Aw come on, Nic, we let you off the first time for English when you came dressed all in pink with pink hair to match, but no bra, I mean even I couldn't keep my eyes to myself.'

On another occasion the same head looked straight into my shocked and frightened eyes as another girl punched me. He turned, into the fortress of his office, pretending not to see. I knew from that point that authority wouldn't protect me. I'd have to look out for myself.

The girl who hit me, I later realised, had suffered. The torn wallpaper and holes in the doors of her home had shocked me but I didn't comprehend their imprint on the individual.

I met my attacker many years later and she had transformed herself. We were completely unalike as she had been driven by a desperate need to escape through acquiring money and had changed her accent to mould it into home-counties English which would fit with her new group of friends. She now owned a ski lodge and spoke about Lech and Oberlech in a language code designed to alienate outsiders such as her housekeeper (who she mentioned frequently) and myself, not part of the Alpine 'in' set.

She spoke about wanting to give something back. But she also spoke about immigration and Brexit. I remember arguing with her that now she had money perhaps she could give something back. Perhaps I was feeling that I too should have sold some principles for money or been hungrier. She mentioned that back in Hall Road School, we had given her the possibility that a different life could be had. We allowed her a glimpse of our family life. She ate tea with us, wore my clothes and really, I had no idea how hard her life had been. But it was difficult to admire the woman, forty years later, sitting opposite me swathed in Versace, scoring points because she paid her staff more than I earned.

I didn't want to retaliate but found myself back in the schoolyard. Looking back, I am pleased that those days opened up the world for some people. If they have now become exuberant exhibitors of wealth with little awareness, I would like to think that this was simply part of the vast spectrum of humanity and that actually she was a fighter and a survivor and given her choices, I should refrain from judging. But what fun would there be in that?

Even the stable family home where I knew that I was loved could not protect me from a sink-hole school in the 1970s. I might have helped some of my friends to see that another life was possible, to have ambition even. But I paid a personal price for being the child of *Guardian*-reading socialist parents.

I felt alone, with nothing really in common with those around me. Had I attended a nice grammar school I probably would have been a good bluestocking girl who stayed in academia and eventually became a university professor or a deputy head. I needed to be a rebel with no fear to survive in Hall Road and there is a side to me even now that knows when a fight will kick off, or that you never show fear when people are trying to bully you. The side that can flip, the side that sees white and stops caring. The side that once stabbed a boy with a broken beer bottle, because he was trying to rape me.

I did not belong and acting to fit in felt weirdly out of control. And actually, that was really damaging to a young person. I became anorexic and bulimic; I could control that. My parents just wrung their hands as if I was the problem. I took an overdose and they paid for me to see a psychiatrist, who also said that I was the problem. I never went back.

I took every drug available and remember loving it. Sex was wildly freeing with Lars. We made love to David Bowie's 'Heroes' in his Riverside flat and played pool to Lou Reed's 'Perfect Day'. We took poppers to dance to Funkadelic's 'One Nation under a Groove' – as in the lyrics, nothing could stop us.

The music was an entry into hedonism and an escape from a small town. When my exam results came through in the summer of 1979, I told the Head to 'fuck off' and left to do my A levels at technical college. I passed my driving test a month after my seventeenth birthday and drove my red Beetle everywhere with a pile of the New Romantics we had then become in the back.

This was a new era where Steve Strange and Rusty Egan came down from London to put on bands such as Spandau Ballet and Chris Sullivan played with his band, Blue Rondo à la Turk, around the corner from where I now live on Barry Island.

By this time, I had found some of my own identity and a lot more confidence, but this only really manifested itself in the knowledge that I was attractive to men. I was tragically having my worth affirmed by snogging a semi-famous band member, or hanging out with the famous on our trips to nightclubs such as Club for Heroes in London.

During the holidays and on weekends, I worked behind the bar with others from Cardiff, in our uniform of mini togas, with every drink costing £1 as we were obviously not being employed for our mental maths.

But even if I was snogging Martin Kemp or standing next to Grace Jones, I also must have had a part of me that wanted to do something for myself and I took my basic portfolio to Camberwell College of Art where I was accepted for a foundation course, only to discover that grants for art foundation were only awarded for study in your home town.

The impatience of youth meant that I needed to leave Cardiff, so I took a place at North London Poly to study a degree in humanities.

The last couple of years in Cardiff while studying was one long round of partying. I had to do my A levels in a year, as I was studying at an establishment that specialised in resits. At no point do I remember getting any reasonable advice or guidance or even being offered the chance to go to another sixth form. So, I slogged through at Rumney Tech with older kids who had flunked. I got dreadful grades and returned the following year to discover that I now had to learn different poems and periods of history.

North London Poly, through clearing, was my saviour.

My gang were the hairdressers and the shop assistants and the bands of Cardiff. Many of us eventually moved to London and my best friends are still from that time.

I worked for Steve Strange running the guest list of the club that he ran with my friend Claudette. The fashionistas would squabble for entry and in the mode of a Roman emperor Steve consented with a nod to me wherein they glided through. Alternatively, a slight head tilt condemned them to the rank of mundane, enforced to queue – a style death sentence. Claudette went on to have a high-profile career as a promoter and organiser of film premier parties and prominent brands.

Electra managed clothes stores for Joseph in Knightsbridge and later returned to Wales, where she ran her own business. She is married to Panos and they split their time between Wales and Greece. Others became poets and finance directors or highly successful casting directors and film-makers. Many are sadly no longer with us. Some became drug addicts and died too young.

This was a point in time where change was pivotal. Up until the 1950s, teenagers were never really a thing. My parents just went from being children to adults and then marrying and having families.

The Sixties brought huge change, but the Seventies tore a strip through the old order and even my children reckon that we had some of the best music. My mother had one sexual partner. I had everything to rebel against and really at the time didn't realise or compute how much sexism I was dealing with or ignoring on a daily basis. Only later, when I completed a counselling diploma, did I come to realise how much this had affected me.

There are points that I remember fondly and there are also parts which are painful to recall. I know that I was not equipped to deal with the world into which I was thrown. I was brought up at home to be polite and manners were seen as an attribute. But I was then hurled into an environment at school which was survivalist and with people with whom I had little in common. Outside I had to slowly equip myself with armour and didn't properly understand that I could say 'no' to a lot of things. I got myself into dangerous situations and now feel grateful to be alive.

I have recently re-connected with others from that period who have named their social media group 'The Last Gang'.

A few of us meet to make music. I get to sing some of the songs.

LAURA AND ME

Gillian Drake

That dress, the one with the memories – was it the one you wore
for your first date, first dance, first job? Did you meet a significant
someone when wearing it, pack it for the holiday of a lifetime, or
spend your student years in it? You may have got married in it, worn
it to that unforgettable party, or just reached for it time and again
because it made you feel happy, pretty or confident.

Clothes can have this effect – that's why so many of us still have
things in our wardrobes that are years out of date, that we know will
never fit us again, are faded beyond belief. But how hard it is to
throw them away. A particular designer can inspire devotion almost
to the point of addiction. In the 1970s, Laura Ashley's peasant
dresses and romantic Victorian and Edwardian designs influenced
the tastes of a generation, and this influence was felt for years after
her untimely death in 1985.

The history of Laura Ashley, the 'kitchen table' company that
became a multinational brand, is well documented. But what about
those who made and bought the clothes? Workers from the early
days of the company, and women from Wales who were dedicated
customers, here provide an insight into Laura Ashley's immense
appeal.

Born Laura Mountney at her grandmother's house in Merthyr
Tydfil in 1925, Laura Ashley returned to Wales with her husband
Bernard and their family in 1960. Trading as Ashley Mountney, they
opened a shop in Machynlleth. Rosina Corfield[1] joined them in
1963, having first been apprenticed at Cardwells in the town. "I
finished school at 15 – you went to work, didn't you? she said." In

the Ashleys' living room they made tea towels, oven gloves and a fisherman's simple smock, with pockets in the front. Bernard Ashley printed the tea towels, surrounded by black dye. "There was only a little partition between him and us ... it was black, we couldn't see each other!" Factories in Tybrith and Carno followed, where they made the nostalgic Victorian and Edwardian-inspired long dresses that came to bear the name Laura Ashley.

"We did the whole garment ourselves," recalls Rosina. It was more rewarding than piecework, as "you knew it was your work." Laura Ashley would buy a pattern, redesign it and give it to Rosina, saying, "Do this the quickest way."

"Nobody showed me – I just picked it up as I went along." The material was cotton. "... tiny little prints and white cotton blouses ... I remember doing smocks with a yoke, two pockets and buttons down the back." Bernard Ashley bought the fabric, which came in big rolls. In the early days there was no overlocker on the sewing machines to neaten the seams so they had to finish them, "sitting on the bins the paint came in." Equipment was in short supply: "We used to take our tights in for him to strain the colours!" A pattern cutter, Antony Sheppard, would do the cutting and was responsible for the packing, orders and distribution: "It kept the Post Office in Carno very busy!"

"We worked hard but we had fun," says Rosina. "If there was an order Bernard Ashley wanted out, we just worked till it was done ... it was like a little family." Laura and Bernard Ashley attended Rosina's wedding. Women were allowed to work at home when they had children[2], and when Rosina's son was born, this is what she did. "My husband used to check it [the work]." Eventually Rosina went into the warehouse on quality control. "They were so different to local people," she says of the Ashleys. "Their style must have hit at the right time. She got it spot on:

tiny little prints... It was marvellous. They had nothing at all when they came."

The company provided work in the local area. People appreciated not having to move away or travel, and families would work there, including Rosina's sister. "If it wasn't for the company," says Rosina, "I wouldn't be living where we are now. We had lovely memories – no one can take that away from us."

Brian Jones[3] was appointed as a print designer in 1972. Laura Ashley interviewed this "ordinary little kid from Newtown who had a natural gift for art," as he puts it. The interview room was full of qualified designers, but as he was leaving the room, he was told that he had the job. He designed the prints from the 1970s to the mid-1980s, working initially "in a tiny studio with Laura and Bernard Ashley and Bill, the studio manager. We were all gifted amateurs," he says, and described himself as 'a clean slate' because he hadn't been to art school. His job was to "translate her ideas into print". Laura Ashley "loved antique patchwork quilts ... the inside of an old book or a piece of broken china would land on my desk ... She loved it when a new print was born." Fabric had been produced in two colours at first, then as the company grew it acquired more sophisticated printing equipment which could deal with more shades.

Like Rosina, Brian describes the company as "a family – we all put in 100%." He agrees that the style was right for the time: "We captured that decade – that myth of Welsh country living ... You could spot a Laura Ashley design – you either loved it or hated it ... We were so different," he adds. "The world came to Carno." Nothing was planned – "it just sort of happened. I was a shy little kid – and this happened and it was just mind-blowing." Brian retired after 26 years with the company and "It still haunts me."

This almost magical sense of excitement, originality and romance that permeated the company found a response in the customers who wore the clothes and used the fabrics and wallpapers to recreate the dream at home. What most people would recognise as 'typical Laura Ashley' was the long, printed cotton Victorian or Edwardian style dress. Usually high-necked, with pintucks, cotton lace and a sash, these prompted Bernard Ashley to remark that his wife had had "the whole world dressed as milkmaids."[4] Although inspired by rustic style and influenced by the Welsh countryside, they were not just 'country' dresses – they were worn by devotees in suburbs and cities all over the world.

Ruth Jenkins was one such devotee, who remembered the urban appeal of a country style dress when she lived in London: "August 1974 was hot, very hot. It was the summer when I discovered that long dresses and long skirts were cool. The *Sunday Times* had a special offer of a long, flowy Laura Ashley dress. It was made of cotton, was roomy and had wide sleeves almost to the elbow, no collar but a slit in the front which looked a bit like a narrow V. I was so happy about the dress. It was wonderful to wear. The material was bliss and the feel of it just right."

Ruth had been invited for a weekend in Radnorshire, and describes rushing down the escalator at High Holborn tube station: "I was wearing high Italian sandals with my blue Laura Ashley dress and it was no surprise that I slipped. I felt myself tumbling and falling but was caught by two men. Both in pinstripe suits with a carnation in the buttonhole and bowler hats. Both held me very gently and led me to a bench. Both spoke softly and smiled and asked whether there was anything I needed, whether there was anything they could do for me. I thanked them but said no. They lifted their hats and disappeared with the next tube.

"Only later it dawned on me that my 'saviours' must have thought I was pregnant and was thankful they were not there to see me blush!

"The dress was ideal for my three actual pregnancies, two of them in Wales. It must be somewhere still, packed away in boxes that haven't been opened for years."

Another urban customer was Constance Hill, who recalls: "The leading fashion magazine of the day was Vogue: pages full of tall, slender, beautiful models wearing elegant garments constructed in luxurious materials by famous designers who worked, usually in Paris, for very rich women. We were not tall, beautiful or rich but we were young, pretty, romantic and mostly in gainful employment. Laura Ashley was our couturière designer.

"By 1976 she had opened a string of shops in the major cities. I was working in London and when shopping with friends on a Saturday morning we would make our way to Kensington where she had a shop just behind Harvey Nichols (we never set foot in there!). Her shop was always crowded. We did not have much money and we did not always buy but we certainly tried on everything we thought would flatter us or enhance our self-image which coincided with her vision of the Victorian girlhood of a more innocent age.

"I had two dresses to wear on special occasions, both of good quality cotton – one purple and mid-calf, the other yellow, long and flowing. I remember going to a party given for some foreign colleagues, one of whom turned up with a lovely bunch of yellow flowers for me, saying he knew I was going to wear that yellow dress."

These accounts say much about Laura Ashley's appeal. The designs were attractive, they were affordable by most and they were made in Wales. They gave women and girls access to flattering, pretty, unusual clothes that they wanted to wear.

Another committed buyer, Caroline Adams, confirms this: "What did we do – girls of eighteen in the early 1970s – when we needed a long dress for a formal dinner? We didn't have much money and we didn't have much choice either. But then came a revelation: at one of the university Christmas dinners there was a handful of girls wearing something quite different. Stylish, modern, yet looking back to a romantic era with frills, flounces, ruffles, soft colours and, yes, long dresses! Laura Ashley as a brand was just beginning but where were the shops? We were in Liverpool so my friend Lin and I had to make a special trip to London.

"We knew that the shop was on Fulham Road which turned out to be a very long road indeed … it was a matter of walking until we found it. At last, there it was – dark green painted frontage and stylish interior. We were in heaven. There were so many dresses to choose from. We each bought a long navy pinafore dress with a square neckline. This could be worn with a blouse or jumper underneath, or, even better, another Laura Ashley dress. Mine was blue and white with a white frill at the neck and cuffs. Our exhaustion was forgotten as we climbed back onto the train bearing our precious dark green carrier bags.

"Of course, we didn't just wear these dresses to stuffy dinners – they were more versatile than that. We wore them to friends' homes, to the pub; they were the dresses for any occasion. Part of the appeal was that they were so comfortable to wear, in direct contrast to any 'evening' dresses which we had tried on. They were fashionable and instantly recognisable."

Later, living in Cardiff: "I went back to Laura Ashley when I was pregnant because I knew I would find something lovely that wasn't a 'maternity' dress. I bought two dresses which were similar in style with long sleeves ending in a ruff and pintucks on the yoke. One was blue and white and the other was rust and cream. I loved them both and wore them everywhere."

It wasn't only teenagers who wore Laura Ashley; women of all ages still wanted to look attractive and to wear flattering, well designed clothes. Laura Ashley realised this, and often reminded her staff: "Now, remember, we're in the camouflage business."[5] Timeless and ageless, the appeal was universal, and suited to formal as well as informal occasions, as Elizabeth Fussell confirms: "I had two Laura Ashley dresses which I wore for every possible occasion because they made me feel special. The blue and white one was a Victorian design, whose neck and sleeves hid signs of ageing while being elegant in movement. The only time the magic did not work was when I arrived at a Swansea Bach Choir concert to find that every female chorister was wearing the same dress!"

John Hugh Thomas, who founded the choir in the late 1960s, remembers: "I was always looking for ways of making the choir look a bit different. The dresses were in four or five pastel shades but unified by the cut and shape ... The choir first wore them at a Monteverdi concert in the Glynn Vivian Art Gallery in Swansea. As we made a grand entrance down the staircase, we noticed that a member of the audience was wearing the same dress!"

Elizabeth recalls another special evening: "My red and white dress, with a wider neck edged with broderie anglaise, was another delight. After a night of feeling unwell, I wore it to a Hertford College ball and the dress, plus champagne, transformed the occasion. It was just right for a Strauss Ball and its swirling skirt wafted well to the music. I still smile when I think of those feminine, beautifully made dresses and long for a revival."

Kirstine Dunthorne recalls with humour the less practical aspects of dressing as a milkmaid in a cold climate: "The Laura Ashley dress I remember is the full-length, Victorian-style frock I bought around 1970. I had just got my first job as a research assistant in the

National Galleries of Scotland and wanted to treat myself with my first salary. The dress was made of quite a coarse blue on white printed cotton and had a high neck, with a white cotton lace frill and full, tightly cuffed, sleeves also trimmed with lace. It had pintucks on the bodice and a sash at the waist which tied in a big bow at the back. To complete the dress' rustic effect, I wore it with a pair of clumpy white clogs. I was very proud of my outfit, which seemed the height of fashion at the time – but it was never really 'me'. I always felt as if I was wearing fancy dress.

> "One of the senior curators at the gallery invited me to a dinner party at his home. There I was, young, junior and inappropriately dressed in a long, cotton milkmaid dress and white clogs among the sophisticated and sombrely dressed curators and connoisseurs of the art world. I blush to think of it!
>
> "The dress really didn't suit me or my career in an art gallery; it was even less appropriate for the Edinburgh climate. Cotton wasn't warm enough in winter and I had to wear a thermal vest under it; the hem of the dress got dirty and soggy; the clogs got muddy and were no good for running for the bus. In retrospect, I was a fashion victim! But I was wearing an outfit that was a true 1970s classic. I wish I'd kept it!"

Laura Ashley said that her clothes were not "for making a splash in a dramatic place; they're simple garments to wear at home..."[6] As Kirstine's story demonstrates, they were not formal career wear and they were mainly suited to warm, dry weather. Later, clothing was produced in heavier fabrics, including Welsh wool flannel made in the Cambrian Mills, a British Legion factory in mid Wales.

The clothes were loved and worn until they fell apart, and often inspired an emotional attachment, a love that fused with life events to give them a significance fondly remembered.

Eleanor Treen, another Ashley fan, remembers "dresses bought in the summer of 1971... A green and white one was followed by a red and white long dress with halter neck, and a dark green-blue sleeveless floor-length dress. I wore them constantly through 1971 until 1976. I particularly remember ... a day in my parents' garden. My mother and I were being silly and frivolous, laughing and taking it in turns to do silly things. I remember it so fondly now, long after my mother died, as one of those close and loving moments that come out of nowhere and stay in your memory.

"Although I loved those dresses it was my blue corduroy skirt that I wore till it fell apart. I had just left school and didn't have much money but the clothes were, in relation to wages, much cheaper than they are now. I wore it everywhere, dressed up or down with a grey pinafore with pockets, with tight black roll neck sweaters and a mutton sleeve blouse.

"I met my husband when I was wearing it, and wore it long after the nap of the corduroy had worn off on the waist panel on my hips. I wore it held up with braces with the zip undone when I was pregnant but finally had to abandon it when the material became paper thin and gave way.

"I loved the way the skirt swished when you walked and the way it was figure hugging at the waist panel before it flared out to the floor.

"For me, Laura Ashley clothes represent those years after school and before serious jobs and family. They caught my mood of wanting to be different and showing off with glorious floating skirts that swished and felt dramatic after miniskirts and tunics."

Several contributors have mentioned that the styles were suitable as maternity dresses. One of these was Liz Pettifor, who bought her dress in 1979: "I had just found out that we were to become parents.

It was a pinafore dress in a pale purple with little red flowers, side seam pockets and a frill at the bottom and was so comfortable – I just added a polo neck jumper when cold and t-shirts in the spring. I loved it so much I seem to remember wearing it throughout the entire pregnancy! I wore it again three years later when expecting our second child. This dress was with me for the two most emotional and life-changing periods of my life."

Laura Ashley was also popular with students. Glynis Buckham remembers a white cotton blouse, bought while in college in Bath, away from home in north Wales: "I wore it for years until it almost rotted away. It was very fine cotton with slightly puffed sleeves and nipped in at the waist. It had lacy panels down the front and on the cuffs. I felt at the time I was the bee's knees!

> "I had another Laura Ashley garment, a full-length skirt with a Wedgwood blue and white floral pattern. I loved wearing the two articles together. The skirt had a v-shaped band around the waist and it fitted me really well.
>
> "I was living in a flat in one of those gorgeous Georgian houses and Laura Ashley had just hit town (it would have been 1974). I met a motorbike crowd that I hung out with more than going to college. I had two personas. One was as in the photograph, with eyebrows neatly arched and wearing that lovely blouse and skirt. The other was getting on the motorbikes at the weekend and riding down to the coast."

Glynis' blouse was the 'Mexican', famous for having been styled by the *Sunday Times* in a much more daring way than the Laura Ashley tradition.[7] Like Glynis, the blouse had more than one 'persona'!

There were many versions of the blouse. The Victorian style was worn by the ladies of the Swansea Bach Choir after the earlier dresses were abandoned, being hot to wear onstage and difficult to iron. The blouses, chosen because, as John Hugh Thomas observes, "they had a style", were high maintenance too. Choir member Delyth Holland remembers: "After maybe ten years of members becoming frustrated with ironing the pintuck pleats of the blouses, and as it became more difficult for new members to get the same design, we moved over to a plainer high-necked blouse. Around the year 2000, we switched to some horrid Crimplene red round-necked tops with sparkles on the front, and matching Crimplene jackets." No more ironing, but the end of the distinctive style! "Now we wear black tops of varying designs, and the men wear open-necked black shirts."

Glenys Walters, who wore Laura Ashley for years, also remembers her "archetypal Laura Ashley Victorian blouse ... with high neck, and sleeves gathered into a tight cuff, the front and neckband covered in white lace." It is easy to see where the inspiration came from: "My grandmother, married in 1905 in Caernarfonshire, wore a similar blouse for her wedding."

"We find anything with a nostalgia about it goes; it's always a winner,"[8] said Laura Ashley in 1976. Nostalgia – and literature, too. Laura Ashley famously revived the long, white cotton nightdress. A girl could feel like a romantic heroine in one of these, as Jean James recalls:

"The year was 1973. Over the previous few months, I had been working as a chambermaid in a small Swiss hotel ... the work kept us busy, although not too busy to stop me from thinking of my ultimate aim: spending some hard-earned cash on something I had been desiring for a long time.

"Perhaps it was Jane who began it. Or was it Tess or Cathy? These were the women who had leapt alive at me from the pages of those finely drawn novels; the characters who appeared in my mind as real people, often to be found holding a candle in the darkness, hair tumbling out of a thick braid, standing on a landing clothed in a voluminous white cotton nightie, while the wind whistled keenly outside or a fire smouldered in the attic. This was my quest: a nightie fit for a romantic heroine.

"Thus it was that when I eventually reached the streets of London it was not pavements of gold that I went in search of, but instead a shop on the Fulham Road – Laura Ashley's. My feet carried me past the crimson, green and blue flower-sprigged dresses; there was only one target and there it hung in all its finery: a Victorian-styled nightdress made from the finest white cotton muslin, so thin it was almost transparent. It was a creation of frilled ruffs, puffed sleeves and mother-of-pearl buttons. The ends of the sleeves were gathered into exquisitely deep cuffs, the yoke was inset with delicate lace and the edged hem rippled to the floor. The moment had come. I did not even need to look at the price tag for this was what I had been saving for – the past in the present: nostalgia.

"All those days I should have been doing the dusting, when instead my nose was deep into Charlotte Bronte, Emily Bronte or Thomas Hardy, had brought me to this place. I dressed in that nightie so much that it wore through and my mother had to darn it for me. Eventually she told me that it was beyond repair, and she was glad of it because now I could "buy a decent flannelette nightie and the Laura Ashley would make good dusters."

By the end of the 1970s the Laura Ashley dress was becoming more refined, losing some of the homespun look but keeping the nostalgic, romantic, historical influences.

Glenys Walters remembers a beautifully made dress: "the evening dress in fine sprigged cotton has a separate jacket and a wide tie belt. The fully-lined bodice, which has narrow shoulder straps, is covered in tiny horizontal pleats and there is an overskirt which divides in the centre to reveal the second layer of the full skirt beneath. The jacket has 'leg of mutton' sleeves and is shaped by many small pintucks on the front and at the cuffs. The jacket, belt and overskirt are trimmed with white lace, and even the miniature shoulder pads inside the jacket have a tiny, pleated lace edging, in a place where they will never be seen. The full skirt is edged with several rows of small pleats in the traditional Laura Ashley style. The workmanship in this dress is unsurpassed." Glenys has happy memories of wearing the dress to Glyndebourne and on many other occasions.

Laura Ashley is reputed to have said, "I reckon that women looked their best at the turn of the century",[9] and many of her shorter, day dresses evoke the Edwardian seaside. Glenys' first Laura Ashley dress was in this style, and is still in excellent condition. Glenys also had a blouse in fine white cotton with a striped 'sailor' collar in soft lilac.

Pam Davies was another fan of the sailor style: "My favourite piece was a 1920s-type white cotton dress with a drop waist and sailor collar," bought in Exeter where she had planned to visit the cathedral. "On the way there I clocked a Laura Ashley shop down one of the streets. I am afraid that fashion won out over culture – though we did eventually get to the cathedral! I really loved that dress and wore it for a number of summers till it became more grey than white. I finally abandoned it for one of a similar design, this time in a soft blue print, which also lasted for years. I must have bought lots of Laura Ashley clothes over the years, but those two dresses were my favourites."

Laura Ashley also produced clothes for children. Elaine Francis wore her dress as Sunday best in a small Welsh mining village: "Every Easter the village would have a singing festival, and new clothes were bought for the children ... It was during one of these Easter festivals that I had the pleasure of wearing a Laura Ashley dress.

"It was absolutely gorgeous – white background with delicate pale blue and darker blue daisy flower pattern, and ... a lovely white underskirt which made me want to swirl and swirl around. The fabric was exquisite, made from a fine cotton. It had a sweetheart neckline and puff sleeves. I wore it to chapel on the Easter Sunday and I knew immediately that it was a success as I had admiring looks from the congregation.

"Once the Sunday services were over, the dress immediately had to return to the wardrobe until the following Sunday. In those days I attended chapel for a morning service, Sunday School in the afternoon and a further service in the evening... Hence the phrase 'Sunday best.'"

Glenys Walters sums up the appeal of the Laura Ashley style: "Laura Ashley made clothes for women who wanted to look pretty, and this is what attracted her many admirers. They are extremely flattering to most figures, the fabrics are soft and comfortable, and there is never any restriction when wearing them – they can be put on and forgotten about.

"They were very feminine clothes, concealing rather than revealing, and when we wore them, we did indeed feel pretty, rather than glamorous or highly fashionable, and the prices were extremely reasonable considering the workmanship that went into them. When Laura Ashley so tragically died and her guiding hand was lost, we who had bought nearly all our clothes from her were left to struggle through racks of unsuitable garments in other places. Laura Ashley made it all so easy for me – I always knew I would find what I wanted in her shops, and I have never felt that way since."

Laura Ashley's designs had a profound influence, both on 1970s fashion and on the women and girls who made and wore them. For those who worked in the company's factories, it was an opportunity to earn money without having to move away from mid Wales, an area with few other job opportunities. For those who wore the clothes, they represented self-expression, freedom, comfort, fun. The influence never really went away and is having a revival now at a time when, ironically, the Laura Ashley company – changed in ownership over the years and removed from its beginnings – endures increasingly hard times. But the originals are still available in vintage shops and online, and what has become known as the Laura Ashley style, with its rural and Welsh influences, continues to be recognised all over the world.

Notes

1   Rosina Corfield, telephone interview, May 15th 2020.

2   There were never any night shifts and the working week finished at Friday lunchtime, in order to prepare for the weekend. See Anne Sebba, *Laura Ashley: A Life by Design* (London: Weidenfeld & Nicholson, 1990).

3   Brian Jones, telephone interview, May 14th 2020.

4   Sir Bernard Ashley, quoted in *The Laura Ashley Story* (news.bbc.co.uk, Wednesday, September 22nd 1999, UK).

5   Sir Bernard Ashley, quoted in interview with Martin Wood, 7–8 December 2007. Martin Wood, *Laura Ashley* (London: Frances Lincoln, 2009), 64.

6   Laura Ashley, interview with Fyfe Robertson BBC Wales 1976, quoted by Martin Wood in *Laura Ashley* (London: 2009), 58.

7   Martin Wood, *Laura Ashley*, 61.

8   Laura Ashley, interview with Fyfe Robertson BBC Wales 1976, quoted by Martin Wood, *Laura Ashley*, 58.

9   Quotefancy.com

Acknowledgements

Rosina Corfield, Brian Jones, the Jenkins family, Constance Hill, Caroline Adams, Elizabeth Fussell, John Hugh Thomas, Kirstine Dunthorne, Eleanor Treen, Liz Pettifor, Glynis Buckham, Glenys Walters, Sian Walters, Delyth Holland, Jean James, Pam Davies, Elaine Francis.

The Laura Ashley Archive, Newtown, Wales.

Swansea Bach Choir

Caroline Adams

Glenys Walters

Glenys Walters 1915 wedding blouse

Eleanor Treen

Glenys Walters

Elizabeth Fussell

Laura Ashley Romantic nightdress

Glynis Buckham

Liz Pettifor

THE WONDER OF WOOLWORTH
What I Learned as a Saturday
Girl in the Early 1970s

Jane Salisbury

On that first Saturday, at 8.45am, I was so pleased to wear the lemon wrap-around nylon overall and to stand behind the loose biscuit counter with scrubbed hands and the required smile. Such was the popularity of Barry's Woolworth that the store operated a waiting list for senior school girls wanting Saturday employment. With encouragement and help from my mother, in October half-term 1969, I wrote a letter of application to 'The Manager' hoping to be hired for the busy Christmas period. An application form arrived in the post. It informed me that my name had joined a waiting list and not to expect an invitation to interview until Spring 1970, when I would be fifteen.

And that is precisely what occurred. With freshly plaited hair, I arrived for a 4.30pm interview in school uniform, sporting a leather satchel and well-polished shoes. I recall an easy mental arithmetic test and a conversational interview about politeness and cleanliness. I left with a spring in my step after stating my dress size for a uniform! Norman Greenbaum's hit record 'Spirit in the Sky' was playing through the store speakers. I felt modern and trendy and put my bus fare money towards a pair of new tights (American Tan), watching the hosiery sales assistant closely in anticipation of my newly acquired job.

A mix of pride and delight followed at 5.30pm on very that first Saturday as a Woolworth employee. I was ushered from the shop floor upstairs to the office hatch where I was handed a windowed brown envelope which framed my name, JANE DONOVAN, on the white printed payslip inside. This felt so very official with its Staff Pay Roll digits and National Insurance Number. Of course, it was legitimate, formally recognised employment, unlike my two previous summer jobs at Barry Island.

In 1968, aged just thirteen but pretending to be fifteen, I'd worked as a weekend waitress in The Ponty Cafe for twelve shillings and sixpence a day! A year later I'd improved my liquidity by ten shillings selling beach balls, buckets and spades in Ben Jones Beach Shop where I earned £1 2s. 6d. Cash in hand had been my only experience, so I felt the importance of the pay packet keenly and some twenty years later was able to acknowledge the wage ritual as an important *rite de passage* into Wales' formal economy.

Woolworth was a large employer in the late 1960s and 1970s, with over a thousand shops across British and Irish high streets. At the Barry store on a Saturday, some thirty or so women faced the public, while four men worked in the stockroom. The manager and assistant manager were both men. The gender divide was so apparent. Yet a modicum of power rested with section supervisors and floor walkers. These women kept us all under surveillance. Looking back, I see they were guardians of the required courtesy and policed the wholesome presentation of staff. A loose strand of hair could get you sent from the shop floor to 'tidy up your appearance'. Chewing gum could result in a warning and scolding lecture on etiquette.

'How can you say "May I help you?" when you are blowing bubbles and chewing the cud?' Lengthy chats to browsing friends were not tolerated and offenders would find themselves last to be allowed off the shop floor at the end of the day. The immaculate staff Ladies' room had framed messages on the back of each toilet cubicle door! So even when spending a penny, we women were reminded of the Woolworth concept of service.

'Courtesy costs little, but means a lot!'

'Customers FIRST always!'

And,

'Now wash your hands.'

After working just three months (i.e. 12 Saturdays), the store was reorganised to self-service, with the majority of enclosed four-sided rectangular counters removed. Only the Pic 'n' Mix Sweet counter and Cheese and Bacon counter remained, with two assistants each. Imminent decimalisation was the trigger for this massive change. The country's centuries old duo-decimal currency of twenty shillings to a pound and twelve pence to a shilling was to be replaced by the hundred penny system in use today. We Saturday girls were told that Woolworth would spend thousands on hundreds of new cash registers and pricing stamps, but in truth we were more interested in the new uniform.[1] All of us much preferred the bright cornflower and sky blue chequered overall which was lab coat style and straight. It was easy-care nylon and bore a machined embroidered Winfield logo on a chest pocket. In our new attire we continued to serve courteously and found ourselves covering different areas of the store than we had hitherto.

At school, subject teachers made an effort to prepare us. Our history teacher taught us that plans to change the pound had been announced by James Callaghan back in 1966, when he was Chancellor of the Exchequer. In maths we were given monetary problems to solve like calculating compound interest. Seam allowances for dressmaking in our needlework classes were no longer 5/8th of an inch but 1.5cms; yards were replaced by the more generous metre. In cookery/home economics, where we girls were in training as future wives and mothers, we were advised to memorise that 500grams was roughly 1lb in weight (Salisbury, 2003). Our lively music teacher had us listening to and critiquing the rather banal song lyrics by Max Bygraves titled 'Dec-im-al-i-sation'. The song's function was to be an aide-memoire to teach the population the fact that a hundred new pennies now equated to a British pound note.[2]

A huge media campaign prepared the public. Posters, leaflets and BBC programmes explained the new system. All Woolworth staff undertook compulsory training and we Saturday girls were required in small groups to attend a two-hour session after school about a month before the official changeover date. In fact, half of the coins had been put in circulation well before February 15th – known as Decimalisation Day or more popularly as D-Day. Training involved practising with a new converted cash register. We were also given 'What if?' hypothetical scenarios to discuss. These focussed on how we should behave courteously with difficult customers. We also had great fun engaging in role play exercises with the male assistant manager who was brilliant at being a cantankerous customer.

On my first Saturday working with the new money, I was allocated to the frozen goods section. This had its own new till and a large laminated conversion chart. All price labels still held both decimal (new pence) and shillings / old pennies, and we were instructed to accept payment in old coins but had to supply change in new ones. I recall that it was largely older shoppers who took the longest to retrieve from purses and check the printed receipts. It was not unusual to be asked 'What's the total in old money, please?' and 'What do I owe you in real money, my darling?'

Woolworth, like all stores, had 'rounded up' fractions to the nearest pence with the result that prices were effectively raised. Some shoppers complained that a new £1 didn't buy as much and some were baffled that a sixpence piece was now only worth two and a half old pennies! The full hierarchy of manager, assistant manager and supervising floor walkers patrolled the store on that first Decimal Saturday and I felt confident that help was always nearby. George Harrison's melodic hit single 'My Sweet Lord' was played on the hour throughout that day and may well have diffused potential monetary frustrations.

In the 1970s, popular straplines and musical jingles voiced by various celebrities were used to promote Woolworth across different media. These three are firmly engraved in my memory:

'That's the wonder of Woolworth!'

'That's the wonder of good old Woolies!'

'Everybody needs Woolworth!'

Recollections are fragmented but tinged with nostalgia, for 1970 to 1973 were happy times for me. Woolies was part of the community. People browsed and toured the store: boyfriends, neighbours, and aunties visited the counters to say hello. My memory is one of collective sociability, especially fostered among the women staff, with older full-time employees looking out for us Saturday girls.

A small staff restroom and subsidised canteen on the first floor provided low-cost lunches and snacks. Only women used this room – the manager, assistant manager and storeroom men ate elsewhere or left the building for their breaks. The lunch breaks of one hour operated in a staggered way from 11.00am to 2.00pm so that there were always adequate numbers of sales staff downstairs in the shop. I so enjoyed the lunch breaks, when risqué humour and bedroom stories generated much laughter. These were times when we Saturday girls were entertained by a handful of older women and often shocked by the detailed conversational topics. The Problem Pages in women's magazines often provided the stimulus for what I can only describe as 'performances'. The star of these gatherings was Gina, a 35-year-old passionate Led Zeppelin fan; she had all their albums and had seen them perform at Cardiff's Capitol Theatre in December 1972. We girls envied her this experience, but she was a credible adult and we admired her assertiveness. Though married with two school-aged sons, she admitted to us that she loved coming to work not only to escape domestic drudgery (Gavron, 1966) but to have her own separate friends. Gina's views on modern life seemed bold at that time. Her views on contraception were so easily memorised:

'The pill is most effective if you hold it between your knees!'

On the notion of sexual intercourse during menstruation Gina was adamant:

'If a bloke can't wait a week, he's not worth knowing!'

And, on reading aloud to us a magazine Agony Aunt's suggestion of an alternative pleasuring of a husband via arm pit intercourse, Gina's booming voice was emphatic:

'A woman's body is hers! No means no. Just remember that you girls!'

Gina was not vulgar in any sense. But she was highly vocal and pragmatic in her advice. She deployed a different set of vocabularies to those used in sex education at school. They were also in stark contrast to those terms carefully chosen by our mothers whose steerage on chastity and 'keeping yourself for the man you intend to marry' were not untypical, even in the 1970s.

The building formerly occupied by Woolworth still remains but it is now a Poundland – a bargain store I occasionally visit for serviettes, candles and tea lights. It is a soulless place, pumping out tinny Musak and with none of the social interactions and polite etiquette that characterised Woolies. The aisles are far narrower now and the store layout is different, yet the original shop flooring and wall shelving remains, and I can recognise the distinct areas where I once stood to serve customers. Feelings of sentimentality and attachment surface and quite surprise me.

Retrospectively, with the perspective of a 65-year-old and with so much life and learning under the bridge, I know for certain that those Saturdays at Woolworth were an important element of my socialisation into womanhood. I learnt first-hand about servitude and civility and that the latter cost nothing but was the KY Jelly of successful interaction with purchasers! I learnt – albeit vicariously – about sex, and that a woman could say 'No' to it, even within marriage. But I also acquired disquieting knowledge that women earned less than men, that married women typically worked a 'double shift' (Sharp, 1976) – after a day's shopwork, the norm for Woolies' women was to return home to make the tea and service the home and family.

Woolworth is perhaps a distinct symbol for me of an era before I became fully alert to the gross inequalities of the labour market and the life-limiting assumptions about a woman's place. It was a relatively naive period for me and in fact, some ten years passed before I actually read *Spare Rib* magazine or attended a Consciousness Raising (CR) Group. However, the seeds of my later feminism were planted firmly during my work as a 1970s Saturday girl.

Notes

1   Subsequent records report that Woolworth spent over £5 million on decimalisation.
    http://www.woolworthsmuseum.co.uk/1970sdecimalisation.html

2   'Decimalisation', a song by Max Bygraves can be accessed at
    https://www.youtube.com/watch?v=jCiEzQ4EGk4

References

Gavron, H., *The Captive Wife: Conflicts of Housebound Mothers* (Harmondsworth: Penguin, 1966).

Salisbury, J., 'Sixties Schooling', in D. Beddoe, ed., *Changing Times* (Honno Press, 2003).

Sharp, S., *Double Identity: The Lives of Working Mothers* (Michigan: Penguin, 1984).

PAINTING THE
BEAUTY QUEENS ORANGE

Lynne Parry-Griffiths

Wednesdays are the same as Tuesdays. They come from the Wirral, Little Neston, New Brighton, all white nylon one-piece costumes and matching stiletto points. Clutching Carmen rollers, chiffon scarves, plastic trays of spidery lashes, Elnett hairspray, and those tubes that paint orange stripes of legs. None of them pay me any attention. Why should they? I'm eight years old and deep in a *William*. All they care about is making sure their lines are clear and crisp, the hair sprayed into submission, and not falling over in front of the judges. Blank, smiling skull masks, pencilled eyebrows, and all wrapped up in a cloud of Charlie.

They bring their mothers, aunts, and in the summer holidays, their small sisters. Many of them make the journey six times, some more. Tuesdays for the little ones' Miss Rhyl Rosebud, Wednesdays are Miss Sunny Rhyl, Thursday night is Miss Prestatyn and Friday, one more for the little one, Miss Prestatyn Princess Charming. They'll be back until it's finals weeks and the holidays are over. Wendy, Yvonne, Sue, Hazel, Sharon, Dawn, Judi, Carol and Diane. Dad knows them all and they call him Jack, which is how I come to be sitting reading as they snap their straps and squeeze tangerine feet into impossible shoes, practising Bambi steps until Mrs Kay tells them to stand still.

I'm quite good at maths but can't work out how Hazel, Wendy and the girls are all still twenty-three. They have to put their ages on the orange entry forms Dad has in his office and I've been helping him sort them out since I was six and a half, so I know everything the judges know. And more, because I see the forms every week.

The forms are simple: name, address, age, vital statistics, and occupation. I think I was the first person in my class to be able to spell occupation; I've seen it often enough.

'Why are they always nurses?' I say and Dad laughs.

'You won't be a nurse, will you Fan?'

'I'm going to be a barrister.'

'Good girl.'

This week, Mrs Kay has peach fluffed hair; last week it was lilac. Perhaps next week it'll be pale turquoise. It doesn't dare move, defiant in the face of the famous sea breeze. Mrs Kay smiles as she watches the girls' attempts with their extra-large cans of Elnett, or Boots' own.

'Girls, girls!' Mrs Kay is clapping her hands. She reminds me of the headmistress in the *St Trinian's* films I love even more than the Norman Wisdom ones they show on Saturdays. Miss Fitton, that's her name, but my sister said it was really a man dressed up.

'Elegance, elegance,' says Mrs Kay, demonstrating how to stand. 'Bottoms in, shoulders back and no slouching and unladylike displays.'

She doesn't need to explain what she means, but even so the girls smirk and giggle. Behind her pink pointed glasses Mrs Kay's eyes narrow, but she knows what she's talking about. She's a retired professional ballroom dancer and it shows. Not so long ago she and her dancers appeared in *Holiday on the Buses*, the one set in Prestatyn Pontins.

'When you are ready, you will line up and numbers will be distributed. You must make sure your number is always clear for the benefit of the judges. You slip the band around your wrist and hold it by your side. Is that clear? By your hip. Nowhere else.'

Dave, who works for Dad, does the numbers, but it is Chrissy, one of his secretaries who comes in with them.

'Wotcha, cock,' she says to me, grinning.

'All right, Chris.'

'What're you reading this time?'

I show her the book jacket.

'Good, is it?'

'Yeah.'

'Your dad says do you want anything?'

'I'm ok, ta.'

'Right. Come and sit with me when it starts, ok?'

I'm always glad when it's Chrissy's turn, with her fire red hair and matching nails. She's known me since I first started coming to work with Dad, on Sundays, when he had to man the Tourist Information Centre once a month. They all have to do it, even the bosses like Dad and Smithy.

'The numbers, please, Christine,' says Mrs Kay, holding out a small, fat hand. Chrissy's scarlet tips hand them over and again I wonder how she manages to type with those nails.

'Sorry, Mrs Kay,' says Chrissy. 'Good luck, girls. Break a leg. Or maybe not.'

I giggle, but no one else does. I'd love it if one of them slipped and ended up in the water because watching them parade around the pool like the sheep and cows in St Asaph auction is boring. How they can stand and smile for so long takes practice and Dad says most of them have been coming since they were little and in the Rosebud. They have to be over sixteen to enter Miss Sunny Rhyl and under ten for Rhyl Rosebud, so there's a few years of practice to get in before they begin the circuit all over again. Most of them take dance classes run by ladies like Mrs Kay and learn Pitmans and touch-typing. A good typist will always find work, though they will finish when they have their first baby, so the life isn't too long.

'And don't forget, girls, smile!' Mrs Kay bares her dentures. There's a tiny trace of Max Factor smearing one of her plastic canines.

'Seeing a pretty girl always puts a smile on people's faces, so let them take a good look at you. You stop when you reach the judges' table and turn around so they can see you properly. All the time you make sure you are smiling. Am I clear?'

'Yes, Mrs Kay.'

'Wait until Dave calls you for a few words and don't forget to speak up, and be clear and precise. Then you make your way to the line-up and stay there until everyone has been called. Stand still and smile. Do not fidget or shuffle your feet. Keep holding the number in place because the judges may take the opportunity to inspect you further when the next contestant is at the furthest end of the pool. Do I make myself clear?'

'Yes, Mrs Kay.'

'The judges will call for the placed girls first from the line-up and then you take your places on the podium. The winner will be given a sash and the top three must then remain for photographs. The rest of you should then make your way back here, handing your numbers back to Christine who will be waiting, won't you, Christine?'

'Of course, Mrs Kay.'

'You do not need to speak; we have all your details. After the photographs, the winners return here and hand in their numbers. Is that clear?'

'Yes, Mrs Kay.'

All that walking and smiling for a sash and place in the final. Dad writes the sashes in poster paint and there are sponsored prizes. Mum says it's no wonder Dad's on sixty a day and we haven't had to buy bottles of Schweppes or cans of Baxters for years.

Finals Week has top prizes, including jewellery, and we do well out of it too. As Dad says, it's all part of the business.

Most of the girls are ready before time and stand like racehorses in the starting stalls practising smiling and taking deep breaths. They arrived an hour and a half earlier in various tones of orange, ranging from peach to tangerine but don't put on their full faces until the final twenty minutes.

'Am I streaky?'

'Oh God, don't say I'm patchy. I'll die if I am. Can you see?'

'Have I missed a bit?'

They peer at the backs of each other's legs, their elbows, the small of the back, making sure they don't wrinkle too much in case of lines. Some of them are dying for a ciggy; a faint whiff of Embassy and polo mints adorn their chatter about who won New Brighton the other day and who's in for Prestatyn tomorrow. Mrs Kay disapproves of gossip and the girls are careful to censor their tittle-tattle as small ears are present. A lot of them have younger sisters and know when to stop.

Every week I watch them transform from orange chrysalises to fully painted butterflies. Arriving in belted macs and headscarves, all of them clutch vanity cases and make-up boxes, their hair wound tight around a range of rollers. Some of them have new Carmen heated rollers and plug them in – if they can find the single plug – as soon as they arrive, much to Mrs Kay's annoyance. No one wears tights, some have shortish skirts and platform sandals, one or two are in shorts and even denim flares. The eyelashes have usually been glued into place at home, and tested. The last thing a girl needs is to smile for the judges and discover a faint tickling on the cheeks as a bottom or top lash makes a bid for freedom. They pull contorted faces before adding further layers of mascara until I think they must have to summon up reserves of hidden strength to even blink.

Max Factor and Nivea will hide a multitude of sins beneath their powder puff enhancements, along with what they call blusher and Mrs Kay still calls rouge. She says they don't know how lucky they are with their mascara wands. Back in her day they had blocks of mascara and had to use water to work up a paste before they could even think of adding it to their lashes. The girls all smell of Charlie, Rebel, Tramp and the occasional Chanel Number 5.

If they're regulars, the costumes are already under their clothes which they hang neatly on the pegs like we do in school, although they don't have stickers by them. Bikinis and large, dangling earrings are banned. Plastic clip-ons seem to be preferred to match the ubiquitous white shoes and costumes. One or two of the more daring are wearing red, green, lemon or navy, but no one likes black; it doesn't show off the bottled tan. If the weather's been decent, they've managed a couple of hours on the sun lounger in the back garden.

'Oh, what do you use?'

'Olive oil.'

'Really?'

'Yes, me mam gets it from the chemist's.'

'Is it better than Boots?'

'Cheaper. You don't get through so much.'

'Oh, right.'

'I've only used olive oil for me ears.'

'Try it. They don't use anything else in Spain.'

'Ooh, I love Spain.'

'The fellas are so dishy.'

'Bit cheeky if you ask me.'

'And that's enough, girls,' says Mrs Kay clapping her palms together. 'Fifteen minutes, fifteen minutes.'

'Yes, Mrs Kay.'

I go back to the world of William Brown – things make more sense there – and not for the first time yearn for housemaids, cooks, and giddy young men. Most of the girls painting their faces in front of me would have been maids in William's time. Lipstick and powder applied in secret on the half-day off when you went walking out with your young man and an overly short skirt was more than frowned upon. No parading around an open-air swimming pool in little more than their underclothes for the delights of day trippers and holidaymakers with nothing else to do apart from sip tea darker than the girls' legs and chew on Sunblest butties.

Lips are perfected, blotted and pouted. A final application of powder fixes the runs and they're ready. Perhaps one day I'll be able to draw such perfect pouts, though when I'm their age I'll be at university with other things to think about.

Good old-fashioned scarlet slashes are still preferred, although coral is making a bid. The girls laugh about the pale baby pinks they used to wear back in the Sixties and how one or two even tried white or black. The eyes are lightly ringed with kohl copied from Elizabeth Taylor's Cleopatra, ignoring the fact that the look was fashionable thousands of years ago. I could tell them how Nefertiti and Hatshepsut painted their eyes but I don't think they'd be that interested.

Topping the kohl are various shades of shimmering shadow, mostly turquoise and lilac, definitely no browns and purples. 'You'll look as if you haven't had a good night's sleep,' says Mrs Kay and no one wants that, do they?

'Ten minutes, ten minutes.'

The headscarves are all off, the rollers unwound, leaving fat and skinny sausages to be teased and pulled. Hairpieces are unpopular after one landed on the judges' table. Curls and ripples are enough.

Mrs Kay goes through the final routines. She'll stand them in order, tugging at costumes to make sure not too much is on show and any tan lines are addressed. A lot of the costumes have cups sewn in 'to enhance what nature never intended,' says Mrs Kay, and cotton wool and tissues are strictly forbidden. All their measurements have been given to the judges on their entry forms and most are uniform in their regularity.

34-22-34, 35-23-36 or even the perfection of 36-24-36. The forms don't have anything about educational qualifications even if the girls have a smattering of CSEs, O Levels and City and Guilds.

Chrissy tells me Dad's looking and I wave.

'All right, Fan?'

'Yeah, I'm fine.'

'Want a drink or anything?'

'I'm all right, ta.'

'Crisps?'

'No, ta.'

'I'm a bit busy now, so stay with Chrissy. Mind you don't get in the way.'

'All right.'

I never get in the way and if I'm bored, I can always rely on William.

The baths are about three-quarters full. Once the peak weeks kick in it'll be crammed with families drawn to the crystal water seven feet deep in the middle, diving boards and a range of refreshments. We never have to sit near the holidaymakers and have the best views of the girls and judges.

'Good afternoon, ladies and gentlemen, boys and girls,' booms Dave the compère.

Chrissy chats as we watch Mrs Kay gently shove each girl on her way. 'She's a regular,' she says. 'Oh, that one's new. Haven't seen her before. What do you think of that cossie? Those shoes look painful.' I tell Chrissy she's far prettier than any of the girls with their artificial tans, nails and eyelashes, and she laughs. There's a joke entry form for Chrissy pinned on the wall of Dad's office saying she's two foot five, and twenty-five stone.

'And here we have contestant number four, Hazel from Little Neston,' says Dave, reading from his clipboard. On the judges' table, I watch Dad shuffle papers and laugh at something the female judge says. She's one of the singers from Tito's cabaret. For finals they always bring in the star of the summer season, and TV people like Arfon Haines Davies. This year Dad says they've got Faith Browne again. The last time she came she wore a huge floppy hat and sunglasses so I still don't know what she really looks like.

'Give her a round of applause, ladies and gentlemen, boys and girls,' urges Dave and the crowd obliges. When Hazel reaches the far end of the pool, cheers and whoops are raised. She seems to beam more at that section before fixing her lips and continuing with her parade as Dave reads aloud what he calls her vital statistics. Occasionally, a girl changes circuits and goes to the Morleys so she can compete for Miss United Kingdom and Miss World, as Rhyl and Prestatyn are tied in with Miss Great Britain. Wendy, 23, made it to the finals of Miss UK a few years ago, but she's back now.

Dave shares some more information about Hazel, 22, from Little Neston, as she makes her way towards him, still smiling. The judges study her as she stands in front of them and slowly turns around. I don't mind the competitions, but sometimes I do wonder why we don't have the same type of thing for boys apart from the Junior Tarzan. I'd never have the nerve to do what the girls do, or the patience to paint my nails and do all the things they seem to think is necessary to impress the judges.

'Hello, Hazel from Little Neston. How are you today?' says Dave.

'Hello, Dave. It's lovely to be here in Rhyl,' says Hazel speaking slowly and carefully.

Dave laughs. 'And on such a sunny day in Sunny Rhyl,'

The conversation continues and we learn that Hazel is training to be a nanny and how she loves children and animals. I go back to William flooding Ginger's house under the nose of a fluffy maiden aunt as Hazel makes way for Judi.

When all the girls have taken their turn around the pool, they wait in a smiling line of lipstick until the judges reach their decision.

Chrissy asks me who I think will win.

'Number seven.'

'To win?'

'Yeah.'

'And in third place,' says Dave making each word last till teatime. 'It's contestant number two.'

A section of the crowd applauds and whistles. I don't recognise the girl; she must be a visitor.

'And in second place, it's contestant number five.'

'Still think it'll be seven?' says Chrissy.

I shrug.

'She won Prestatyn last week.'

'And the winner of this week's heat of Miss Sunny Rhyl, is...' Dave pretends to shuffle the papers on his clipboard. He does this every contest and Jackie, Smithy's secretary, stands forward with flowers.

'Why don't you do the flowers, Chrissy?'

'I'd rather see to you,' she says and means it.

'Contestant. Number. Four.'

'Wrong again,' I say.

Hazel from Little Neston steps forward and Dave pecks at her left cheek. She is still smiling as he helps her onto the winner's rostrum as all the other numbers clap politely. Phil the photographer is immediately in place and Bob from the *Journal* writes up the results. Most of the crowd lose interest as soon as Dave thanks the ladies and gentlemen, boys and girls, the judges, the sponsors, but most of all the girls themselves. The judges share a final joke and Dad, Jackie and a couple of others start to clear everything away until next week.

'You all right here for a bit, cock?' says Chrissy.

'Yeah.'

'Don't talk to anyone, will you? I won't be long.'

'All right, Chris.'

It'll be another hour or so before Dad can take me home and I'm glad it's a new *William* I've brought today. Chrissy helps Jackie and the other secretaries and Mrs Kay leads the girls away back to the changing room behind us. A drink will arrive for me once Chrissy has finished and I can hear Dad laughing with Phil and Dave. The winner and her family go with Smithy and Jackie and Dave to the Westminster, but we don't because we go on Tuesdays after the Rhyl Rosebud.

I prefer Tuesdays. The Rosebud is in the bandstand where the Rhyl Silver Band play on Sunday evenings. Smithy's in the band and sometimes we pop in to listen because Dad says you can't beat a bit of brass. I frown and try to work out the connection between silver and brass.

The Rosebud isn't that different from Miss Sunny Rhyl, apart from the frilly dresses and lisps. Most of the contestants seem to come from the same places on the Wirral, but we also get a few locals, Towyn, Colwyn Bay, Abergele. I'm more or less the same age as the older ones though Mum calls them the little ones and their world is a universe away from mine. Their dresses stick out thanks to the layers of petticoats and some are so short glimpses of matching frilly knickers are clear to everyone. A lot of preening and brushing seems to go on, but make-up is strictly banned, not that everyone seems to follow that rule; I've seen Mrs Kay stare very closely as yet another blonde Kerry from the Wirral bats strangely black eyelashes at her. In spite of their years, most of the mothers still seem to take Shirley Temple as their model, and I have to say I am envious of their sausage ringlets. Even when Mum ragged my hair, I ended up looking like my Action Girl after I left her in front of the electric fire.

Dave is on compère duty again but it's a lot less formal than Miss Sunny Rhyl. All the girls seem to want to be 'a nurth' when they grow up and one or two insist on lisping a few notes of Lena Zavaroni though none of them can sing.

'Perhaps we'll be hearing a lot more of you in the Junior Talent,' says Dave and I cross my fingers and say I hope not. Mum tells me to shush, I'm only jealous.

The Junior Talent Show's got a bit edgy since that family from Colwyn Bay turned up. Dad says they're a bloody nightmare.

Mum had to make up the judging table last year and they caused a fuss because their girl didn't win because she was obviously trained to sing properly. They gave her third prize and it was Mum who had to do it. She was just about to hand over the prize cheque when they called the girl off the stage and Mum was left clutching the envelope. No one was impressed and Mum told Dad she would never do it again.

When it's all over, Dad takes us across the road to the Westminster with the heat winner for proper afternoon tea. It's the poshest hotel in Rhyl and they cut the crusts off the triangle sandwiches and serve cress with the egg. Mum tells me not to eat everything though I get to drink warm coca-cola from a bottle with a paper straw. I eat tuna fish and mayonnaise triangles but prefer the taste of salad cream. Tea is served in stainless steel pots on a big silver tray with wooden handles. The small plates have circle borders and green serviettes. It reminds me of Pam's wedding last March when I was a bridesmaid: butterfly cakes, bara brith, scones, sponge fingers and slices of chocolate cake a bit like the iced squares we have in school with sauce.

'Don't have a scone,' says Mum. 'You know you don't like them.' And she's right, I don't. The currants look like flies.

Dave makes jokes and keeps everyone going. I'm glad it's only the winner of the Rosebud who's allowed to come and they're always the first to leave. Everyone else is used to each other, and we'll do it all again on Friday at the Royal Lido.

At the Lido, we always sit in the best booth, the middle one with the red velvet padded seats, and the reserved sign, to watch the Miss

Prestatyn Princess Charming and Junior Tarzan. I get to drink more coca-cola and sit through the different acts. Brioni the magician always gets his tricks wrong. Dad told us last week how Brioni managed to lock himself into a wicker basket and had to be let out after half an hour. I quite like the man who sings 'Ring of Fire' but it's always much better when everything's over and the families have all gone home. All of the artistes are friendly and I know the Minting girls well by now. Ken who plays the Hammond Organ is always happy to show us magic tricks. The only one who doesn't really have much to say to us is Brioni.

The competitions are the same each week. Dave asks the same questions he asks on Tuesdays and gets the same answers about wanting to be 'nurtheth'. Most of the girls wear different frilly dresses, though one or two turn up in the same outfits and shoes. You see them if you go to the loo, the mums all tugging and spraying, though again Mrs Kay makes sure none of them try to get away with make-up.

Mum quite likes Princess Charming, but often I'm bored and glad I've brought a *William* or *Famous Five* or *Five Find-Outers and Dog*. We don't sit on our own for long though, sometimes Chrissy and her boyfriend join us, sometimes Smithy who chats with Mum more than me.

Dave introduces the judges to everyone, and Dad's adjudicating as always. He makes sure the judges aren't exactly the same as the Rosebud's so no one can accuse anyone of favouritism. Each week one of the acts has to judge, along with some of the sponsors. Mum says there's no way on God's earth she'll be caught again and besides, she can't leave me on my own. The prizes are different as well because no one wants to have two Burbank baby dolls. One year they had the Holly Hobby dolls as prizes. I had the full range and we hung some of them on the Christmas tree along with the plastic mice and pipe-cleaner men.

After the Princess Charming, Dave moves us on to the Junior Tarzan which is much more fun with the tummy rolling little boys in swimming trunks showing off their matchstick muscles and pale chests. All of the boys have to make the Tarzan noise and most of them are so rubbish everyone laughs. Like the Rosebud and Miss Sunny Rhyl, you get the same faces every week and a mixture of what Dad calls the pros and the locals. The nightmare family from Colwyn Bay turn up; Dad says the father's a bloody drip of a man and often says he's almost landed him one.

The competitions don't take more than an hour or so and we have a break before the cabaret starts. When I was little, I thought they meant Cadbury and was wondering what happened to the chocolate. The acts are ok, and usually the same type. Magicians, lady singers in spangly dresses and big earrings, men in three-piece suits, huge round-pointed collars, velvet bow ties and frilly-fronted shirts.

With the competitions over, Dad and a few others come and sit with us for a bit. It's good being able to sit in the middle booth with the red padded seat and orange lamp. Once or twice cheeky holiday makers have tried to sit in it, but the staff have to tell them they're sorry but it's reserved for VIP guests. Mum doesn't like to make a fuss and will say it's fine, it doesn't matter, but Mr Fred Jackson the Lido boss says if it's reserved, it's reserved.

The holiday makers and contestant families clap along to the songs we hear every week, but I prefer my book, unless we have company as I know it's rude to read when someone's talking to you. There's usually a raffle and I don't know why Mum buys a ticket as most of the prizes come from Dad's cupboard. Once the raffle's done, the people start to think about going home.

The regulars are always the last to leave. 'Goodnight Jack,' I hear them call to Dad and he's at the bar now, shirt sleeves rolled up, pint and fag in hand. The tie will be off as well and Mum makes a tutting noise because he stuffs it into his pocket. We always end up having to look after his jacket.

The bar staff begin to clear the tables and collect glasses and we leave the middle booth and join Dad in the bar area though there's a big sign that says 'Strictly No Under 18s are Allowed in the Bar Area'. Dad gets us more drinks and we hear him laughing at something someone has said. Smithy chats with Mum and Phil the photographer's wife, or Chrissy, or Dave Christely, or Ruth his fiancée, and I go off and play with the other children. Often, we go to the big curtained function room they don't use on a Friday and leave the adults to get on with their chatting and drinking and smoking. Sometimes Lorraine Minting and I pretend we're giving concerts and everyone claps when we finish, even though the microphones have been switched off. She teaches me all the words to Would You Like to Swing on a Star and for a few minutes we're on *Top of the Pops* or the *Eurovision Song Contest* and there's no big brother to call you names and take the mickey out of everything you do. After a while Mr Fred Jackson appears. He's the dead spit of Frank Cannon and Dad says the bar staff call him Cannon behind his back, though no one can cook a whole salmon like him. Dad says it melts in your mouth and it's served with scales made out of cucumber. He always says hello, how are you, did you have a good night, and we smile and say yes, thank you, even though once Mr Jackson appears, we know we'll be going home sooner rather than later.

Most of the time, I'm still playing or singing when Mum calls me and says come on, it's time, we have to go now, and she's got my coat ready. I have no idea what the time is, but it has to be late. Dad's been drinking pints of bitter, and Mum's had a port and lemon – the only thing she drinks apart from shandy. Sometimes I have my coat on and we're ready and Dad's still talking and laughing. Aunty Mill says he jangles worse than any old woman once he gets going.

Most of the time he's chatting with the sponsor reps, doing what he calls a bit of business. More crates of soup, tonic water, pineapple juice, and my favourite, bitter lemon. Finally, he's ready and we say goodnight, see you all next week, meaning Tuesday or Wednesday.

THE CURE

Bridget Taylor

They thought it was going to cure me. It didn't, of course. I knew it wouldn't. But I went because there wasn't an option. In fact, that brief interlude turned out to be one of the only positive memories I have of the 1970s – a decade I would much rather forget.

It had all been a bit of a shock, really. Rather than living the cloistered, prosaic life of a 'mental patient' (permitted terminology in 1975), I was travelling down the M40 in the back of our Cortina. I remember staring out of the window and wondering what was going to happen to me.

My parents had responded without question when summoned by the Professor of Psychiatry – doctor was God in the Seventies. My mother told me afterwards that the meeting was brief, brusque and very uncomfortable. I wasn't included of course; the idea of patients' rights didn't include the mentally ill until 1983.

Apparently, I was to be transferred to a hospital better equipped to manage chronic mental illness. After nearly two years of intensive treatment with no improvement, it was time to move me on. I was to be admitted to Banstead Hospital. I knew all about Banstead – and so did my father – it came under the category of 'bin'. He was adamant: no, I was not going to a long-term institution, not now or ever. He refused to be persuaded and signed the 'against medical advice' form. I was hauled out of occupational therapy, given a bag full of mind-altering drugs, and we were off.

I missed it: not the place, not the staff, but my fellow patients. I met some wonderful people 'inside'; we were a mutual support group, without which I was lost.

It wasn't long before my father made his announcement; he and I were going on a holiday. One of his Welsh students had offered him use of a cottage in a place called Mumbles. It was very kind of Davies, he was an excellent chap, and my father felt he couldn't refuse – not that he wanted to. He thought that to get away from sad memories was just what I needed and the fascinating geology of Gower could take my mind off ... off what? Off food, off weight, off death? I didn't think it was just what I needed at all, but seemingly it had all been arranged and I had lost the right to an opinion.

Although the academic year had ended, the school term still had several weeks to run; this meant my father was free but my mother was not. This holiday would be just me and my father, on our own, for ten days. The thought sent me into a mild panic. I felt nervous – almost shy. Looking back, I realise he too must have felt apprehensive. After all, taking a depressed, hopelessly anorexic daughter to an unknown holiday destination can't have seemed much fun.

The car was loaded up with maps, books, cameras, clothes for every conceivable climatic condition and, of course, food. My mother had filled her entire Tupperware collection with nourishing refreshment she hoped I might eat; poor Mum, she cared so much.

My father was a great fan of Radio 4, which he continued to call the Home Service; it was tuned in before we reached the ring road with the *Today* programme having just started. This is fixed in my memory because Britain had just voted to stay in the European Community and Barry Norman was getting extremely excited about it. Not quite as excited as John Simpson forty-one years later, on the day we voted to leave.

Our first and only stop was just before the Severn Bridge at the impressive Aust Services. Entering the enormous café was like going into the jaws of hell for me: nothing but food as far as the eye could see, sending my mental calorie counter into overdrive – and then I saw the view. I have no recollection of what I actually ate, but the sight of the River Severn with its graceful bridge facing towards Wales is imprinted on my memory. The place is a bit neglected now and the services have shrunk, but the view is the same: the sloping banks; the wide, slow river; and the 'old' bridge leading to the country I now call home.

I had never previously been to Wales. The first sign we saw after crossing the bridge was to Pwllmeyric: it was then I realised I was in a different country. Of course, I had known Wales was separate but that ancient, romantic name spoke of another culture. It would have taken much longer to reach the Mumbles than it does these days; it must have been late afternoon as we approached Oystermouth. I was greeted by a great expanse of glistening muddy sand. There is something otherworldly but soothing about that low tide shoreline. I felt it when I saw it the first time and I have felt it every time since. My father gave me a brief tutorial about Swansea Bay tidal flow as we drove through the village looking for our destination. The cottage was at the south end of the village, an area called – somewhat unimaginatively – Southend. It was at the top of a row of similar cottages built into the side of the cliff. The only access appeared to be via a steep flight of steps.

We had to leave the car at the bottom and climb the considerable number of steps to reach the very last house. I was delighted by the requirement for such intensive exercise and ran up and down to the car rather more than was necessary. The cottage had belonged to the excellent chap Davies' uncle, who had died some years before. It didn't look as if much had changed since the uncle's day; it had a quaint fifties air – almost a slight whiff of Vim! The elevated position gave a panoramic seascape from nearly every window. I chose the smaller of the two bedrooms, at the top of a precipitous flight of stairs, and the whole of Swansea Bay belonged to me.

There appeared to be a fairly tight schedule. This was

unexpected, as my father wasn't usually the most organised of men. I presume it was a plan to prevent me having time to do or think … whatever it was he thought I was going to do or think. We were to unpack, explore the local vicinity and then perhaps a meal or – quick afterthought – a snack.

I loved my bedroom; the furniture was too big and any reasonably sized person would have had difficulty in moving around. No such problem for me. I spread out my belongings with ease, filling the musty drawers with my shapeless, skeleton-making clothes. I had another 'poor Mum' moment when I saw that she had hidden a Tampax box amongst the bed linen; hope really does spring eternal – unlike my menstrual cycle which hadn't sprung for some time.

By the time we began our exploration of the local vicinity, it was early evening and the bay had taken on an entirely different persona. The mud had disappeared and, in its place, there was an endless, gently undulating stretch of blue-grey water. I can clearly recall my first walk along the seafront into the village: the narrow quay with its row of sailing boats patiently waiting for action; crazy golf; several shops that seemed to sell more or less everything; the amusement arcade; and, eventually, the sight of Oystermouth Castle. I'm sure that my father gave me a potted history of the castle but I didn't listen. Perhaps it was the silhouette against a golden sky or the commanding power of the ancient stone walls. Whatever it was, something about that majestic ruin penetrated my apathy and ignited a small flame of anticipation.

Extreme aerobic activity was one of my weight reduction measures, so my father's belief that vigorous exercise was an essential ingredient of health worked to my advantage. We almost jogged back down Mumbles Road, weaving our way past Friday night drinkers spilling out of a surprising number of pubs. As this was a pre- hen party era, there were no scantily dressed females with L plates or 'pink willy headbands'; the predominately male clientele was just enjoying the atmosphere. We passed the bottom of 'our' steps and sprinted on as far as Knab rock and Mumbles head. I thought it was all beautiful: the old Victorian lifeboat station; the squat, octagonal lighthouse; the sweep of the bay with Swansea the other side; even the flares from the steel works and the bikinied monkey on the pier. It wasn't because of the drugs or malnutrition that Mumbles struck a chord with me; it was unpretentious, non-judgemental, a place where mad people could be accepted without question or patronisation. The place has changed. It is now a gentrified suburb of Swansea with a new lifeboat station, fewer pubs, more flats, trendy shops and a Marks and Spencer – but it has kept its unique character, its tolerance, friendliness and charm. It is still beautiful.

It had to come of course – the meal. The memory of my father's understanding and sensitivity can still bring tears to my eyes. He laid out the content of each Tupperware container onto the small kitchen table and told me to take whatever I wanted – as long as it wasn't only lettuce. He didn't check my plate or watch me eat; we sat together in that shabby, cosy sitting room, peering at the vintage television.

What would have been on BBC 1 – my father wouldn't have entertained ITV – on June 5th 1975? My memory isn't sufficiently long term, but I do remember we laughed at something, maybe *The Two Ronnies* or Dave Allen. I know we saw the news because my father explained each item as if my incarceration had precluded any access to current affairs. Actually, there was a rather sophisticated television set in the patients' day room; my scant knowledge of life events was gleaned from the tail end of the news before *The Good Life* or *Fawlty Towers*.

My father was not a fan of Margaret Thatcher and, in her new role as leader of the opposition, she appeared frequently on both television and radio. She joined us at 10 o'clock most evenings, her strident, premodulated voice driving my father to distraction. He was left wing anyway but Maggie converted him into a radical socialist!

Apart from instructing me in a fairly unbalanced view of politics, my father introduced me to the history of the Gower by what he termed stratigraphy, and I called rock formation. Geology was my father's passion; he enjoyed nothing more than sharing it with anyone willing to listen. On family holidays, the mere mention of igneous rocks or crystalline would send my brother and me on an urgent mission. Now, much to his delight and my surprise, I was genuinely interested.

The sudden fine weather meant we could probe the depths of Gower for hours without the encumbrance of waterproof clothing. My father would stride along in a pair of long shorts, an aertex shirt and, beneath his hairy legs, a pair of white socks and sandals. I trotted along beside him in a baggy tee shirt, jumbo shorts and a pair of Doc Martens beneath my equally hairy legs.

We followed our holiday schedule to the letter; it involved a mixture of bay and valley walks. It is sometimes difficult to separate my Gower memories of 1975 with those of twenty years later when I took up a more permanent residence there – although I don't think a great deal had changed.

The days tend to merge together: I know that 'doing' the coastal path from Mumbles Pier to Caswell Bay and back across the cliff behind the cottage was high on the agenda. Pennard and Pobbles Bay followed and then, perhaps, it was Three Cliffs. The Three Cliffs trip is particularly clear in my mind because it involved food. We walked through woodland, passed Pennard Castle and crossed the beach towards those stunning, iconic cliffs. After a lively conversation about limestone and a jog over the dunes, my father thought we should try the Gower Inn for lunch. My immediate reaction was one of blind panic. What the hell was I going to do? Prior to the Three Cliffs day we had taken a picnic – sandwiches for my father, a leaf medley for me.

The menu was worrying: chips seemed to accompany almost everything but – a glimmer of hope – some dishes were 'served with salad garnish'. My father had cod and chips and I asked for only garnish. The very nice food lady brought me a large plate full of lettuce, watercress and tomato; she brought the dressing separately. It was as if she knew.

It was a very happy lunchtime. Some of the locals, who were having a pint, began chatting to my father. His barely discernible Irish accent became a thick brogue whenever he talked to the Welsh: I don't know why; perhaps it was to demonstrate Celtic bonding. I was acutely embarrassed at first but, as it seemed to bring out his usually lacking social side, I didn't comment. The beauty of Three Cliffs Bay was intensified by the charm and kindness of those people in the Gower Inn.

Rhossili was my absolute favourite place and remains so. I was amazed by the endless stretch of pristine sand; we walked for miles along that beach and back along the headland (Devonian Red Sandstone) before risking a scramble over to Worm's Head.

My father leapt over the rocks, with me following in his exact footsteps as if I was a child. One of the many theories proposed in the Seventies for the onset of anorexia nervosa was a fear of adulthood. The skeletal, prepubescent state which results from starvation was seen as a means of avoiding independence and sexual maturity. Anorexia is now known to be more complicated, but I have a suspicion that, in my case, the 'little girl' theory could have been a factor. If I had regressed much further towards childhood, I would have been asking Daddy for a bedtime story.

Worm's Head was the end of the world. There was no boundary between the sea and sky, the emptiness couldn't and shouldn't be filled. I am sure that it was this feeling of infinity that gave me back my desire to take part in life. It was an unconscious desire and remained dormant for a very long time; but from that moment, in that place, it was there.

It was a wonderful holiday. My father was nauseatingly self-congratulatory about the way he had managed everything – meaning me. My mother was relieved to see that I hadn't completely disappeared.

The connection between mental health and the natural world is not a new concept. Most mental hospitals had some garden space and encouraged patients to 'get out there and do some digging'. Even in central London I was given a tiny patch of earth to 'cultivate'. I obediently planted a few bulbs, but watching a spindly tulip struggling to survive didn't fill me with hope. My good friend and fellow anorexic said the tulip had turned out like its planter – spindly and struggling to survive. I frequently visited my patch, not to nurture the bulbs but to smoke.

Nowadays the positive affect of being in the natural world is used therapeutically and, since Thatcher closed most of the mental institutions (my father would have done things differently!), patients live in the community and are able to walk freely in the countryside.

Before my Welsh experience I was very sceptical. Not just because of my pathetic tulip; I had spent time in the countryside before but it hadn't prevented my mental illness.

Gower was different; perhaps it was the wildness, the beauty, and the sense of being part of something that can and will exist without human intervention. I felt small and insignificant (both of which I was!) but I needed to keep being part of that something.

So no, it wasn't a cure. It wasn't even the beginning of the end. But I do know that it gifted me the will to live – and I'm still here.

CONTRIBUTORS

Sue Bevan

Sue won the international Alpine Fellowship Theatre Prize 2020 with *Hiraeth*, exploring the place for forgiveness and retribution in the context of the Aberfan disaster, where she found herself as a ten-year-old first-aider. She also won The Drama Association of Wales International One Act Play Competition with *Mum's the Word*, a raw exposé of the exhausting and often challenging transition to early motherhood. Sue's own Valleys story of losing her child to adoption when she was fifteen is told in her memoir, *That Picture Of You*, and was the subject of an award-winning BBC R4 documentary.

Kate Cleaver

Kate Cleaver is an Anglo-Indian writer studying for a PhD with Swansea University. She is researching the lives of ordinary people who found themselves incarcerated in the Briton Ferry Insane Asylum, Vernon House. She has begun to create stories and has found that linking her stories to historical fact is a way to bring people from the past to life; she is asking if those ghosts can be recreated into stories, into creative history. In 2019 she was long listed in the New Welsh Writers Award and in 2020 had a memoir published by Parthian in *Just So You Know: Essays of Experience*.

Gillian Drake

Gillian Drake was born in Barry and now lives in Swansea. She has written since childhood but began to write for publication in the 1990s when her teen novels, *Rhian's Song* (winner of the Tir na n-Og Award) and *The Girl in Green*, were published. Other published work includes articles on local and social history, poetry and short stories. Gillian is a graduate of Aberystwyth University, and gained an MA in Creative Writing from Swansea University in 2005. She has worked in the voluntary sector in areas as diverse as archaeology, mental health, and education.

Nic Hafren

A graduate of the University of Bristol, Nic worked as an actor performing new writing. She has collaborated on modern adaptations of Greek classics and undiscovered Elizabethan texts. She was a founder member of a theatre company specialising in improvisation. This was followed by work as an editor and screenwriter for independent television and also a lecturer in media studies. Currently, Nic works as a freelance writer and counsellor where she has written and led workshops dealing with mental health and wellbeing. She is a member of the band Electric Church Music where she sings and contributes the odd lyric.

Sue Davies

Sue started life in rural Cheshire but left her Girls' Grammar School to run away to sea at 17. Since then, her professional and personal lives have been alternately delicious and disastrous. She's been married, pregnant, divorced, redundant, employed, unemployed, sacked and self-employed but the recurring theme throughout has been the sea and from running a boat business in Cornwall to returning to Anglesey nearly 20 years ago, her work has included Search and Rescue Coordination for HM Coastguard, working with homeless youngsters and training lorry drivers, and now she writes (whilst looking after lighthouses on Anglesey for Trinity House).

Sue Jones-Davies

She is best known for her role as Judith in the film *Life of Brian*. She was a founder member of the feminist group Raving Beauties who performed on the opening night of Channel Four. The audience's response to the poetry led to a book deal with the Women's Press. Their first anthology *In the Pink* was a bestseller and led to the group compiling two more poetry books and one prose. Their most recent book *Hallelujah for 50ft Women*, was published by Bloodaxe in 2015. Currently Sue teaches yoga and works in her woods.

Ruth Dineen
Born in 1950 in Cardiff, Ruth had a glorious adolescence of *Jackie* magazines, cheesecloth shirts and dancing round handbags. She bumped in to Women's Lib in the late 1960s but it wasn't until her pregnancy that she truly registered the impact of sexual discrimination. She's not a writer but this was the one story that she felt she needed to tell. She's variously been an English teacher, graphic designer and lecturer. After leaving academia she co-founded the Co-production Network for Wales to encourage greater democratic accountability and citizen power in our public services. She remains a (thoroughly) radical feminist.

Eluned Evans
Born in Wales in 1949 to a Welsh father and an American mother, Eluned spent her childhood in the US, moving back to the UK in 1960. Since then, she has lived in various parts of Wales settling, finally, in the village of Cwmystwyth. She has worked in the public and voluntary sectors, finishing her working life as an administrator in adult education at Aberystwyth University. Following her father's death in 2015, she moved back to the family home to help care for her mother. This led to the discovery of the letters which inspired the article in this book.

Phyllis Kinney
Born in Pontiac, Michigan on 4 July 1922, Phyllis studied music at

Michigan State College before winning a fellowship in Voice at the Juilliard Graduate School in New York. In March 1947 she came to the UK and joined the Carl Rosa Opera Company as Principal Soprano, touring Britain during 1947–8. In April 1949 she married Meredydd Evans, settling in Harlech, but continued to sing in concerts and on BBC radio in London. Her daughter Eluned was born in 1949 and in 1952 the family moved to the United States where, in 1955, she created the role of 'The Girl with the Tablet' in the first performance of Roger Sessions' opera *The Trial of Lucullus*.

From 1955-1960 she was Instructor in Music, Voice teacher and Choir Director at Lasell College for Women, Auburndale, Massachusetts. However, in 1960 the family moved back to Wales where Phyllis continued to lecture in music, teach singing at the University Colleges of Wales in Bangor and Cardiff, and to publish music for children.

She became increasingly interested in Welsh traditional music and, along with her husband, spent more than four decades researching the subject. In 1991 she received an Honorary Masters degree from the University of Wales, Bangor for her work in the field of Welsh music. She became a Fellow of the University of Wales, Bangor in 1997 and in 2011 her definitive book on the subject *Welsh Traditional Music*, was published by the University of Wales Press.

Following her husband's death in February 2015, Phyllis donated all their joint research papers to the National Library of Wales. The Meredydd Evans and Phyllis Kinney Papers are being catalogued and made publicly available as part of The Welsh Music Archives.

Phyllis is now 99 years old and enjoying a very full and well-deserved retirement in Aberystwyth!

For more information see: https://blog.library.wales/phyllis-kinney-the-musician-from-michigan/

Catrin Gerallt

A former Current Affairs Editor at BBC Wales, Catrin Gerallt combined her journalistic career with writing. Her short stories have been broadcast on Radio 4 and the BBC World Service. In Welsh, her writing has featured in various collections, including the highly acclaimed *Clymau* (Gomer). In 2017, her adaptation of a T. Llew Jones children's novel was longlisted for the CLIP Carnegie Medal. Catrin now works as a full-time writer and was awarded a Literature Wales bursary to work on her first novel.

Lynne Parry-Griffiths

Lynne grew up in the shadow of Rhuddlan Castle and was educated on the site of a Norman graveyard. A love of history was developed at an early age although she went on to study English Literature and Drama before undertaking a postgraduate course in creative writing. She has twice been short-listed and once named runner-up for the Cheshire Prize for Literature. In 2017 she was longlisted for a New Welsh Writing Award and has had short stories published in a several anthologies. She lives and teaches in north Wales and is very fond of tea and *The Archers*.

Philippa Guest

Philippa was born in Cardiff on June 10th 1961, Prince Philip's 40th birthday. Her mum named her after him! She has had a lifelong career teaching English in secondary schools in Hertfordshire and Cardiff. She had wanted to be a teacher from the moment she started nursery school, which was fortunate, given the outcome. She now lives with her husband, Edward, near Cardiff Bay, where she sometimes works as a TV extra. She recently fell asleep in bed on the set of *Casualty*! Philippa and her husband have two adult daughters who live nearby, as well as a much-loved cat and rescue dog.

Virginia Isaac

After graduating from the University of East Anglia in 1971, Virginia settled in the Brecon Beacons where she practised self-sufficient farming and founded Brecon Carreg. Moving to Gloucestershire, she became a Director at UCAS and was a trustee of Cheltenham College and the Cheltenham Festivals. She was a governor at the University of Wales, Trinity St David and an adviser to the Welsh Language Commissioner. She became CEO of Inspiring Futures in 2013 but has now relocated back to Carmarthenshire. She is married with two children and four grandchildren and is a daughter of *Small is Beautiful* author EF Schumacher.

Sue Jenkins

Sue Jenkins was born and brought up in Swansea, and currently lives in America. After a promising start to her academic career, she was kicked out of Bristol University for failing her Latin exams. Accused by her mother of being 'on drugs', she was required to do a secretarial course, which opened doors to a solid and lucrative career at Reuters and Dow Jones. When not contemplating starting her unwritten novel, or obsessively, compulsively editing the work of others, she can be found amidst the cats and dogs in her kitchen, testing recipes for her unwritten cookery book.

Rhian E. Jones (Editor)

Rhian E. Jones is a writer, critic and broadcaster from South Wales who now lives and works in London. She writes on history, politics, popular culture and the places where they intersect. She is co-editor of *Red Pepper* and writes for *Tribune* magazine. Her books include *Clampdown: Pop-Cultural Wars on Class and Gender* (zer0, 2013); *Petticoat Heroes: Gender, Culture and Popular Protest* (University of Wales Press, 2015); *Triptych: Three Studies of Manic Street Preachers' The Holy Bible* (Repeater, 2017) and the anthology of women's music writing *Under My Thumb: Songs That Hate Women and the Women Who Love Them* (Repeater, 2017). Her latest book is *Paint Your Town Red: How Preston Took Back Control and Your Town Can Too* (Repeater, 2021).

Liz Jones

Liz Jones is the author of *The Queen of Romance* (Honno, 2021), a biography of the eccentric author, actor and theatre entrepreneur Marguerite Jervis. Shortlisted for the 2017 New Welsh Review writing award and runner-up in the 2019 Hektoen International essay award, she writes for everything from literary journals to women's weeklies. Liz lives in Aberystwyth with her husband where, winter or summer, she likes to swim in Cardigan Bay.

Sheila Kitrick

Sheila is a Londoner with Welsh (Richards and Lloyd) and Irish (Regan) bloodlines. She left school at fifteen and returned aged thirty. She graduated with an honours degree five years later. She is married with two children from a first marriage and six grandchildren. Post-graduation she worked as a research psychologist and, latterly, practitioner (London and Paris). She set up in private practice as a psychotherapist in 1993, specialising in work with children. She moved to Wales in 2010. Her two hobbies are writing and the design and construction of stained-glass art.

Rona Laycock

Rona's writing is influenced by the countries in which she has lived and travelled but her real creative source is to be found in the country of her birth, north Wales. The late Welsh poet, Nigel Jenkins, introduced her to Japanese haibun and haiku which she uses for travelogues. Her work has been published by Gomer, Honno, *Acumen*, *Mslexia* and *Magma Poetry* amongst others. Her first poetry collection, *Borderlands*, was published by Cole Press and Musicmasters as an audio CD. She is the editor of *Graffiti* magazine, founder member of Cirencester based writing group Catchword, and a creative writing tutor.

Carolyn Lewis
Born in Cardiff in 1947, Carolyn's work has appeared in previous Honno anthologies. Her first novel, *Missing Nancy*, was published by Accent Press in 2008. She gained an MPhil in writing at Glamorgan University (now the University of South Wales). Her stories have won major and local prizes and have appeared in the *New Welsh Review* and *Mslexia* amongst others and her second novel was published in 2020. She's worked as a creative writing tutor for many years and two text books have been published based on her teaching methods. Currently she's taking a PhD at Swansea University.

Rhiannon Lewis
Rhiannon Lewis is the author of *My Beautiful Imperial*, which was listed by the Walter Scott Prize Academy as one of its 'recommended' historical novels in 2018. Her novella, *The Significance of Swans*, came runner up in the dystopian novella category of the New Welsh Writing Awards in 2019. Short story successes include, the Bristol Prize, 2018 (shortlisted), Hammond House International Short Story Prize, 2017 (3rd), and Frome Festival 2017 (winner). In 2020, *The Last Flight* was shortlisted by the HG Wells Short Story Competition, and *Piano Solo* won the William Faulkner Short Story Contest in New Albany, Mississippi.

Christine McLennan
Christine McLennan is a teacher and mother of four, who has worked with the Centre for Alternative Technology for more than

forty years. She is a passionate sustainability educator and pioneer of alternative energy. She lives with her husband in Machynlleth, where they bike a lot and continue to impart their knowledge to the next generation.

Barbara Michaels

Barbara Michaels has been a journalist and writer all her life and is published by Honno in the anthologies *Laughing, Not Laughing*, and *My Cheating Heart*. She is now finalising the draft of her debut novel *Last Flight from Kai Tak*, poetry collection *Poetry for our Time*, and a memoir spanning 60 years of writing. Her children's book, illustrated by artist Sian Bowman, *What's the Matter with Slithers?* was screened recently on YouTube. She is Editor of *BIMAH*, circulating tri-annually to the Jewish community in Wales and reviewing theatre, opera, ballet and books. A mother, grandmother and great-grandmother, she lives in Cardiff. www.barbaramichaels.co.uk

Jane Salisbury

Jane Salisbury (née Donovan) was born in Barry in 1955. Before recent retirement, she coordinated postgraduate research studies for the School of Social Sciences, Cardiff University, and lectured in educational policy, qualitative research methods and post-compulsory education and training. Jane has published papers on classroom ethnography, vocational education and training and the sociology of work. Jane is a Trustee and active member of Wales Assembly of Women (WAW) and an Executive member and Trustee of The Contemporary Arts Society for Wales (CASW). She has one daughter and lives with the painter Alan Salisbury in Barry and Limousin.

Rose Simpson

After leaving York University in 1967 to join the Incredible String Band, I lived and played with them until 1971, when I moved to

Wales. After a varied, often eccentric, working life, including a year as Mayoress of Aberystwyth, I returned to academia in 2006, progressing to a PhD in German Literature and my present post as Honorary Lecturer at Aberystwyth University. I have published in academic journals and my memoir of the Incredible String Band years *Muse, Odalisque, Handmaiden* appeared in December 2000.

Sue Sky

Born in London, Sue studied Social Sciences at Leeds Polytechnic and took a postgraduate professional social work course at Cardiff University. She was a social worker in Barry before becoming a full-time unpaid worker with Cardiff Women's Aid and helping establish Wales' first refuge in 1975. For 20 years she worked for Cardiff community organisations. She joined the newly-devolved Welsh Government in 1999 and for eight years was the Welsh National Breastfeeding Coordinator. In 2019, Sue and her partner were among the first in the UK to obtain an Equal Civil Partnership. They have two children and two grandchildren.

Bridget Taylor

After several years of mental illness, I was – surprisingly – able to resume my nursing career. In 2010 I retired and, with my Welsh husband, exchanged London for Carmarthenshire: chosen for its space, beauty and coastline. A desire for a new experience resulted in my undertaking a local adult education Creative Writing course. Much to my disappointment, numbers dwindled and the course closed. Determined to carry on, four of us from the course started our own creative writing group. The group has grown and the encouragement of these friends has given me confidence to develop my embryonic writing skills.

Carolyn Thomas

Carolyn Thomas is originally from the Neath valley but has lived in Tyneside since reading English at Newcastle University. She is now retired after a career of teaching in Further, Higher and Adult Education. She has reviewed for *Stand* magazine and contributed poetry to collections published by Sunderland University's Spectral Visions Press, an enterprise run by students studying English and Creative Writing, but this reflection on life as a gay woman in the 1970s is her first published prose work. Stereotypically, she has a cat, still considers Wales as home and sports a dragon tattoo.

Liz Vining

Liz was born in Aberdare in 1953 but spent her formative years in Penarth. Throughout her life she has lived in several locations in south Wales and finally settled in Swansea having returned there in 1997 to study ceramics. To fit in with motherhood, she has had an eclectic working life: hotel work, modelling, childcare officer, archaeological finds recorder, arts centre worker, although her main source of income was as a self-employed antiques dealer. She was inspired to write her essay 'Concealment' when she reconnected with a college friend who knew nothing of those intervening 48 years.

Sue Williams

Hailing from Swansea docks, Sue represented Wales at both netball and squash while at school. After working as a probation officer in some of London's highest crime areas, she eventually became Head of Youth Justice for Wales. She's written three novels that have been longlisted for literary prizes including the Debut Dagger, but 'Chwarae Teg' will be her first published work. She is ridiculously proud of the fact that during the Covid lockdown she successfully trained for a half marathon by running around the back roads near her home near Llandeilo, which she shares with a small assortment of sheepdogs.

ABOUT HONNO

Honno Welsh Women's Press was set up in 1986 by a group of women who felt strongly that women in Wales needed wider opportunities to see their writing in print and to become involved in the publishing process. Our aim is to develop the writing talents of women in Wales, give them new and exciting opportunities to see their work published and often to give them their first 'break' as a writer. Honno is registered as a community co-operative. Any profit that Honno makes is invested in the publishing programme. Women from Wales and around the world have expressed their support for Honno. Each supporter has a vote at the Annual General Meeting. For more information and to buy our publications, please write to Honno at the address below, or visit our website: www.honno.co.uk

Honno Press
D41 Hugh Owen Building
Aberystwyth University
Aberystwyth
Ceredigion
SY23 3DY

Honno Friends
We are very grateful for the support of all our Honno Friends. For more information on how you can become a Honno Friend, see: https://www.honno.co.uk/about/support-honno/